DESIGNING *and* PLANTING YOUR GARDEN

DESIGNING
and
PLANTING
YOUR GARDEN

with Arthur Hellyer

COLLINGRIDGE

ACKNOWLEDGEMENTS

We should like to thank the following contributors for
the illustrations in this book:
Drawings of garden designs: Norman H J Clarke
Line drawings: Virginia Noakes
Colour photographs: Pat Brindley and Harry Smith
Black and white photographs: *Amateur Gardening*,
Pat Brindley, R J Corbin, Ernest Crowson, John Cowley,
Denis Hardwicke, Humex Limited, Elsa Megson,
Kenneth Scowen and Harry Smith

Published by Collingridge Books
an imprint of Newnes Books
a division of The Hamlyn Publishing Group Limited,
Bridge House, 69 London Road, Twickenham, Middlesex TW1 3SB
and distributed for them by
The Hamlyn Publishing Group Limited,
Rushden, Northants, England
© Copyright The Hamlyn Publishing Group Limited 1935,
1975, 1986

First published 1935 under the title "Your New Garden" by
W H and L Collingridge Limited.

Fourth edition 1975
First softback edition 1986

ISBN: 0 600 33323 X

Set in 9 on 10½pt Monophoto Times New Roman 327
Printed in Italy

Contents

Introduction

Whether a garden has to be made from the chaos left by the builder or from an existing garden that does not match one's taste or requirements, it is usually wise to take one's time over it. That is why I have divided the chapters of this book into three sections, the first two each representing a year's work and the third dealing with some of the maintenance work that is necessary in any garden and which has not been covered in the previous sections. However, this measured progress need not be followed if there are overriding reasons for greater haste. Thanks to the development of powerful yet safe herbicides and the ready availability of plants in containers which can be planted at any time when weather and soil conditions permit, it is possible to take many short cuts. Though I do not think that 'instant gardens' are, in the long term, usually the best gardens, they are a possibility and so, at each appropriate stage, I have indicated how such short cuts can best be made.

Gardens that are entirely new provide some problems that are rather different from those common to all gardens. There are, for example, many questions connected with the treatment of untilled soil that will not arise once you have got the land into good order. Closely linked with these is the very important matter of rate of development. You may feel that this should be governed mainly by your pocket, but that is not the only consideration. Adequate preparation is essential for some features and too much haste at the outset has been the ruin of many a promising garden for, once permanent features have been installed, it is very difficult to clear the ground satisfactorily of weeds and pests, to improve its natural drainage and to break up subsoil.

Garden planning may actually be easier in a completely new garden than in one that is already made but does not meet one's requirements. Here one can start with an entirely open mind, unhampered by considerations of expense or difficulty of alteration. It is a little ironical that trained garden architects are usually left to demonstrate their skill on comparatively large and therefore easy plots whereas small town gardens, which fairly bristle with problems, are generally planned by amateurs or, worse still, by unimaginative jobbing gardeners.

You may even need to become quite a proficient builder during the first few years. It is always useful to be able to tackle simple carpentry and masonry, but never more so than when starting a new garden which may need a shed, frame, greenhouse, screen walls, terrace walls, steps and other features. These matters are often overlooked in the ordinary garden handbooks which are written principally from the standpoint of garden maintenance rather than garden making.

A gardener's year does not start on January 1. Some may contend that it starts in spring, when growth begins anew, but the usual practice is to regard the gardener's new year as beginning in October, when growth is over and the ground must be cultivated afresh. That is the view I have taken in this volume and so the sections, or years, should be regarded as extending from October 1 to September 30. It is quite likely that you will not take possession of your garden precisely at the beginning of the gardener's year, and this may necessitate some modification of the plan. But if you can start gardening some time during the autumn or early winter you may be able to get most of the first year's work done, while if you start much after the calendar new year you will be well advised to take things easily the first season, merely digging the ground and sowing some annuals or planting some potatoes, waiting until the autumn before you make a real start. If any features have to be left out of the first year's programme I suggest that these might be sundry vegetable crops other than potatoes, the fruit garden and the lawn and that they should be omitted in the order in which they are named.

I do not suggest that even in subsequent years it will be necessary, or even advisable, to follow the plan slavishly. Some modification will almost certainly be made necessary by conditions and requirements known only to you. But I hope it will indicate the general lines upon which you should proceed in order to convert an uncultivated plot or an unsatisfactory garden into a beautiful and profitable place without unnecessary delay, expense or disappointment.

Arthur Hellyer

CHAPTER 1

Taking Stock

Disposal of rubbish – Common soil pests – Weeds – What to do with turf – Soil analysis

You are faced with that most depressing sight, a garden plot defaced by the builder! Where you had pictured flower beds there are heaps of brickbats and broken glass, an old mortar bed occupies the very place previously earmarked for a rock garden, while the site of the lawn-to-be is scarred with hastily filled trenches. Even the ground upon which these outrages have been worked holds malign and hitherto unsuspected possibilities in the shape of hungry pests and persistent weeds.

But none of the difficulties is insuperable, and sensible treatment at the outset will usually result in a rapid and final removal of all of them.

Disposal of Rubbish. Your first problem will be the disposal of rubbish left behind by the builders. Most of this can be turned to some account. Brickbats should be collected in an out-of-the-way corner, for they will make an ideal foundation for a path or may even be needed later on for a land drain.

Wood, shavings and sawdust can be burned and the ashes retained as they are rich in potash, one of the three most essential plant foods. They can be kept in a sack in a dry place until they are needed as a dressing for the soil. They will be especially useful in the fruit and vegetable quarters.

Only pieces of glass and metal are valueless and, if the dustman will not take these away, it is best to pay to have them removed to a rubbish dump.

Common Soil Pests. Now comes the question of the disposal of turf – or the mixture of coarse grass and even coarser weeds that masquerade under that name. Do not be misled by talk of the merits of 'virgin' land. That is all very well when the ground in question is good pasturage that has been well cared for by the farmer and has been fed with chemical fertilizers as well as by the droppings of cattle, but it is a totally different matter when one has to deal with a neglected building plot that has been impoverished by crop after crop of hungry weeds. The 'virgin' nature of the unmade garden plot is far more likely to be a danger than a blessing,

An imaginative design for a small garden. Clever use has been made of all available space; the curved path leads the eye to an attractively planted raised bed and the different planting levels add height and interest. In time wall shrubs will conceal the paling

for it implies that no steps have been taken to rid the soil of such natural inhabitants as pests and weeds.

Dig up one or two turves and lay them on a large sheet of newspaper. Then break them up into small fragments and search for any insects or weed roots. You will not find it difficult to recognize two of the commonest soil pests, wireworms and millepedes, even though you have had no previous experience of gardening, for both are very distinctive in appearance. Wireworms measure from a quarter to three-quarters of an inch in length and are of a truly wire-like thinness, and they have shiny yellow skins that make them rather conspicuous. Do not confuse them with centipedes, which are also yellow. There is really no need for doubt on this point, for centipedes have numbers of legs right down their bodies and they are always active, whereas wireworms have only three pairs of very small legs near the head and a 'stump foot' at the tail and they move about quite slowly.

Millepedes are greyish or blackish in colour, long and thin, but more variable in size than wireworms. One type has the curious habit of rolling itself up into a coil like a watch spring the moment it is disturbed. All millepedes have numbers of legs like centipedes, but are distinguishable by their sober colouring.

Leatherjackets are sometimes very numerous in grassland, and they are not very easy to detect. They are an inch or more in length, in shape rather like fat caterpillars, but without legs and very sluggish in their habits, scarcely stirring when disturbed. This last characteristic, combined with their blackish-green colour, makes them inconspicuous, and so you should search carefully through the soil and particularly in the grass roots quite close to the surface, where they are fond of feeding.

Weeds. At the same time take stock of the weed roots you find. Couch grass is one kind that may cause trouble. It is, as its name implies, a kind of grass, and it has coarse, harsh blades and wiry white roots that penetrate the ground far and wide. They are so sharp pointed that they will bore right through the roots of other plants.

Bindweed, also known as bellbine and wild convolvulus, is another possible source of trouble. This has thicker, more brittle roots than couch grass, which drive deeply down into the soil instead of keeping quite close to the surface. In consequence, it is more difficult to destroy. The roots are often in coils.

Other weeds for which you should keep a watch are dock, thistle and nettle – but these can generally be seen more clearly above ground than in the soil.

Informal borders of mixed shrubs and perennials make a delightful foil for a house in rural surroundings

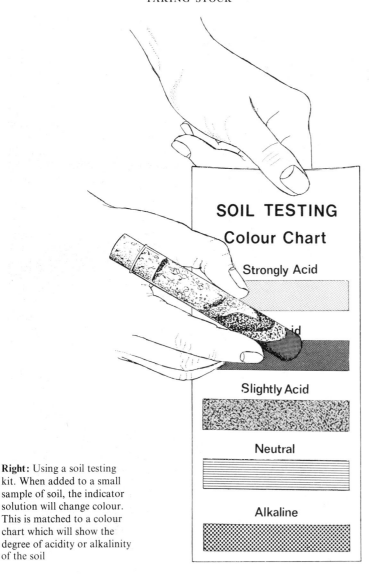

SOIL TESTING
Colour Chart

Strongly Acid

Slightly Acid

Neutral

Alkaline

Right: Using a soil testing kit. When added to a small sample of soil, the indicator solution will change colour. This is matched to a colour chart which will show the degree of acidity or alkalinity of the soil

What to do with Turf. The point of this preliminary inspection is that, having found out what pests and weeds predominate in the soil, you can decide upon a plan of campaign more intelligently. The options you are faced with are likely to fall in the following categories:

If there is a lot of weed it will be wise to strip off the turf and stack it in an out-of-the-way place to rot or, alternatively, to spray it with a herbicide that does not poison the soil. Paraquat (sold as Weedol) and glyphosate (sold as Tumbleweed) are herbicides of this kind. Paraquat is a contact herbicide and will kill weeds in a few days if the weather is warm and sunny. Glyphosate is a translocated herbicide, which means that it moves around the plant in the sap. It may take several weeks to kill weeds but is more effective in killing the roots as well as the top growth. When the grass and weed is clearly dead, it can be dug in. An alternative is to dig the whole plot at least 18 in. deep and pick out all weed roots as you go along but this is back-breaking work and takes a long time. Rotary cultivators tend to make matters worse by chopping up weed roots and distributing them all over the place where many will soon start to grow again.

Similarly, if leatherjackets, wireworms and millepedes are present in force you will be well advised to strip and stack turf, treating it at the same time with some good soil insecticide such as bromophos or gamma-HCH powder. Like couch grass and nettles, these pests have a preference for the top few inches of soil and can be destroyed in great numbers by this method.

If it turns out that the soil is reasonably free of pests and surface-rooting weeds, it will be more economical to dig the turf in than to strip it off. Cut up with a sharp spade into pieces about 6 or 8 in. square and buried, grass side downwards, beneath at least 8 in. of soil, it will soon rot without trouble and will enrich the ground and improve the drainage of heavy land.

If you are in any doubt as to which is the wiser policy – to strip the turf or to dig it in – seek the advice of an expert. A mistake on this fundamental matter may cause a great deal of trouble later on.

Soil Analysis. One other matter which it will be wise to consider in this preliminary stocktaking is the nature of the soil. Dig out deep holes in two or three places and find out how far the good soil continues and what lies beneath it. You will probably be able to glean much useful information about its fertility from people who have lived in the district for some time, or simply by keeping your eyes open and noting the kind of plants that succeed in neighbouring gardens. But if, after all this, you are in doubt as to the nature of the soil, send a sample to an expert analyst (or consult your County Horticultural Adviser) and get a brief report from him on its principal qualities and deficiencies. You can easily carry out a test for free lime yourself by the simple process of obtaining small samples of soil from different parts of the garden, placing them one at a time in a beaker or tumbler, and then pouring a little hydrochloric acid on them. If there is an immediate and considerable effervescence it is a sign that the soil contains plenty of lime, but if there is no effervescence the soil contains little or no free lime. This is rather important, as it may materially affect your later treatment of the soil and also your selection of plants. A more accurate test can be made by ascertaining the acidity or alkalinity of the soil with one of the simple soil-testing outfits that are available. These give a tint that has to be matched with a tint card, the result being given in terms of what is known as the pH scale. A reading of 7 represents neutrality, that is a soil that is neither acid nor alkaline; below 7, increasing degrees of acidity and above 7 increasing degrees of alkalinity. For general purposes pH 6·0 to 6·5 is ideal. Soils below pH 5·00 are excessively acid and unless well limed to raise the pH are only suitable for a limited range of acid-soil plants such as rhododendron, camellias, heathers and gaultherias. By contrast soils of pH 7 and over are unsuitable for these plants, though they are excellent for many vegetables and for lime-loving plants such as cherries, whitebeams, pyracanthas, lavenders and clematis.

Top: With low-growing perennials in the foreground, the dividing wall and steps give the illusion of two separate gardens. An attractive tiled path leads invitingly to the lawn above

Left: Flowering shrubs will make a splendid show and give a sense of welcome to the immediate surrounds of the house. Once established they will require little attention

CHAPTER 2

A First Clearance

Dig the whole plot – Stripping and stacking turf –
Lime and chalk – Land drainage – Excluding rabbits

Having decided between the rival merits of stripping, weed killing and digging in turf, the next task is to dig the whole plot as thoroughly as possible. You may feel that this is a waste of energy and time, and that it would be better to decide upon a plan first so that you need only dig those portions that are to be made into beds or borders, or are, at least, to be sown with grass seed. Practice proves that this is false economy. Not only are better results obtained by digging all the ground irrespective of the use to which it is to be put, but, in the long run, time is actually saved by this means. For one thing it is much easier to dig a fairly large area of ground than a number of small patches and strips, and for another the task of levelling or terracing is greatly simplified when the whole area has been roughly dug.

Stripping and Stacking Turf. If stripping is decided upon, remove all the turf and stack it before starting to dig. It will be sufficient to remove the turf with from 2 to 3 in. of soil, for this will contain most of the surface-rooting weeds together with the pests that feed in their roots. The stack should be built in an out-of-the-way corner where it can remain undisturbed for at least a year. Begin by building a low wall of turves, grass downward, in the form of a square, and fill in the centre with more turves which need not be arranged with such precision, though it is as well to keep the grass side down. Then build the wall higher and throw more turves into the centre, continuing in this manner until the stack is completed. Upon each layer of turves scatter a thin sprinkling of sulphate of ammonia and a small quantity of gamma-HCH or brom-ophos insecticide. The first-mentioned will hasten decay; either of the latter will destroy soil pests.

Digging Rough Ground. To dig ground effectively it is necessary to make a trench into which the soil can be turned and to keep such a trench open in front of one throughout the digging operation. If the plot is small the first trench can be dug right across one end and the soil removed to the other end where it will be required to fill in the last trench. If the plot is large it will almost certainly be more convenient to mark it out in an even number of strips of equal width, each of which will be dug separately. The first trench is then opened across the end of one outside strip and removed to the same end of the last strip at the opposite side of the plot. Digging then proceeds down one strip, back up the next and so on until the whole plot has been dug, the soil at each turn being thrown sideways to fill the open trench in the last strip.

The trench needs to be about 1 ft. wide and 10 in. deep. If the soil is very weedy or difficult it may be necessary to work with a trench 2 ft. wide and 20 in. deep but this involves a great deal of extra work and is seldom used nowadays. When such 'double digging' is employed each spit or 1-ft. deep layer of soil is kept in the same place as before, the top soil on top and the subsoil down below. This is done by digging out the top spit and then breaking up the subsoil beneath before opening the next trench.

But for all normal purposes plain digging to the full depth of the blade of a spade or the tines of a fork is sufficient. Which tool is used depends on the nature of the soil. If it is turf covered a spade will be essential to chop through the turves and a spade is also best for very light, sandy soil which slips through the tines of a fork. But for rather stiff soil without a great deal of weed or grass cover a fork may be just as effective and a great deal easier to use.

Always dig with the trench in front of you, turning the soil spadeful by spadeful (or forkful by forkful) into the open trench. Do not make too big a 'bite' each time and try to invert the soil completely

Digging plan for a plot. The plot should first be divided into easily worked strips. The soil from the first trench is barrowed to the end of the plot and used for filling in the last trench. The gardener then works backwards, throwing the soil forward into the open trench in front of him

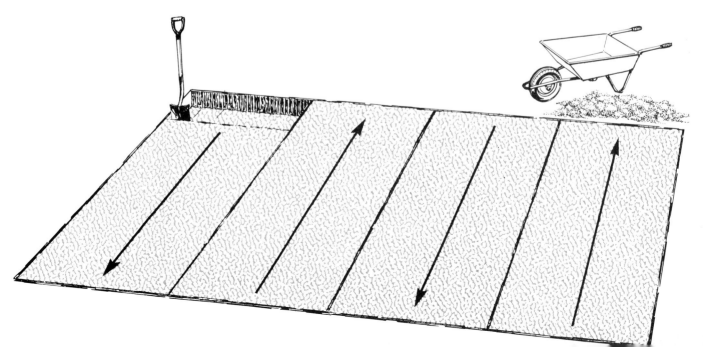

as you toss it forward so that any grass or weeds are completely covered. This not only looks tidy but it makes it much more likely that the weeds and grass will die.

If you see the roots of persistent weeds such as couch grass, bindweed, docks, thistles and nettles, pick them out as you go and burn them later on.

Digging can be done at any time of the year, but the work is much heavier in summer, when the ground is hard from lack of rain. Autumn is really the best time, as then the newly turned clods will be exposed to the alternate frosts and thaws of winter and will, in consequence, be thoroughly broken up. For this reason it is sound policy to leave the surface as rough as possible at first so that a large area of soil is exposed to the weather. If the soil is very stiff and unyielding, you may even find it worth your while to throw it up in a series of steep ridges, for in this way an even larger surface can be exposed.

You will not require any manure during the preliminary digging. This is better applied later on when the plan of the garden has been settled upon and the positions of beds, lawns, etc., have been marked out. The same treatment will not suit every part of the garden, for some things require one food and others another. There are even plants, notably alpines, that flower better and are in general more satisfactory when they have no manure whatsoever.

Lime and Chalk. But what can often be given with advantage at the outset is a dressing of lime or chalk, especially if the soil is known to be acid. The chemical effect of both is similar, their value consisting in their ability to improve the texture of the soil and to liberate some of the food materials that may be locked up in it. Lime tends to lighten stiff clay and to make it more workable. Chalk has a similar effect and, rather curiously, can also be used on sandy soil to make it more retentive of moisture during dry weather.

Hydrated lime is the form commonly used in gardens. It is a fine white powder which can be used at rates varying from 2 to 8 oz. per square yard according to the degree of correction required.

Chalk can be obtained newly quarried in lumps, but although this is cheap it is not really economical, as years must elapse before the lumps break up and the chalk has any very noticeable effect upon the soil. What the gardener requires is ground chalk – and the finer the grinding the better. Rates of application can be as high as 1 lb. per square yard to produce an effect equivalent to that of hydrated lime.

There is yet another form in which lime can be added to the soil, and that is as powdered limestone. This has practically the same value as ground chalk, but it does not hold water so well and is therefore not so useful on sandy soil. Against this must be reckoned the fact that good quality limestone is long lasting and very steady in action. Rates of application are the same as for ground chalk and this also applies to magnesium limestone, a special form which is useful on soils that are deficient in magnesium. But before using such a specialized dressing as this it would be advisable to seek the advice of an expert as to whether it is desirable.

There is no point in applying lime, chalk or limestone to ground that is already of a chalky nature or if it effervesces freely when treated with acid. Nor should any of these substances be used at this stage if you intend to grow rhododendrons, azaleas, heathers or other plants which dislike chalk and lime. If these are to be included, you should wait until the garden has been fully planned and then apply lime only where it can do no harm.

Land Drainage. Another point that should be considered carefully at this stage is the drainage of the plot. If the soil is light and sandy or the subsoil consists mainly of gravel or chalk, this is not likely to be a problem, but heavy clay soil, or stiff loam overlying a clay subsoil, may need some assistance. It is sufficient usually to mix some straw or very strawy manure (more straw than manure for preference, for the reasons already given) with the soil from 1 to 2 ft. beneath the surface. Dead bracken will serve the same purpose if straw is not available, the important point being to use something that will decay slowly and keep the soil from binding together too closely.

Only on very heavy or very low-lying land will drains be required, but you should not hesitate to make them if you find that surface water collects badly during the winter, for it is quite impossible to garden successfully under such conditions. The cost of draining swampy or waterlogged land may easily be repaid in a few years.

It is not essential to have a brook or main drain into which to divert the surplus water. The problem of the ordinary garden can often be solved by a series of shallow land drains, connected at their lowest point with a soakaway. This is prepared by digging a hole about 4 to 6 ft. in diameter and sufficiently deep to penetrate the impervious subsoil into something more porous below. The hole is then filled to within a couple of feet of the surface with stones, clinkers, and any other large, hard rubble that may be at hand. During very wet weather surplus water will collect in this hole and slowly percolate from it into the lower strata.

Land drains are made at the depth of the culti-

A dressing of hydrated lime improves the texture of a heavy clay soil and is the best method of correcting acidity

vated soil since water collects on the comparatively solid pan of undisturbed ground that lies immediately beneath. Each drain must have a fall of at least 1 ft. in every 20. In absolutely level ground it is necessary to make this fall artificially by digging the drainage trenches more deeply at one end than the other.

The simplest form of land drain is made by digging out a narrow trench of the required depth, filling the bottom 9 in. or 1 ft. with stones and clinkers, covering these with gravel or cinders and then filling up with turves, grass side downwards, and soil. A better drain is made with special earthenware pipes which you can obtain from any dealer in agricultural sundries or through most builders' merchants. These are laid end to end on a bed of gravel or cinders. Stones or clinkers are then piled around them and the drainage is finished off as already described.

Excluding Rabbits. A problem that you must consider if the surroundings are very rural is that of rabbits. These destructive creatures become extremely bold when food is scarce and will destroy most garden plants if not kept at bay. They also tear the bark from trees in their efforts to sharpen and shorten their teeth. The only satisfactory method of excluding rabbits is to place wire netting around the whole garden. This should not exceed 1½-in. mesh or baby rabbits will squeeze their way through, and you must bury it at least 2 ft. deep to prevent larger rabbits from burrowing under it. Usually a height above ground level of 3 ft. is sufficient, but if there are many hares in the district it will be wise to have at least 5 ft. of wire.

Top: (1) Cross-section of a pipe drain. Earthenware pipes are laid in rough rubble and clinkers
(2) Outline of the herringbone pattern in which drains are laid to slope down to a deep pit or soakaway. This should be about 4 to 6 ft. in depth and filled with stones, clinkers and coarse rubble

Top right: Laying a pipe drain. The joints are covered with crocks to prevent soil from clogging them and stones or clinkers are then piled round them

Right: Even a small, narrow garden offers scope for many attractive features. Here, a rectangular pool and irregularly shaped island bed add width, while the fence is used as a support for espalier-trained fruit trees

CHAPTER 3

Choosing a Plan

Style in relation to surroundings – Aspect – Choose plants to suit soil and situation – Views – Paths – Contour – The long narrow garden – Width of beds and borders – Lawns – Banks and dry walls – Rock gardens – Sunken gardens – Ornamental pools – Fruit and vegetables – Greenhouse and frame

We now come to the task of choosing a plan for the garden. You may decide that this is so important that it is necessary to call in the services of a garden architect. Even if you do, it is hardly probable that you will want to leave matters entirely in his hands. You should at least have a say in the choice of style and decide upon the principal features, even though you do not rely entirely on your own judgement as to where these shall be placed. To some extent the garden should be an expression of your own personality, and this it cannot possibly be if it is planned entirely by another person.

Style in Relation to Surroundings. A frequent mistake made by beginners is to choose their garden plan without relation to the architecture of the house and the general surroundings. If this were not so we should not so frequently see the anomaly of crazy paving, which is definitely rustic in character, brought into close association with the formal outline of a modern house. Such a building calls for formal treatment in its immediate vicinity, and concrete slabs or squared paving blocks are more in keeping with its style. As one gets further away from the house the atmosphere can change, becoming wilder or more picturesque. However, by no means all houses are formal in character, and what may suit a dignified mansion could look ridiculous near a rustic cottage.

The Question of Aspect. Two further points that have a great bearing on design are the aspect and contour of the plot. It is partly on this account that ready-made designs are seldom of much use except to suggest general ideas. For example, you may see a plan in a book or magazine that pleases you greatly and yet find, when you come to apply it to your own plot, that if you follow it too slavishly your principal border will be situated in a completely shady place, or that you will have a pool at the top of a slope instead of at the bottom where it would look more natural.

When gardeners speak of a border with a south aspect, often abbreviated to 'a south border', they mean that the border is on the south side of some fairly high obstacle such as a fence, wall or hedge. Conversely a north border is one that is on the north side of such an obstacle. The reason for stressing this is that, in a garden bounded by fences on three sides and a house on the fourth, the border with a south aspect will be on the north side of the garden, the border with a north aspect will occupy the south side, the border with a west aspect will lie on the east side, while the border with an east aspect will be found on the west side. Obvious though this may seem, it not infrequently involves the beginner in a great deal of confusion.

Many plants prefer a sunny position to a shady one. Some are so insistent on this that it would be folly to attempt to grow them in any but an open spot, and this you must bear in mind when making your garden plan. Most alpines are sun lovers and, in consequence, you should make quite certain that at least the greater part of any site chosen for a rock garden is quite clear of the shade of trees or neighbouring buildings. Roses also need plenty of light and air if they are not to suffer from mildew and kindred troubles. Water lilies demand sun, but most ornamental fish like to retire into the shade during the hottest part of the day in summer. These contradictory claims can be reconciled by constructing the pool right out in the open, but arranging a few large stones or marginal plants to give shady nooks for the fish.

After all this you may feel that there is nothing left with which to fill the inevitable shady places. That is not so. If you plan them as shrub borders, herbaceous borders, and ferneries, with hardy bulbs for extra colour, especially in spring, you will have no difficulty in planting them effectively.

Choose Plants to Suit Soil and Climate. The nature of the soil may also have a bearing on design. It has

A formal pool and stone-flagged patio area make a dignified setting for an older style house

Top left: Design for a small courtyard on the north side of a house. A shelter is linked to a store shed where it will catch the sun. In such a small area paving is preferable to grass. Levelling of slightly sloping land allows the construction of a low wall and steps which add interest. The planting consists of specimen foliage shrubs and herbaceous plants in straight-edged borders

Left: An alternative design for a similar courtyard. The use of small blocks or brick paving allows greater variation in the outlines of the plant beds than the slab paving in garden (1) and the planting is more varied. A light-foliaged ornamental tree gives dappled shade over the paving and a small pool reflects the sunlight

Top: A simple yet highly effective alternative to the conventional plan of regular borders around a rectangular lawn so often applied to gardens of medium size. The design, set at an angle to the house, gives variation in the widths of the borders which allows greater variety in planting. The roses, placed behind a screen hedge, have an element of surprise. To preserve the firm edges which such a design requires, mowing stones are used and these also play a part in the design

Bottom: The long, narrow plot is a common problem and such gardens need to be divided into smaller areas. Interlocking views through the garden and changes of direction greatly increase the interest. Whether paving or grass is used will depend on the size of the various enclosures, each of which becomes a little individual garden with its own planting scheme

17

Top: Curved, irregular outlines of beds and grass enliven the appearance of a tiny garden, while the planting of roses with annuals in front provides a variation in height

Right: An effective way of treating a long, narrow garden. The screen and climber in the background allow an intriguing glimpse of the garden beyond

often been said, with considerable justice, that the most successful gardeners are those who have been willing to recognize the limitations of their site and to grow only those plants that have proved themselves satisfactory under these particular conditions. There is little sense in trying to grow rhododendrons and azaleas if the soil is impregnated with lime when there are plenty of equally beautiful shrubs that enjoy such conditions, including buddleias, spiraeas, flowering currants and mock oranges.

Even roses are not likely to be very successful on thin chalky soils, such as are to be found on many downlands, and so their place, in the more formal parts of the garden, may well be taken by annuals, flag irises and the many tender bedding plants such as dahlias, pelargoniums and begonias that will grow in such places and make a cheerful summer display.

Similar restrictions are placed on the gardener by other peculiarities of soil or climate. Sandy soil used to present a difficult problem, but nowadays there are so many glorious flowering and berry-bearing shrubs that will grow well in such places that sand is hardly a drawback at all if you are sensible enough to accept its limitations. Further on in this volume classified lists of plants will be found with information as to the kinds of soil and situation in which they succeed best. You will do well to consider these carefully before proceeding much further with planning your garden, for obviously the types of plants you intend to grow will affect the style of the garden layout.

Views. Do not forget that the garden should be a constant source of delight from the house, and that the position of the principal windows should therefore be taken into account when preparing your plan. Try, as far as possible, to create a pleasing view from every living-room, and also, if practicable, from the more important bedrooms. You may think that this is an ideal that can only be achieved in a large garden, but this is far from being true, as some of the plans included in this chapter will indicate. It is also well to remember that the most interesting gardens are almost always those that have the greatest number of different and preferably contrasting views, and that here again it by no means follows that the big garden comes off best. Even in a tiny plot it is often possible to arrange several quite distinct pictures by grouping a few shrubs here, placing an arch there, or arranging a small rose- and clematis-covered screen in such a way that the whole plot is not apparent at the first glance.

Paths. Unnecessary paths are a frequent trap for the amateur garden designer and are the particular favourites of jobbing gardeners and garden-making builders, who never seem to tire of having at least three paths where one would serve. In many a small suburban garden paths might well be eliminated altogether, except immediately round the house and from the front gate to the front door. Sometimes a series of stepping-stones set in turf may be far more effective than a formal path without taking up one-quarter the room. There are occasions, particularly in town gardens, when one path might be placed close to a fence or wall with a northerly aspect, for there are not many plants that will thrive in such a place. If one or two holes are left for climbing plants the unsightly bareness of the fence can be covered quite satisfactorily and the path will not be monopolizing valuable space.

Much argument has centred around the rival merits of straight and curved paths. This is really a matter for individual taste, though it may be governed to some extent by the character of the surroundings. In a general way, straight lines or regular curves are more appropriate in a formal setting, whereas random curves and irregularity are better suited to rustic surroundings.

Contour. Do not grumble if your garden happens to be on the side of a hill. This will probably add to your labours at the outset, but it is much easier to make a really effective garden on sloping ground than in an absolutely level place, where there is always a danger that the finished result will reflect the flatness of the site and be comparatively uninteresting. It is true that a great deal can be done to provide an artificial contour by grouping trees and shrubs of different heights and also by the inclusion of herbaceous borders, pergolas, arches, screens, and built-up rock gardens, but in all these matters the hillside gardener starts at an advantage.

The Long Narrow Garden. In towns the back garden is sometimes excessively long in proportion to its breadth, and this provides the landscape architect with a further problem. There are various ways in which such bad natural proportions can be masked, one of the simplest being to dispense almost entirely with wide borders on each side, replacing these by strips of cultivated soil just wide enough to take rambler roses, clematis, jasmines, and other climbing plants that can be trained on trellis work or screens to clothe fences and provide some privacy from adjacent gardens. All the principal flower beds are then placed horizontally across the plot, which is further divided into several distinct sections by means of shrubs, either in informal shrubberies or planted as hedges, or with creeper-clad screens.

Width of Beds and Borders. This leads us to another important point – namely, the ideal width for beds and borders. This question must always be settled to some extent in relation to the particular requirements of the job in hand. But you should keep two points constantly in mind: firstly, that the beds or borders must be sufficiently wide to allow you to make an effective arrangement with the plants you intend to grow; and, secondly, that if they greatly exceed 6 ft. in width it will be very difficult to hoe between the plants and perform other necessary routine operations without a great deal of trampling on the soil. I do not suggest that it is wrong ever to walk on a bed once it has been made, but it does save time if most jobs can be done from the pathway, and it is certainly more pleasant in wet weather.

Most beginners err on the side of making mixed borders of shrubs and herbaceous plants much too narrow, with the result that they never get a really

Scalloped edges to an herbaceous border break up the long, straight lines of a narrow garden, lending it a softer aspect

effective display of colour. There are very few hardy perennials or shrubs that bloom for more than a few weeks at a time and so, in order to maintain a bright display, it is necessary to arrange groups in such a way that as one variety passes out of flower another grows up and takes its place. This is quite impossible to do satisfactorily if the border is only 3 or 4 ft. wide. From 6 to 8 ft. is satisfactory and in parks and large gardens borders usually exceed this considerably, but then more hands are available in such places, and the problems connected with weeding, hoeing, and general maintenance do not arise so acutely as they do in the owner-gardener establishment.

Lawns. A lawn plays an important part in almost every garden. Properly placed it can be an immense asset, for it provides the groundwork upon which everything else is built up and is an ideal foil for the brilliant colours of flowers. From the purely artistic standpoint it is usually an advantage if lawns can extend right up to the principal flower borders, but this increases labour, since the verge must then be cut by hand, and plants flopping over it may kill the grass or make mowing difficult. For this reason many gardeners prefer to have a path, even if only a narrow one, alongside every long border, or at least to place a line of paving slabs along the edge so that mowing stops short at a distance of about 15 in. from the border.

Top: A medium-sized suburban garden should not be a scaled-down copy of a much larger country garden. This design for a wide plot shows the use of a bold yet simple shape for the lawn with a generous area of terrace near the house and plentiful tree and shrub planting to create an illusion of greater space. There are mowing stones around the lawn both for good finish and convenience. A partly concealed ornament and a summerhouse draw attention to the partly screened garden inviting exploration

Bottom: This design for a seaside garden makes use of transparent screens not only to give an essential protection to the planting from salt-laden gales but also as a design element. Seaside gardens also need boundary protection for which wattle fencing is ideal and within which trees and shrubs specially selected for use in such situations must be used

Top right: In the larger garden one can plan for a greater range of subjects and this design includes trees and shrubs, fruit trees, vegetable and rose gardens and waterside plants. The sloping site is contoured naturally and the design adapts itself to these contours with levelling confined to the area round the house. A meandering path leads from the terrace down to a pool with a weeping willow in the lower part of the garden

Right: An economical alternative to the traditional type of outcrop rock garden. A few large boulders, selected for their shapes, can be interesting features in the small modern garden if placed to form bold groups whilst rock plants can be grown in a prepared and well-drained scree bed of gravel or stone chippings as the sketch shows

For a bank in a lime-free garden, heathers make an excellent covering. Varieties can be chosen to provide flowers almost throughout the year and the winter-flowering *Erica carnea* varieties can be grown in moderately alkaline soils as well as those which are neutral or acid

Steep Banks and Dry Walls. You will be well advised to avoid any steep grass banks, for these are extremely troublesome to maintain in good condition. They generally suffer badly during dry weather, and are difficult to roll and mow at all times. If you must have banks in the garden it is best to set rock garden stones upon them and plant appropriately, or else to grow suitable varieties of cotoneaster, the deciduous barberries, genistas, the smaller shrubby hypericums, helianthemums or lavenders, and, if the position is fairly mild, many kinds of cistus. In lime-free gardens heathers often make the best possible covering for a bank. If a wise selection is made it is possible to have bloom practically throughout the year, and there is plenty of variety both in colour and habit.

It is often better to dispense with banks altogether and to replace them by dry stone walls. These can either be vertical or else may have a very slight slope backwards, known technically as a 'batter'. This is a form of gardening that has delightful possibilities, for if the wall is carefully built and plenty of good soil is rammed between the stones, it will be possible to grow a surprising variety of really choice alpines which will make a floral picture second to none in the garden. The whole subject is dealt with more fully further on in this volume.

Rock Gardens. Rock gardens proper can also be fascinating. Here is a real possibility for you to enjoy a great number of treasures in a small space. Though some rock plants are difficult to grow there are many others which are easy. A selection can be made of kinds that will thrive in ordinary garden soil without elaborate preparation, or rock beds of special soil can be prepared for less-adaptable plants.

Nevertheless the rock garden is a feature demanding careful consideration, for the essence of its charm is naturalness, and this it cannot possess if it is badly placed. It is a good general rule to keep rock gardens as far away from the dwelling-house as possible, for they belong to informal rather than to formal surroundings. But this is a counsel of perfection that you may not find it possible to follow; in any case, in garden planning it is not wise to adhere too slavishly to any set of rules. If the house is built on a hillside it may even be possible to surround it completely with rock gardens in an entirely natural and satisfying manner. So here again is a chance to show your own artistic sensibilities. The fact that most alpine plants need all the sun and air they can get may seriously limit the number of possible sites. It is easier to make an effective rock garden on sloping or undulating ground than on the flat but mounds and valleys can be manufactured satisfactorily with no help from nature at all. It is even possible to make a charming moraine bed for alpines by the simple process of bedding large, flattish stones in level soil and covering the surface with stone chippings.

Raised Rock Beds and Sink Gardens. It is also possible to grow rock plants in raised beds made by building unmortared walls with stone or brick and

filling with prepared soil. Since such beds make no pretence of being natural they can be used in quite formal surroundings, even as objects of interest in tiny patio gardens. So too can stone sinks and troughs filled with soil and planted with alpines. These features are dealt with in greater detail in Chapter 22.

Sunken Gardens. In direct contrast to the rock garden, which calls for informal treatment, the sunken garden almost invariably requires a formal setting. A sunken garden is often very pleasing in the immediate vicinity of the house, and is frequently used for the cultivation of roses, though it is equally suitable for bedding plants and annuals. The old Elizabethan knot garden, with its intricate patterns drawn in box and thyme edging and its brilliant mosaic of colour, was almost invariably made below the surrounding ground level so that the pattern could be clearly seen.

But the sunken garden holds one very serious pitfall for the unwary – since it involves the excavation of a great deal of soil, it may be subject to serious flooding in wet weather. You will be well advised to think this over carefully before embarking on it, particularly if the subsoil is clay or the ground is low lying. You may be able to overcome such a possibility by means of well-placed land drains, but this means extra labour and expense. There are many gardens in which it would be far better to dispense with a sunken garden proper, and create a similar effect by surrounding a suitable plot with a raised path or borders.

Ornamental Pools. An ornamental pool or water garden, well stocked with aquatic plants and gaily coloured fish, can be a delightful feature. It can be made to fit in with almost any style, for there are water gardens of all types, formal and informal, these often making use of rigid polythene or glass fibre pools or heavy-duty plastic or rubber sheeting. In a tiny garden a charming feature can be made of a butt or half-barrel sunk level with the ground, filled with water and stocked with one water lily and a few goldfish. At the other end of the scale is the ornamental lake which plays a part in

the landscape architect's more expensive dreams. If you decide to include a sunken or a pseudo-sunken garden, a formal pool might prove to be its most attractive central feature, while if a rock garden figures more prominently in your thoughts you should not overlook the possibility that an informal pool may add to its effectiveness. But whatever plan you eventually decide upon, do not forget that the exact position and construction of the pool must be governed by two practical considerations: firstly, that water lilies require a fair amount of sunshine if they are to be kept in full health and open their flowers freely; and, secondly, that most ornamental fish appreciate a little shade during the hottest part of the day. As I have already remarked, these opposite requirements may be reconciled by constructing the pool in an open position and arranging overhanging rocks or edging slabs to provide protection for the fish. Water plants and small, spreading, evergreen shrubs near the pool margin may also play a part.

Fruit and Vegetables. Fruit and vegetable quarters warrant as careful planning as the flower garden, though they rarely get it. You may think that you have no room for either, but I would suggest that you consider the matter further before coming to a final decision. There can be no doubt that fresh vegetables and fruits add greatly to the pleasure of a garden, and can be a considerable convenience. You must also take into account the fact that by using dwarfing rootstocks it is now possible to grow quite an extensive collection of apples and pears in a small space. Cordon or espalier fruit trees can make an attractive permanent screen between one part of the garden and another, while fan-trained plums and cherries may be almost as decorative as flowering climbers on some of your walls or fences.

Unless you have plenty of ground at your disposal you will probably be well advised not to grow any but early potatoes and to make no attempt to supply the kitchen with vegetables throughout the year. But these are not arguments against the inclusion of any vegetables, for even in small gardens it may be possible to find a corner for parsley, mint and thyme, and at least one bed in

which to grow crisp summer salads. Do not forget that there are few vegetables or fruits that will thrive in the shade. Notable exceptions are summer spinach and Morello cherries, but even these do not relish the dense shade and drip caused by large overhanging trees. So if you do decide to have a vegetable garden or a small orchard, choose a good open spot and one that is not likely to be affected at a later date by neighbouring trees.

A Place for Greenhouse and Frame. Later on you may require a greenhouse or frame. The former will almost certainly need to be in a sunny position – tender ferns are practically the only greenhouse plants that require permanent shade. Should there be room for several frames, it may be wise to have one in the shade for cuttings, cyclamen corms during the summer and similar purposes, but if only one frame is to be built it should get plenty of sunlight. Shade, when needed, can be provided artificially.

Greenhouses are of two principal types – lean-to and span-roofed. The former must be built against a wall – for preference a wall with a southerly or south-westerly aspect – while the latter are placed in the open. It is an advantage if the ridge bar of a span-roofed house can run north and south, for then each side will get an approximately equal share of direct sunlight.

There are also now some circular or octagonal greenhouses which require no particular orientation and because of their shape offer interesting possibilities as ornamental as well as utilitarian structures.

Yet other possibilities are the conservatory, garden room and house extension, all of which may be used as living rooms as well as places in which to cultivate plants. Since they are usually attached to the house it may be possible to heat and light them directly from the domestic system.

It is possible that you will decide not to install a greenhouse or frame in your new garden for some considerable time to come, but that is no reason for ignoring them altogether when you are preparing your plan. If you do not make due provision for them at the outset it may be very difficult to place them satisfactorily later on.

Left: Containers planted with bright annuals blend well with a modern patio, providing much colour in a small area

Right: Trained fruit trees used as screens can be as decorative as many climbing plants

CHAPTER 4

Levelling and Marking Out

How to obtain true levels – Remove surface soil first – Dry walls for terraces – Steps – Marking out right angles – Circles and ovals – Irregular outlines

Having decided upon a plan for the garden, your next step will be to carry it out. For this some elementary understanding of the simplest principles of levelling and surveying are, if not essential, at least helpful. Quick but reliable methods of marking out right angles or drawing circles, ovals, and ellipses will enable you to complete a job so well that it will bear comparison with the work of professional garden architects.

First, about levelling: I would repeat again what has already been said in the preceding chapter – namely, that sloping ground is not necessarily a disadvantage. There are times when it is even better than level ground – as, for example, when a rock garden is to be made. But it is essential that all lawns that are to be used for games should be absolutely level, and it is also advisable to terrace ground if it slopes so steeply that it would be difficult to carry out ordinary cultivation such as digging, hoeing and grass cutting.

How to Obtain True Levels. The simplest method of obtaining levels on very uneven ground is with a set of three or more 'boning rods', a 10-ft. straight-sided plank, a plumb-bob, and a spirit level. A boning rod is simply a 6-ft. piece of straight timber sharpened at one end with a T-piece nailed across the other end. A nick or saw cut is made in the timber 1 ft. from the point. To level any given piece of ground, find what appears to be the lowest part and drive in one of the boning rods vertically until the nick is just level with the soil. Then drive in a second rod 9 ft. away and place the straight-sided plank on edge across the two T-pieces. Rest the spirit level on top of the plank and raise or lower

the second boning rod till the bubble shows that the plank is dead level. The rods should be checked from time to time with the plumb-bob to make certain that both are vertical. Now by sighting across the tops of the two T-pieces a level can be obtained right across the plot in this direction and further rods can be driven in at any convenient point. It is wise to take levels in two or three directions.

By measuring upwards from the nick in the upright to soil level you can ascertain the difference in levels between various points and decide upon a mean to which the whole plot shall be levelled. In evenly sloping land this mean can be found by dividing the difference in level between the highest and lowest points by two, but if the ground consists of a number of unequal mounds and depressions allowance must be made for this. Where the differences in level are only slight, long boning rods can be replaced by short stakes driven into the ground at 8- or 9-ft. intervals and levelled with the aid of the spirit level and straight-edged plank.

Remove Surface Soil Before Levelling. When levelling ground, never dig out the surface soil from the highest point and tip it on top of the existing soil lower down. This would give one part of the garden an extra ration of fertile top-spit soil at the expense of another part. Soil to the depth of at least 1 ft. must first be removed and stacked on one side. Then it will be at hand as a topdressing when the work of levelling the lower layers has been completed.

Dry Walls for Terraces. If the level of the ground varies greatly and the land has to be terraced for some particular purpose, it will be necessary to devise some method of retaining the soil in the terraces. Probably the simplest method is to have a steep bank of soil joining each successive level, but there are some severe drawbacks. If such banks are covered with grass they are extremely difficult to mow, though the advent of the air-cushion mower has eased this problem. If the banks are planted the soil may be washed down during heavy rain storms. One possible way out of this difficulty is to treat the whole bank as a sort of rock garden on rather more formal lines than usual, with stones set in groups or diagonal lines across the bank in such a way that nowhere is there an unobstructed slope of soil from top to bottom. These stones, if well bedded in, will help to hold the soil up until the plants fill it with roots and so bind it together. Rock banks can be most effective, and on page 22 I have shown such a bank planted with heathers.

Another effective method of holding up terraces is to build what are known as dry walls between one level and the next. This is simply a wall which is built of unmortared stones. Such constructions are freely used in many upland parts of the country for agricultural purposes, and in time they become most attractive, because numerous plants grow in

(1) Levelling ground using pegs, a levelling board and spirit level. Further pegs are inserted and driven in to the level of the first, and so on across the plot. Soil is then added or taken away until all the pegs are covered to the same depth

(2) Measuring differences in level. This can be done with a line and spirit level, but if the slope is steep a board and spirit level can be used in several stages, in which case the difference in level is the sum of the heights

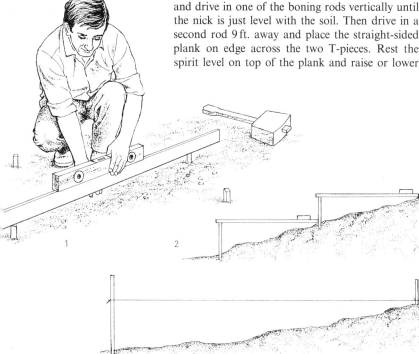

the crevices between the stones and conceal them.

Dry walls require rather careful construction if they are to be really secure. It is easiest to work with stones that have been roughly shaped, though it is quite possible to construct a wall with any largish stones that come to hand. The really essential thing is to start with some big stones for a foundation and to bed these firmly into the soil; moreover, each stone should be given a slight backward and downward slope, and this should be continued throughout the construction, so that all the stones tend to bind together by reason of their own weight. If the wall has to hold up a great weight of soil it may be advisable to give a slight backward slope to the whole structure as well as to each individual stone in it. Technically this slope is known as a batter. Still further strength can be given by constructing buttresses every few yards. These should have a much more pronounced slope than the wall itself.

Good soil should be rammed into all the crevices. It will not only serve instead of mortar and help the stones to bed firmly one upon another, but will also give plants a much better chance of establishing themselves both in the face of the wall and on top of it. It is possible to plant small things in a wall after it is completed, but it is easier to build the plants into position as one goes along, laying the roots in position on one stone with a little soil around them and then placing the next stone on top so that the plant is held securely.

Steps. Differences in level usually involve the construction of steps. These should be in keeping with the surroundings and, if practicable, should be faced with the same material as that used for paths or terraces in the vicinity. It is quite easy to build up concrete steps with the aid of boards laid on edge to act as 'shuttering' to hold the concrete up until it dries. Curved steps can be formed with strips of plywood as shuttering, as these can be bent easily to any desired shape. Sometimes steps are formed of grass. This can look delightful in the right surroundings, but suffers from the disadvantage that grass wears badly and grass steps are rather difficult to keep in order. Grass steps and also those formed of gravel should always be held up by 'risers' of wood to keep the edges firm.

Marking out Right Angles. In order to mark out accurately the outline of beds, borders, lawns, and other features you will require a supply of strong wooden pegs about 18 in. in length and plenty of stout white twine. I recommend white as it is so much easier to see than coloured twine.

Right angles usually play an important part in garden design. You can mark them out accurately in the following manner. First stretch a line to mark one side of the angle (lawn edge, bed, or border). At the corner drive in a peg and attach it to a piece of string exactly 3 ft. in length. From the peg measure along the base line 4 ft., drive in a second peg, and attach a piece of string 5 ft. in length. Draw the loose ends of the 3-ft. and 5-ft. strings together and at the point at which they meet drive in a third peg. A line stretched between the first and third peg will make a right angle with the base line.

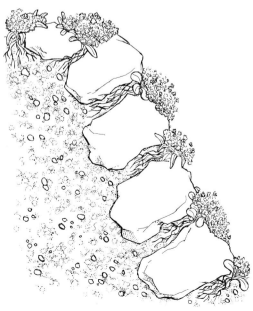

Top: A well-planted dry stone wall can be an enormous asset to a garden. The slight backward slope to the wall helps to support the weight of the soil behind

Left: Section of a dry wall supporting a bank. The foundation rocks should be bedded well into the soil and the stones set in place with a slight backward slope for added strength. Good soil rammed into the crevices will aid the binding of the stones and provide a home for plants

Marking out a circle and an oval. Stout twine, pegs and a pointed marker stick for scratching the outline are all that is required. The method is described in the text

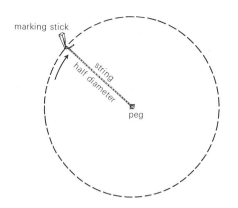

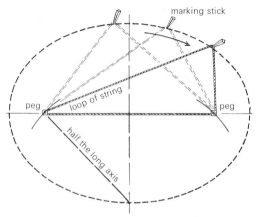

Circles and Ovals. A circle is very simple to make, as it is only necessary to drive in a peg at the centre, attach to it a piece of string half the diameter of the required circle and, with the string held taut, scratch out a circle with a pointed stick or indicate it with a trickle of powdered lime.

An oval bed is a little more difficult. First peg down two lines bisecting each other at right angles to mark the extreme length and breadth of the bed. Then the two focal points are found by attaching a string half the length of the oval to one of the pegs marking the extreme width and drawing the free end round so that it touches the length line first on one side and then on the other of the width line. Strong pegs are driven in at each of these points. A piece of twine twice the length of the distance from one of these pegs to the further extremity of the bed is then knotted into a loop, thrown around the two focal pegs and, with the twine held taut, the outline of the oval can be scratched in the soil with a sharp-pointed stick held inside the looped twine.

You can make many other shapes and designs by variations on these simple basic methods.

Irregular Outlines. These cannot be drawn geometrically. Instead you must mark them out roughly with small sticks and then outline them more definitely with finely powdered lime poured from a bottle or through a narrow-necked funnel. Then if the curve does not please you it is easy to brush the lime away and mark out a different line.

Constructing paved steps. (1) Hardcore or rubble is used for filling in the base. A garden line indicates the angle of rise. (2) Cementing bricks to form the first riser. The support for the step consists of broken paving or flat stones bedded on cement. (3) Paving slabs are laid on the prepared base and cemented into place. A spirit level is used to check that they are level. (4) The completed steps. A slight overhang to the paving stones gives a better finish

CHAPTER 5

How Much Shall I Need?

Measuring superficial areas – Estimating bulk – Gravel – Paving slabs – Walling stone – Soil for filling – Concrete for pools – Volume of water in pools – Turves – Estimating plants

At this stage of your efforts as an amateur landscape gardener you will probably find that an elementary knowledge of quantity estimation – that is to say, the calculation of the amount of material required for any particular purpose – will be of service. It is true that most of the supply firms will gladly give you information on this and allied matters, but it is useful to be able to work out the probable quantities required in advance and so gain an idea as to the cost of any suggested scheme. Here, then, are some simple rules and data that may be used as a basis for calculations.

Measuring Superficial Areas. A measurement should be made across the widest and the narrowest part of the plot and the two figures added and divided by two. Two similar measurements are made across the greatest and least length of the plot and treated in the same manner. The average width and average length obtained by this means are multiplied together to give the approximate superficial area – in square feet if the measurements were in feet, or in square yards if the measurements were in yards. Square feet can be reduced to square yards by dividing by nine, and square yards can be converted into square feet by multiplying by nine.

Estimating Bulk. Measurements of capacity or bulk are made in cubic feet or cubic yards. Three, instead of two, sets of measurements must be obtained – one for average length, one for average breadth, and one for average depth – but these are made in the manner just described. All three are then multiplied together, the answer being in cubic feet if the original measurements were in feet, and in cubic yards if

they were in yards. Cubic feet can be reduced to cubic yards by dividing by twenty-seven.

Gravel. A ton of gravel contains from 19 to 20 cu. ft., but gravel is usually sold not by the ton but by the 'yard' (i.e., cubic yard). A thickness of from 2 to 3 in. of gravel is required for surfacing a path, and at this rate a ton of gravel will cover from 9 to 13 sq. yd., while a 'yard' of gravel will cover from 12 to 18 sq. yd.

Paving Slabs. Crazy paving is proportionately heavier than gravel. A ton contains from 13 to 14 cu. ft., and the covering area depends upon the thickness. Usually 'crazy' is sold in two grades, 'thin' varying from $\frac{3}{4}$ to $1\frac{1}{2}$ in. in thickness, and 'thick' from $1\frac{1}{2}$ to $2\frac{1}{2}$ in. thick. The former has a covering capacity of from 14 to 16 sq. yd. and the latter from 8 to 9 sq. yd. per ton. York paving slabs cover 10 to 11 sq. yd. per ton. There are also many artificial slabs available and these are usually sold at so much each or per hundred.

Walling Stone. Walling stone may be natural or artificial. A usual thickness for natural blocks is 6 in. and this has a covering capacity of about 3 to 4 sq. yd. per ton but artificial walling stone is most likely to be priced per hundred and manufacturers should state the covering capacity. Failing this, it can be calculated by measuring the face to be exposed. For example a stone with a face 6 in. by 4 in. will cover 24 sq. in. so 6 bricks will be required for each square foot of wall and 54 for each square yard.

Soil for Filling. Soil for filling up beds, etc. varies in bulk according to its texture and the amount of water that it contains. Sandy soils are naturally the lightest and may reach 26 or 27 cu. ft. to the ton, while heavy clay barely touches 18 cu. ft. for the

APPROXIMATE QUANTITIES OF MATERIAL REQUIRED FOR 10 FT. LENGTH OF PATH

WIDTH OF PATH	2 FT.	$2\frac{1}{2}$ FT.	3 FT.	4 FT.	6 FT.
Bricks (flat)	71	89	107	143	214
Bricks (on edge)	107	134	160	213	320
	CWT.	CWT.	CWT.	CWT.	CWT.
Crazy pavement, $\frac{3}{4}$ to $1\frac{1}{2}$ in.	3	$3\frac{3}{4}$	$4\frac{1}{2}$	6	9
Crazy pavement, $1\frac{1}{2}$ to $2\frac{1}{2}$ in.	5	6	7	9	14
York paving slabs	$4\frac{1}{2}$	$5\frac{1}{4}$	6	9	12
Gravel (2 in. thick)	3 ($\frac{1}{6}$ yd.)	4 ($\frac{1}{5}$ yd.)	5 ($\frac{1}{5}$ yd.)	7 ($\frac{1}{4}$ yd.)	10 ($\frac{2}{5}$ yd.)
Gravel (3 in. thick)	5 ($\frac{1}{5}$ yd.)	6 ($\frac{2}{9}$ yd.)	7 ($\frac{1}{4}$ yd.)	10 ($\frac{2}{5}$ yd.)	15 ($\frac{3}{5}$ yd.)
Concrete (2 in. thick)					
Gravel	3	$3\frac{3}{4}$	$4\frac{1}{2}$	6	9
Sand	1	$1\frac{1}{4}$	$1\frac{1}{2}$	2	3
Cement	1	$1\frac{1}{4}$	$1\frac{1}{2}$	2	3
Concrete (3 in. thick)					
Gravel	$4\frac{1}{2}$	$5\frac{1}{4}$	6	9	13
Sand	$1\frac{1}{2}$	$1\frac{2}{3}$	2	3	$4\frac{1}{4}$
Cement	$1\frac{1}{2}$	$1\frac{2}{3}$	2	3	$4\frac{1}{4}$

A steep slope can be transformed by the construction of a series of level terraces with supporting walls to create a garden of unusual interest

same weight. The average for good fibrous loam is about 23 or 24 cu. ft. Peat varies considerably in weight, light sphagnum peats giving about 9 cu. ft. per cwt., closer sedge peats between 6 and 7 cu. ft. per cwt. Leafmould is still lighter, though it varies considerably according to its age. Some of these materials may be sold by the 'load' instead of by the ton, in which case you can estimate the volume of a 'load' as approximately 27 cu. ft. (1 cu. yd.).

Concrete for Pools. Later on, if you decide to make a pool, you may need to calculate the quantities of gravel, sand, and cement required for preparing concrete. A rough but simple and reasonably accurate method of doing this when using base concrete consisting of 3 parts of gravel, 1 part of sand, and 1 part of cement is to provide enough gravel to supply the whole required bulk and then add the sand and cement as extras. Their bulk will be lost in mixing and the shrinkage that takes place as the concrete dries.

The bulk of fully dried concrete required for a rectangular pool is obtained by multiplying the length by the breadth and this by the thickness of the concrete. This gives the volume of concrete for the bottom. Twice the length is then added to twice the width, the figure so obtained is multiplied by the depth and the result is multiplied again by the thickness of the concrete. This gives the volume of concrete for the sides. The sum of the two calculations is then added together to give the total volume of concrete.

A circular pool is a little more difficult. The volume of concrete for the bottom is obtained by measuring from the centre to the side and multiplying this by itself. The result is then multiplied by $3\frac{1}{7}$ and this, in turn, by the thickness of the concrete. The volume of concrete for the sides is obtained by doubling the measurement from the centre of the pool to the edge, multiplying this by $3\frac{1}{7}$, this in turn by the depth of the pool, and the result by the thickness of the concrete. The sum of the two calculations is then added together as before.

The simplest way of dealing with an irregular pool is to measure out a circle or rectangle which approximately covers it and calculate the volume of concrete for the bottom on this basis. The length of the sides can be measured with string.

Do not forget that all measurements must be made in the same units – yards, feet or inches. You must not have some measurements in yards, some in feet, and some in inches.

Nowadays most small pools are bought ready made in glass fibre or rigid plastic or are lined with special plastic or rubber sheeting. When ordering sheets for this purpose they must be in one piece sufficiently large to cover base and sides of the pool and extend at least a foot over the edge so that they can be firmly anchored in place and concealed with soil, paving slabs or rocks.

Volume of Water in Pools. The volume of water in a rectangular pool or tank is obtained by multiplying together the length, breadth, and depth, all in feet, and then multiplying the result by $6\frac{1}{4}$. This gives the volume in gallons. For a circular pool or tank the measurement from the centre to the side (in feet) is multiplied by itself, and the result is multiplied by $3\frac{1}{7}$. The figure so obtained is multiplied by the depth (in feet), this giving the volume in cubic feet. To obtain the volume in gallons multiply by $6\frac{1}{4}$ as before.

Turves for Lawns. Turves are sold at so much per hundred and are almost invariably cut in strips 1 ft. wide and 3 ft. long. One hundred of these will cover $33\frac{1}{3}$ sq. yd. of ground. The very best turves for bowling greens, etc., are sometimes cut in 1-ft. squares, as there is then less variation in thickness and it is consequently possible to lay them more evenly. Such turves have a covering capacity of approximately 11 sq. yd. per hundred.

Estimating for Plants. When planning herbaceous borders an average of four plants per square yard may be adopted as a rough guide to requirements, though, of course, in actual practice the distance of planting will vary from the front to the back of the border as the smaller marginal plants can be set much more closely than the larger kinds used in the background. It is even more difficult to generalise about shrubs since they vary so greatly in ultimate spread but a rough idea of the number required could be based on an average spacing of 3 ft., i.e. 1 sq. yd. per plant.

You will find further information of a similar character in relation to bulbs, fruit trees, etc., in the chapters devoted to those plants.

CHAPTER 6

Garden Carpentry and Masonry

Choice of wood – Arches and pergolas – Arbours and summerhouses – Screens and trellises – The potting shed – The tool shed – Garden frames – A greenhouse – Glazing – Greenhouse staging – Seed trays – Window boxes

The ability to do some constructional work will facilitate and cheapen the job of making and maintaining a garden. I propose to deal with the whole matter in this chapter.

All garden carpentry has to stand a lot of wear and every kind of weather, and it is a waste of money and labour to buy wood which will not stand up to the elements. Even supposing that your early attempts are not fully satisfactory and structures have to be refashioned after a few years, you will still be able to use the good wood again, whereas poor wood will be a loss under any circumstances.

Choice of Wood. For arches, pergolas, and screens many people prefer to use 'rustic' wood – that is, poles with the bark left on. If this is favoured, be certain to obtain larch poles which have been felled during the winter. These will retain their bark for several seasons, but, if cut at any time from early spring till the leaves fall, the bark will work loose in a short time and, quite apart from the untidy appearance, a number of pests will certainly find shelter beneath it. Silver birch, ash, pine and hazel poles are sometimes used, but even when cut in winter none is so satisfactory as larch. If these woods are much easier to obtain you will find it best to scrape off all the bark before starting the carpentry. This can be done with a stout knife and spokeshave, after which the wood should be treated with a preservative.

Personally, I prefer squared timber and rely on obtaining the desired effect from the climbers draping themselves around it. It only takes a couple of years to clothe an arch or pergola of ordinary size. Oak, teak and western red cedar are the pick of the woods for outdoor work. They need no preservatives and weather delightfully. Unfortunately they are not cheap but owing to their lasting properties are economical in the long run. Good quality yellow deal, preferably creosoted under pressure or otherwise protected against decay is suitable for pergolas and arches. Frames, greenhouses and any other closed structures inside which plants are to be grown are more satisfactory if painted, as creosote gives off fumes which injure soft growth.

Arches and Pergolas. The width and height of an arch or pergola will naturally be governed by the position for which it is intended, but you should remember that the space originally occupied will be considerably exceeded when the timbers are smothered in foliage and flowers a few years after planting. A radius of 15 in. all round each upright is a modest estimate for plant growth. Spiny rose

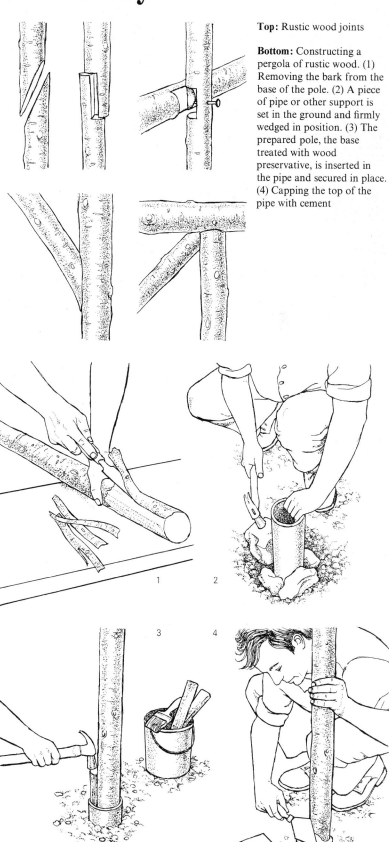

Top: Rustic wood joints

Bottom: Constructing a pergola of rustic wood. (1) Removing the bark from the base of the pole. (2) A piece of pipe or other support is set in the ground and firmly wedged in position. (3) The prepared pole, the base treated with wood preservative, is inserted in the pipe and secured in place. (4) Capping the top of the pipe with cement

shoots should be given more room and wisterias require a pergola of extra height because of the hanging flower trails which can be 2 ft. in length.

The uprights should extend at least 18 in. below soil level. They are less likely to rot and will be considerably firmer if placed on a footing of concrete and partially embedded in the same material or in brickbats. You will find that slightly charring the end of rustic wood is more satisfactory than creosoting it, but creosote or other wood preservative serves well for squared timber. The diameter of the wood used will depend upon the size of the arch and the distance apart of the uprights, but uprights should never be less than 3 in. in diameter or 3 by 2 in. if squared. Up to a point the larger the wood used the better will be the effect, and it is usual to employ stronger timber than is absolutely necessary in order to ensure an appearance of solidity. In any case you will probably tend greatly to underestimate the weight of well-grown climbing plants, so it is wise to spend a little extra and be on the safe side.

The design must fit in with that followed in other woodwork in the vicinity, but whatever form the arch or pergola takes it is wise to remember that any structure with braces – that is, wood arranged in triangles – is considerably stronger than one of similar material unbraced. In an arch the bracing can take the form of slanting cross-pieces joining two uprights and of corner struts. The wood may be joined simply by nailing one piece on top of another, but this joint relies for its strength solely upon the the nails and does not usually give a good finish. Half-lap joints are easily chiselled out, and if fitted carefully take little strength from the wood cut into. It is impossible to make satisfactory joints between two curved poles or a flat and curved surface, and all joints in rustic wood must either have both faces made square or one must be scooped out to receive the other. All nails must be well galvanized and of correct length, as galvanized nails cannot be bent over satisfactorily.

Arbours and Summerhouses. Many arbours are, from the point of view of construction, little more than deep arches filled in at the back and supplied with a seat. This form is generally intended to be more or less completely covered with climbers. For this purpose the climbers should either be thornless and spineless and capable of withstanding clipping or the seat should not be built into the woodwork of the back and sides but should be a separate structure. It is wise to make the back of such an arbour with plenty of strong cross-pieces on to which the growths can be trained securely.

The ground under and immediately in front of the seat must be well drained, and can with advantage be paved to give a dry foot rest and withstand the heavy wear it is likely to receive. A shady site under the drip of trees is particularly liable to become waterlogged.

If you decide to build yourself a more elaborate summerhouse, the materials used should, as far as possible, be chosen to suit the style of the house or other neighbouring buildings. Some of the most satisfactory summerhouses are being made of western red cedar, a practically indestructible Canadian wood which weathers a delightful grey, and which is so soft and unobtrusive that it will harmonize with almost any other material. Unlike oak, western red cedar is very easy to work. A shelter built in this wood can be roofed appropriately with shingles (wood tiles) of the same material.

You will find it well worth the time and money to concrete the foundation of a summerhouse, for rot at the base in winter does more to shorten the life of wood than any other factor.

The framework of the walls is easily assembled on the ground out of 2 by 2 in. or 3 by 2 in. timber, the uprights being 16 in. apart. All braces should run right through, the uprights being cut to fit them.

If no braces are used, it is wise to mortise and tenon the principal uprights. Diagonal tongued and grooved boarding on the inner wall makes a strong job, and can be used instead of bracing. Feather-edged weather boarding is suitable for an open arbour or summerhouse intended solely for use in fine, warm weather, but if the structure is to form a playhouse for children in all weathers you will be well advised to use some form of rabbeted (grooved) siding or storm boarding and fit the openings with removable sashes or folding doors. The floor joists should either be laid on thoroughly creosoted sleepers or small brick piles, and must be well ventilated below. The floor can be built first and the walls erected on it, but it is really better for the joists to extend into the walls and be nailed to the uprights. This makes a slightly stronger job and means that any floor board can be removed without disturbing the walls.

Unless the roof extends well over the walls or is thatched it is always worth while providing a gutter running to a drainage sump or rainwater butt, for the drainage from even a small roof can make the walls very damp. Iron roofs are to be avoided as unless expensively lined they make the summerhouse very hot in summer and noisy in every shower and give so little shelter from cold in winter that the house will not even serve as covering for sprouting potatoes. If shingles are used they can be laid directly on open battens, but must be fixed with galvanized or copper nails, as should all cedar or oak since the acid in the wood soon eats into iron nails.

In very modern surroundings summerhouses constructed largely or wholly of corrugated PVC or other plastic sheeting can look well. This is an easy material with which to work; it is long lasting and light and can be nailed or screwed to any desired framework. Some manufacturers offer plans for its use in the garden in various ways.

Screens and Trellises. A light screen is most simply constructed out of expanding or square trellis, bought ready-made, fixed to strong upright posts, well secured in concrete below soil level. The whole is made considerably more rigid by the addition of a firm head bar of 2-in. squared wood, or larger according to the height of the screen and distance apart of the uprights. As such trellis is almost invariably of deal it requires either thorough creosoting or, better still, painting with a good outside paint.

If the screen has to act as a windbreak and carry heavy creepers, trellis alone is not strong enough to withstand the wind pressure when fully clothed, and a stouter structure built up with squared wood adequately braced will prove well worth its cost.

Even stronger and more permanent are screens made from the precast pierced concrete screening blocks available in a variety of patterns and colours. These are particularly suitable for gardens designed in a modern style. The screen blocks must be cemented together with a good smooth-working mortar (3 parts sharp sand to 1 part cement is one popular formula) and care should be taken to keep the faces of the blocks quite clean while erection proceeds. Special blocks are available with which to build pilasters at the corners into which the blocks are slotted and pilasters can also be used about 10 ft. apart to stiffen high screens or to break up long ones into a series of panels, but this will depend to some extent on the character of the blocks used. Manufacturer's instructions should be obtained whenever possible and also all blocks and pilasters used should be of the same type to ensure correct bonding.

The Potting Shed. In all but very small gardens a tool or potting shed is likely to be required. The construction of this differs little from that of a summerhouse if it is to stand isolated, though you will probably find it most convenient to build this shed as a lean-to structure against the garden or outhouse wall or abutting the north end of a greenhouse. (There is no reason why the shed should not be built at once and the greenhouse added later on.) If you have a choice of site, one which allows the window to be built on the north side is an advantage, as it gives a more uniform light. This is a great advantage when sprouting potatoes.

It is well to make a good job of a potting shed, for if the walls are stoutly built of 3- by 2-in. framing covered on both sides the shed will suffer much less from fluctuations in temperature. This is important both in summer and winter, for you will be much annoyed in warm weather by a close heat in which seedlings flag faster than you can prick them out, and during the winter it is most useful to have a practically frost-proof place (except, perhaps, in exceptionally cold spells) in which root crops, gladioli, and dahlias can be stored and potatoes set to sprout.

The bench should be built of good tongued and grooved 1-in. floor boards, supported on a stout framework of not less than 2- by 2-in. deal. It is best to have this directly under the window, and to have the sides boarded up. Below the bench bins for loam, leafmould, and peat should be provided, and suitable storage made for flower pots and seed trays. The divisions can easily be constructed of plain or match-boarding.

The bench must be wide enough to accommodate a couple of seed boxes (or a box and several pots), a couple of small piles of compost (fine and coarse), and a pile of broken crocks for drainage. It is useful to have a small shelf somewhere close to hand on

Top and left: Modern precast walling blocks make excellent screens, and are available in many attractive designs

Bottom left: Setting a wall screen block in place. It is important to check frequently with a spirit level to ensure that the blocks are straight

which to keep plant labels and pencil and any packets of seeds in use at the time.

Where the greenhouse is not immediately adjoining the potting shed it is helpful to have a nest of racks to take seed trays that have been filled with compost and watered ready for seed sowing on the following day. If this rack is made with removable slatted shelves it can be utilized for potato sprouting by removing alternate shelves to ensure adequate lighting of the tubers.

It is unwise to have any felted roof with an angle of less than 30 degrees, while a tile roof is more satisfactory at 45 degrees unless special low-pitch tiles are used. With lower slopes the water does not get away fast enough and creeps back under the overlap, frequently rotting the wood below.

The Tool Shed. The outer framework of a tool shed need differ little in construction from a potting shed, though there is no reason for a north window, unless the shed is to be used as a workroom. Inside it is wise to build in certain fitments at the start or you may find the shed will develop into a lumber-room. On one wall a number of suitable long hooks or nails should be placed to hang all spades, forks, hoes, and rakes as well as smaller tools such as trowels, dibbers, and shears, and a permanent open space should be assigned to the mower and roller. If the tool shed is to contain a bench this should be placed below the window. The space beneath can then be fitted with drawers divided up to take wood-work tools and also nails, screws, layering pins, labels, secateurs, and other small gardening accessories. If you prefer you could, of course, store these in tins or boxes on shelves. A tin of grease and a rag should also be handy, for rust-free tools save an immense amount of labour.

Canes and stakes are apt to become a menace if you merely stand them in any corner, but the problem is easily solved if you keep them in an old umbrella stand or a couple of small barrels.

Garden Frames. Unless you are a first-rate amateur carpenter I would not advise you to attempt to make frame lights, which require really skilled work on the joints. But as unglazed frame lights can be bought separately there is no reason why the rest of the frame should not be made to fit the standard lights. Teak and western red cedar are again the most satisfactory woods to use and require no painting or preservative, but because of their cost many frames are made of good yellow deal well painted both inside and out with at least three coats of a reliable outdoor paint.

The point at which many amateurs fail is the angle of the frame light. There is a tendency to make this too flat, with the result that water creeps back between the panes and drips on to the plants inside. An angle of 8 degrees is the smallest that can be considered safe. Another common mistake is to make the frame sides too thin. Wood of less than $\frac{3}{4}$-in. thickness will afford very little protection from frost. An alternative is to construct double walls of thinner wood and pack the space between them with thermal insulation. The wood must be well seasoned, and all joints properly made or draughts will result.

A brick or concrete base is most satisfactory, but if you cannot use these materials dig out a trench at least 1 ft. wide and 9 in. deep, fill it with clinker or brick rubble and embed the edge of the frame in it.

A Greenhouse. Most amateurs would also be foolish to try to make their own greenhouse, especially in these days when machine-made ones can be bought quite cheaply. Aluminium greenhouses are, like wooden ones, sold in sections ready to be bolted together. Aluminium needs no painting and, as the glazing bars are narrow, these houses let in a lot of light.

If the sides are of wood this must be of adequate thickness or should be lined inside with asbestos sheeting or be packed with thermal insulation as described for frames. The formation of an absolutely level site of concrete or brickwork is essential. If you wish to grow plants in the soil within the house the concrete or brick can be confined to a 9-in. wide footing and a slat path can be made, but if staging or shelving of a permanent nature is to be fitted it may be wiser to spread at least 3 in. of concrete all over the site.

Glazing. Frames and greenhouses must be glazed with best 21-oz. horticultural glass free from bubbles. The panes of glass are sometimes fixed with small metal nails, known as sprigs, but this is not absolutely essential if putty is spread thinly in the rabbets of the sash bars and the glass is gently but firmly pressed down on to it. More putty should then be spread in the angle of the bar and the glass to prevent any water from lodging there. One disadvantage of ordinary putty is that it tends to get hard and causes the glass to crack owing to the difference in temperatures inside and outside the structure causing uneven expansion. Nowadays there are on the market several reliable plastic or bituminous putty substitutes. The glass in aluminium greenhouses is usually fixed with spring clips, some with rubber seals to make a tighter heat conserving joint.

Plastic-covered greenhouses of various types have so far proved more popular with professional than with private gardeners. Flexible plastic sheeting needs to be replaced after two or at most three years. Glasshouses can also be lined with plastic sheeting in order to conserve heat but plastic of any kind tends to cause heavy condensation which can be a problem.

Greenhouse Staging. Even light staging should not be constructed on a framework of wood less than 2 in. square or the weight of pots may be too great for it. A slatted top is easily made of 1- by 2-in. planed battens fixed from $\frac{1}{2}$ to 1 in. apart. If these are of deal you must paint them like the frames. Wood for shelves should be at least 1 in. thick; $1\frac{1}{4}$ in. will not be too much if big plants are to be supported on them.

Metal staging, usually aluminium alloy, will last a lifetime with little maintenance. Staging is often required only at certain times of year, e.g. in spring for seedlings and growing plants and in autumn to display chrysanthemums in flower. It is then

Top and top right: Climbing plants trained on a wooden trellis form a decorative screen, and a trellis set at right angles to a wall can form an attractive mural corner, as shown above with the sweet peas and kniphofia

Right: Slatted wood staging can be made for the greenhouse from 1- by 2-in. battens fixed from $\frac{1}{2}$ to 1 in. apart

convenient if it can be dismantled or folded up and stored.

Solid staging is almost always built up on corrugated cement sheets and calls for little carpentry. It is necessary for tropical plants that need a humid atmosphere, and is useful in a house that is used principally for propagation or for the cultivation of cucumbers. It is also useful if capillary-bench watering is to be adopted, or special plastic trays can be purchased for this purpose together with the necessary apparatus to keep the aggregate spread in the trays constantly moist but never flooded. Pot plants stood on this moist base suck up water from it as they require it and overhead watering is only necessary to start the capillary action. Alternatively, use capillary matting.

Seed Trays and Window Boxes. The great thing in making seed trays and window boxes is to allow plenty of drainage holes. In the seed boxes this is most easily accomplished by leaving a space of about $\frac{1}{4}$ in. between the pieces of wood when nailing. With window boxes it is more satisfactory to make all joints flush and to drill a row or two of holes in the base. Window boxes must be very securely fixed in position or nasty accidents are liable to occur.

Both trays and boxes can be purchased ready formed in plastic and these have the advantage of being light, durable and pest and disease resistant.

CHAPTER 7

Path Making

*Choice of material – Width and direction –
Foundation – Crazy v. rectangular paving slabs –
Setting in sand – Setting in concrete – Brick paths –
Stepping stones – Gravel – Asphalt – Concrete paths*

It is not essential to make paths right at the outset, but there is certainly a great advantage in doing so, for you can then move about freely in the garden whatever the weather. However, path making is a job that can be done just as satisfactorily at one time of the year as another, so if there are strictly seasonal tasks to be done such as lawn making or tree planting before the best period for each has passed, you may well decide to manage without paths for the time being. They can, if necessary, be added during the summer.

Choice of Material. Choice of material is a matter demanding very careful attention. I have already referred to this in Chapter 3, and would particularly stress the selection of material appropriate to the general character of the surroundings. Another important point is that the type of surfacing material chosen should be capable of withstanding the wear to which it will be subjected. For example, thin paving slabs are suitable for a subsidiary path which is not likely to be used a great deal, but are useless for a main walk. Similarly, gravel drives must be considerably thicker than gravel paths, which may vary according to the amount of wear they are likely to get.

Width and Direction. All main paths should be 3 ft. or more in width. Narrower paths are only service-able as byways or tracks for moving about among plants. In the vegetable and fruit quarters paths should always, so far as is possible, be straight, but in the more ornamental parts of the garden curved paths are often preferable. But do not go to the other extreme of making paths that are all un-necessary angles and twists. Remember, above all things, that the main walks may be used quite a lot for wheeling heavy barrow loads of soil and rubbish and moving the lawn mower and roller from shed to lawn, and that you will soon learn to hate a path that doubles the distance you have to cover with every journey.

Foundations. The first essential to any path, no matter what the surfacing material is to be, is a really solid yet well-drained foundation. For this nothing is better than broken clinker or brick rubble, surfaced with finer material of the same kind, to make a smooth, level surface on which the paving slabs or gravel may be laid. If possible, the path should have a steady slope to one point. Absolutely level paths, or those with a series of undulations, are very liable to get waterlogged in patches, no matter what precautions are taken with the drainage.

On wet ground it is always an excellent plan to treat the path also as a land drain by constructing

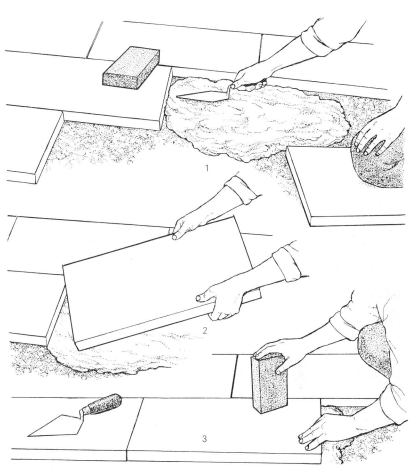

Laying paving slabs for a path or patio surface. (1) Preparing a base of cement. (2) Setting the paving slab on to the prepared base. (3) Tamping the paving slab into place

a deep clinker or rubble-filled soakaway at its lowest point, so encouraging water to pass rapidly through the foundation material and percolate away into the subsoil.

Crazy v. Rectangular Paving Slabs. Crazy paving is most attractive in rustic surroundings, but rather out of place in most suburban gardens. However, it has the advantages of cleanliness, cheapness, and durability, and if suitable creeping plants are established in the crevices between the slabs, it can blend with the rest of the garden in a satisfactory manner.

Rectangular York paving slabs have all the good points of crazy paving and, in addition, a much more dignified appearance. They are ideal for making terraces and wide paths near the house and in the more formal parts of the garden. Imitation paving slabs made of concrete do not weather as attractively as the genuine article, but are consider-ably cheaper and are available in a variety of colours, designs and surface finishes which make them useful for many decorative effects.

Setting in Sand. You can lay either of these paving materials in concrete or in some fine, dry material such as ashes or sand. The latter method has the advantage of cheapness and convenience, and also makes it easier to grow small creeping plants in the crevices between the slabs. It is necessary to have at least a 1-in. deep layer of sifted material into which to bed the slabs, and this must be raked level before starting to set the stones.

Top: For quick results, annuals and bedding plants are most rewarding, giving a summer-long display of colour. Growing in this border are French and African marigolds, *Tagetes signata*, lobelia, sweet alyssum, godetia, petunias, sweet peas and numerous ornamental grasses

Right: *Clematis jackmanii superba* climbing through the leafy growth of a wisteria provides a succession of blooms for many months. The Super Star roses in the foreground are also long flowering

Right: Good ornaments can play an important part in garden decoration. A graceful urn makes a striking focal point against a background of paving

Bottom: Cobblestones in gravel – an unusual path design combining two textures

Each slab must be well bedded into the sand or ash, more of which should be brushed down into the crevices as the work proceeds. The level of the path from one side to the other and also lengthways should be frequently checked with the aid of a spirit level and a straight-edged plank. Irregularities will encourage the formation of surface puddles, and make the path unpleasant and even unsafe to walk on. You will find a heavy, short-handled hammer very useful for tapping the slabs accurately into position, while you should use a trowel to place a little extra sand or sifted ash on any part of the foundation that appears low, or to pack up a slab which may be a little thin at one end. Crazy paving slabs usually have a good deal of clay adhering to them and this should be scraped off before they are laid.

Setting in Concrete. Setting in concrete is a more tedious task, though it undoubtedly results in an even more durable, hard-wearing path. The concrete itself is prepared with 5 parts of builder's sand and 1 part of best Portland cement. These you must mix dry on a hard base. Add water, a little at a time, and turn the heap constantly with a shovel. The concrete is ready for use when it is about the consistency of stiff porridge.

Complete one small section of the path at a time. Throw down sufficient concrete to cover it about 1 in. deep. Spread the concrete evenly with a mason's trowel and bed down the slabs, working a little more concrete into the crevices between them, also with the aid of the trowel. You can leave the final 'pointing' or filling up and smoothing down of the crevices until the foundation layer has solidified. Leave a space here and there in the concrete foundation for planting suitable creeping perennials. Among the best for this purpose are acaenas in variety, cotulas, *Mazus pumilio* and *M. reptans, Arenaria balearica* and *A. caespitosa, Armeria maritima* Vindictive, *Sedum acre aurea, S. lydium, Veronica prostrata* and *Thymus serpyllum* in variety. All these can be purchased in containers from which they can be planted at any time and will require no further attention beyond an occasional trimming up and cutting back if they grow too large.

Brick Paths. Brick paths can be most delightful, particularly if you can obtain some old and well-weathered bricks. These are laid on edge in patterns like parquet flooring, and may either be bedded in sand or set in concrete like paving slabs. But brick has one serious drawback: it gets very slippery in wet weather due to the growth of algae, though these can be kept in check with algicides.

Stepping Stones. In the chapter on garden planning I referred to stepping-stone paths as an excellent method of economizing on space in small gardens where larger paths are not really required – and, let it be added, in many parts of large gardens as well. They are very simple to make, for it is only necessary to obtain some large and rather thick slabs of crazy paving and sink these absolutely flush with the soil. It is desirable, though not essential, to place a shovelful of sharp sand under each slab before bedding it into position. If set in a lawn, be very careful that none of the slabs projects in the least above the surface to avoid risk of damage to the blades of a lawn mower.

Cobbles and Pebbles. Cobbled paths are picturesque and durable but uncomfortable to walk on. However, panels of either cobblestones or large pebbles can often be used very effectively to ornament large areas of paving, as for example on terraces and patios. Further decoration can be given by using pebbles of different colours to form patterns or mosaics. The cobbles or pebbles should always be firmly bedded in concrete as described for paving slabs.

Gravel. If gravel paths are to be a success, it is essential that they should have good foundations of clinkers, brickbats, or other hard rubble. One of the commonest errors is to place a 3- or 4-in. layer of gravel directly on top of the soil without any preparation other than a thorough treading or rolling. No matter how solid this foundation may seem at the time of laying, the gravel will gradually become mixed with it, more particularly during spells of alternating frost and rain, when the soil inevitably becomes loosened by the constant expansion and contraction of the water in it.

Do not make the mistake of rolling the foundation layer too closely and firmly before spreading gravel. It is quite correct to ram the larger clinkers or brickbats in as tightly as may be at the outset, but the smaller pieces on top of these should not be rolled. The reason is that to obtain a hard-wearing surface, it is essential that the gravel should bind closely with the foundation material. If the surface of the latter is too tightly packed before any gravel has been spread, it will be impossible to secure this necessary binding between surface and foundation.

Gravel for path making should usually be of a kind that binds together when rolled. Shingle from a sea beach does not make a good path because it will never bind. It remains loose and is tiring to walk on and needs constant raking if it is to be kept in good order. Small 'pea' gravel and stone chippings can be satisfactory, especially in rock gardens and other places where a natural-looking track is more appropriate than more obviously man-made paths.

When you have spread the gravel as evenly as possible over the foundation layer, rake it smooth and then if it is of the binding kind roll it well with the heaviest roller you can obtain. If the gravel happens to be very dry, you should water it thoroughly before starting to roll. It must be fairly wet if it is to bind properly. Keep a sharp look out for any hollows while you are rolling, putting them right at once by raking them loose again and spreading a little more gravel over them.

Asphalt. Asphalt as a paving material is only suitable for entirely utilitarian parts of the garden, and should never be admitted to the ornamental sections. Asphalt can be purchased ready for laying, in which case it is only necessary to spread it evenly over the consolidated hardcore and roll it. Alternatively small gravel can be spread and a

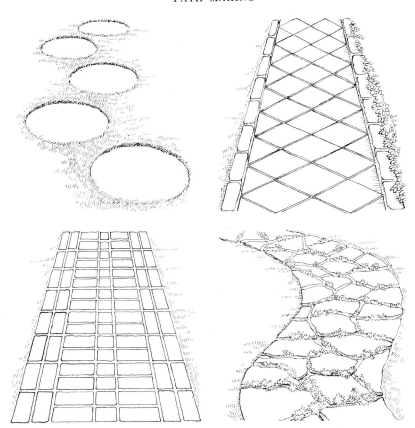

cold bitumen solution poured over it to bind it. Manufacturer's instructions must be followed.

Concrete Paths. Concrete has the recommendation of cheapness and extreme durability and, moreover, it can be laid quickly. It is prepared by mixing dry 3 parts of coarse aggregate, 2 parts sand, and 1 part of cement. Add water, turning the mixture over till it can be worked freely, and then spread it as evenly as possible over the path with a shovel and smooth it down with a mason's trowel. Alternatively, if the quantity required is fairly large, pre-mixed concrete can be ordered for delivery to the site, but this must be used immediately it arrives as it will start to set in a few hours.

The sides of the path can be marked out with planks held on edge by stakes driven firmly into the soil. Spread the concrete over a small section of the path at a time, and smooth it off before passing on to the next piece. Make frequent checks with a straight-edged board and a spirit level so that you do not leave any unexpected hollows or humps.

Concrete can be coloured with special dyes which are obtainable from a builder's merchant. Its appearance can also be varied according to the coarseness and colour of the aggregate used and by various finishing treatments, such as brushing with a stiff broom when the concrete is nearly dry to reveal the aggregate, or raking at a rather earlier stage of drying to make a pattern. If you wish to imitate paving, you can draw lines on the concrete when it is half dry with the point of a mason's trowel and small holes can be scooped out here and there right through the concrete to the soil beneath so that some creeping plants may be grown to complete the illusion.

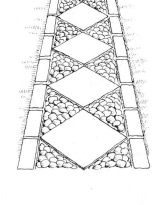

Attractive paths can be made in many textures and a variety of designs using brick, cobble or paving. When setting paving stones in grass care must be taken to ensure that the stones lie slightly below the level of the lawn to prevent damage to the blades of the mower

Top: Roses look well in a mixed border, providing a permanent framework for perennial and other plants which can be grown between them. In this small garden their rich blooms are in pleasant contrast to the cool blue nepeta (catmint) and the yellow eschscholzia in the foreground

Right: Roses in a country garden. Many popular cluster flowered (floribunda) varieties such as Iceberg, Evelyn Fison, and Allgold flower recurrently and will give a continuous show of colour throughout the summer

CHAPTER 8

Ornamental Trees

*The importance of trees – Avoid forest trees –
Some suitable deciduous kinds – Good evergreen
trees – Dwarf trees for the rock garden – General
information – Preparation of the soil – Some points
in planting – Staking – A selection of the best kinds*

Though trees are the most permanent occupants of
most gardens and it is therefore of great importance
to prepare the soil well and clear all weeds before
they are planted, I think that it is worth an effort
to complete this as quickly as possible and then get
the trees in. The reason is that they play a key role
in the design and determine to a considerable
degree where other things are to go. Also they are
the plants which provide the greatest height to the
garden, giving it that solid third dimension which
is so essential except where purely patterned effects
are required. Even young trees, when placed in
position, help one to visualize what the garden is
going to look like when it reaches maturity and if it
seems that mistakes have been made in the plan,
these can be put right at once before proceeding
with other planting.

Avoid Forest Trees. It is rarely wise to introduce
forest trees to gardens that are not fairly extensive.
Either they will monopolize so much room with
their branches and their roots that there will be
little scope for any further gardening in the immediate vicinity, or they will have to be lopped so
frequently and severely that all their natural beauty
will be destroyed. Under this category I include the
common forms of oak, elm, poplar, beech, sycamore, horse chestnut, sweet chestnut, ash, and lime.
I say common forms advisably, for most of these
trees have produced varieties of less vigorous habit
which may, under certain circumstances, be useful.
For example, the golden-leaved elm (*Ulmus procera*
Louis van Houtte) is slower in growth than the
common elm, and so is a beautiful form of sycamore
(*Acer pseudoplatanus*) named *brilliantissimum*, the
young leaves of which are pink and pale yellow.
Most admissable of all are some of the forms with
more or less vertical branches, the fastigiate or
column-forming trees. The best known of these, the
Lombardy poplar, is not very suitable because of
its hungry, far-reaching roots but the Dawyck
beech, the fastigiate oak and the pyramidal hornbeam do not suffer from this defect.

Some Suitable Deciduous Kinds. There is no shortage
of suitable material for even quite small gardens.
The flowering cherries are a host in themselves, and
some forms are so erect in growth that they take
little light from the garden. The best in this respect
is named by the Japanese Amanogawa. Another
delightful variety is *Prunus subhirtella pendula*, a
weeping tree which has been well named the rose-
bud cherry, but Kiku-shidare Sakura, often sold as
Cheal's weeping cherry, is much smaller though
stiffer in habit and one of the best ornamental trees

of weeping shape to choose for very small gardens.

Then there are the crab apples, which are almost
as numerous and showy as the cherries. Their
botanical name is *Malus*, and some of the best
varieties are included in the list at the end of this
chapter. The crab apples flower a little later than
most of the cherries, and so are excellent to supply
a succession.

Closely related to these is the popular mountain
ash or rowan (*Sorbus aucuparia*), which has been
described with considerable justification as the best
flowering and berrying tree for the small garden.
It is extremely hardy, has elegant foliage, pretty
flowers, and brilliant fruits.

The flowering almond (*Prunus dulcis*) has become
immensely popular, and is a first-rate tree in every
way. Its one fault is that the flowers open so early
in the spring that their beauty is not infrequently
brought to an untimely close by frost. But the leaves,
which appear after the flowers, do not suffer, for
the almond is perfectly hardy. The flowering peach
blooms a week or so after the almond, and so is
usually luckier with frosts.

Laburnums make very good specimen trees for
the small garden. You should obtain the variety
known as *L. vossii*, which has much longer trails
of golden-yellow flowers than the common form.

The snowy mespilus, botanically known as
Amelanchier laevis, is a delightful tree with abundant
small white flowers in May and fine autumn foliage
colour. *Cotoneaster frigida* makes a shapely standard with clusters of whitish flowers in early summer
followed by big bunches of scarlet berries. *Prunus
pissardii*, the purple-leaved plum, is one of the very
first to flower, often opening its small white blooms
in early March. The leaves are a good purple. An
even better tree is *Prunus blireiana*, which has
similar foliage and larger double pink flowers.

These are all deciduous trees – that is to say, they
lose their foliage in the winter. You will doubtless
wish to include a few evergreen varieties as well, so
that the garden does not suddenly become bare soil
and branches with the advent of autumn.

Good Evergreen Trees. Among the most striking
evergreen trees are the cedars, but these can grow
as large as elms and beeches and, therefore, are not
suitable for small gardens. Similar remarks apply
to most of the pines, firs, and spruces though some
of these are useful as windbreaks along the boundary
of a fairly large garden. The blue spruces, varieties
of *Picea pungens* which may be sold as *P. p. glauca,
kosteriana* or *moerheimii*, may be planted as
specimens in places where there is room for a spread
of 15 ft. or so, for they are very lovely and comparatively slow in growth. Erect forms of Lawson
cypress (*Chamaecyparis lawsoniana*) such as *columnaris,* Kilmacurragh, Green Pillar, *pottenii* and
ellwoodii, the Irish yew and similar column-
forming conifers are so narrow that it is possible to
include them even in small gardens.

Dwarf Trees for the Rock Garden. You should note that several of the trees mentioned above have produced dwarf species or varieties – some so dwarf that they can be planted in the rock garden. *Juniperus communis compressa* is a perfect miniature tree, no more than 1 ft. in height. There are some dwarf forms of Lawson cypress such as *nana* which in 20 years may be only 2 or 3 ft. high against the 50 to 60 ft. of the parent species. There are many more but it is best to buy these from specialist nurseries or with some expert advice, for not all the conifers sold as 'dwarf' are genuinely so.

General Information. For ease of reference I have grouped these and other suitable trees in a list, giving approximate height and branch spread for well-developed specimens, and some indication of the soil and position they favour if they are at all fastidious. Trees should usually be planted sufficiently far apart to allow for full development of the branch spread. In a few instances this can be restricted a little by skilful pruning, but, more often than not, hard cutting back to keep a big tree within bounds simply means that much of its natural beauty is destroyed.

Preparation of the Soil. The simplest method will be to prepare a circle of ground approximately 6 ft. in diameter for each tree. The soil should be well broken up to a depth of at least 1 ft. (18 in. is better) and some well-rotted manure mixed with it. Failing manure, use peat at the rate of about 20 lb. to each circle plus bonemeal at 2 lb. per circle. While preparing each circle pick out as many as possible of the weed roots you see, as this is the last thorough cultivation the ground will receive so long as the tree continues to grow in it.

Planting. The best time to plant most trees is in the autumn but the work can be done at any time from late October until late March provided the soil is in good working condition, which means that it must not be very wet or frozen and that it must be possible to break down large lumps of soil into reasonably small crumbs. Trees well established in containers can also be planted in spring and summer provided the roots are not broken or disturbed.

The holes prepared for planting must be amply wide so that all roots can be spread out naturally. They must be sufficiently deep to allow the soil mark on the trunk to be fractionally below soil level, or if the soil mark is not clearly visible, to enable the uppermost roots to be covered with at least 2 in. of soil.

A really strong stake should be driven into the centre of each hole before the tree is planted. Choose a stake that when driven in firmly will just reach to the point at which the branches fork out from the main trunk.

Place the tree in position against this stake and if you have no one to help you, tie it loosely to the stake so that both your hands can be free. Then return the displaced soil around the roots, adding some more peat as you go and making quite sure that the soil is worked in around and under the roots. When all are covered, tread the soil down

Top: The flowering cherry *Prunus* Amanogawa is particularly suitable for a small garden, taking up little space with its upright, columnar habit

Left: Planting a tree. (1) The stake should be inserted first. The planting hole should be big enough to allow the roots to be spread out. The stick laid across the hole should line up with the soil mark on the stem. (2) and (3) Soil is filled in round the roots and firmed with the foot. (4) The tree is attached firmly to the stake. A plastic tie with an adjustable buckle is the most satisfactory method

Top: A patio garden is admirably suited to a house of modern design. The formality of paving and Irish yews is softened by the planting of a flowering tree such as this weeping cherry, *Prunus* Kiku-shidare Sakura. Planted as a single specimen in this way, the full beauty of its shape and blossom can be appreciated

Right: The framework of mixed conifers in this formal planting is perfectly set off by a smooth, well-kept lawn. But form is not the only attribute of conifers – they also provide fascinating variations in colour and texture, seen here in blue-green and gold varieties of Lawson cypress, narrowly columnar Irish junipers and striped green and yellow *Thuja plicata zebrina*. An ordinary birch is in the background and in front of it is the much shorter birch known as Young's Weeping

firmly and then finish off with a good scattering of loose soil over the surface which will cover up all foot marks and look tidy.

Then complete the operation by tying the tree securely to the stake. Best for this purpose are the special plastic or rubber tree ties that can be obtained from most dealers in garden sundries. Choose one rather too large for immediate purposes and start by fitting the strap round the stake and running the securing loop hard back against this. Then wrap the buckle-end of the strap around the trunk and make it moderately firm. In subsequent months examine each tie from time to time and rebuckle any that seem to be getting too tight.

A SELECTION OF THE BEST ORNAMENTAL TREES

The height and spread given are those to be expected after 15 to 20 years' growth in normal situations and must necessarily be approximate only, as plants vary considerably in rate of growth according to soil and climate. They can, however, be taken as a guide to suitable spacing. Although some of the trees included might in time become too large even for fair-sized gardens they are included as relatively cheap kinds which might be regarded as expendable when they outgrow their situation.

Acer hersii. Snake-bark maple. Smooth green bark with longitudinal white lines. Deciduous. Height 25 ft. Spread 20 ft. Any soil.
Acer negundo variegatum. Deciduous, white-striped foliage. Height 25 ft. Spread 20 ft. Any soil.
Acer palmatum and varieties. Deciduous, foliage green or purple and variously dissected. Height 5 ft. to 12 ft. Spread 5 ft. to 12 ft. Sunny site, sheltered from north and east. Well-drained but not dry soil.
Acer pseudoplatanus brilliantissimum. Variegated sycamore. Deciduous foliage, coral pink when young. Height 20 ft. Spread 15 ft.
Amelanchier laevis. Snowy Mespilus. Deciduous. Foliage colours in autumn. Masses of white flowers in April. Height 20 ft. Spread 20 ft. Non-limy soil.
Betula pendula. Silver birch. Deciduous. Valued for silver trunk. Ordinary or sandy soil. The best varieties are *tristis*, very pendulous branchlets. Height 25 ft. Spread 15 ft. *B. p. dalecarlica* (Swedish or cut-leaf birch). Similar size. *B. p. youngii.* Weeping habit. Height 15 ft. Spread 15 ft.
Carpinus betulus pyramidalis. Pyramidal hornbeam. Deciduous. Neat conical habit. Dark green leaves. Height 20 ft. Spread 10 ft. Any soil.
Catalpa bignonioides. Indian bean. Deciduous, very large, heart-shaped foliage. Clusters of white flowers, spotted with yellow and purple, are borne in July and August. Height 20 ft. Spread 30 ft. Variety *aurea* has yellow leaves but does not flower so well. It is slower growing. Prune last year's shoots hard in spring to obtain the largest foliage, which otherwise decreases in size as the tree ages.
Cedrus atlantica glauca. Blue cedar. Evergreen conifer, with blue-grey foliage. Height 20 ft. Spread 15 ft. Becoming very large with age and will continue for centuries. Well-drained soil.
Cedrus deodara. Deodar. Evergreen conifer, with drooping branches and green foliage. Height 20 ft. Spread 15 ft. Becoming very large with age. Well-drained soil.

Left: *Acer negundo variegatum*, with decorative cream-striped leaves, is justly popular in urban areas

Right: The rose-purple flowers of *Cercis siliquastrum*, the Judas tree, appear in May before the foliage

Cercis siliquastrum. Judas tree. Deciduous, handsome rounded foliage. Bushy habit. Rose-purple flowers produced in May before the leaves. Height 15 ft. Spread 12 ft.

Chamaecyparis lawsoniana. Lawson's cypress. Evergreen conifer with dark green foliage. Height 30 ft. Spread 15 ft. Becoming very large with age. Any soil. There are many varieties including *C. l. allumii*, erect growth, blue-green foliage; *columnaris*, narrowly erect growth, dark green foliage; *ellwoodii*, columnar habit, feathery grey-green foliage; Green Pillar, erect growth, bright green foliage; *fletcheri*, slow-growing form, with blue-grey feathery foliage; Kilmacurragh, narrowly erect growth, dark green foliage; *stewartii*, bright golden foliage; and Triomphe de Boskoop, with blue-green foliage.

Crataegus oxycantha coccinea plena. Paul's scarlet thorn. Deciduous. Double scarlet flowers in late May. Height 20 ft. Spread 15 ft. *C. o. rosea plena*, double pink thorn, makes a good companion for this. Any soil. Excellent on chalk.

Cryptomeria japonica elegans. Evergreen conifer with feathery, green foliage turning russet red in autumn and winter. Height 20 ft. Spread 12 ft. Any soil. Best in sun.

Cupressocyparis leylandii. Leyland cypress. Evergreen much like Lawson cypress but will grow nearly twice as fast. Broadly columnar habit. Dark green foliage. Height 40 ft. Spread 12 ft., but will easily double these dimensions in time. Any soil. Castlewellan is a popular golden-leaved form.

Cupressus glabra pyramidalis. Arizona cypress. Evergreen conifer with blue-green foliage. Height 25 ft. Spread 7 ft. Narrowly columnar habit. Well-drained soil preferred. Cones freely produced.

Cupressus macrocarpa aurea. Golden Monterey cypress. Evergreen with small yellowish-green leaves. Fast growing and hardier than the green-leaved variety. Height 30 ft. Spread 15 ft. There are also narrower, more columnar varieties with more golden foliage such as Goldcrest and Donard Gold.

Fagus sylvatica Dawyck. The Dawyck beech is a columnar variety of the common beech with green leaves. It is deciduous. Soil well drained. Height 25 ft. Spread 7 ft. Particularly good on chalk.

Ginkgo biloba. Maidenhair tree. Deciduous conifer, with light green foliage, lobed like the maidenhair fern, but much larger. Slow growing. Height 20 ft. Spread 6 ft.

Gleditsia triacanthos Sunburst. The golden-leaved honey locust. Ferny, golden foliage. Deciduous. Height 25 ft. Spread 18 ft. Good drainage.

Ilex aquifolium and its varieties. Holly. Evergreen. Grown for berries on female plants, and for variegation of foliage in some varieties. Height 15 ft. Spread 10 ft. Any soil. Sun or shade.

Juniperus communis hibernica. Irish juniper. Evergreen conifer, with blue-grey foliage and columnar growth. Height 10 ft. Spread 3 ft. Well-drained soil – excellent for chalk.

Juniperus virginiana Sky Rocket. Evergreen conifer with blue-grey leaves and spire-like habit. Height 15 ft. Spread 2 ft. Well-drained soil. Excellent for chalk.

Laburnum vossii. Laburnum, with extra long racemes of flowers. Deciduous, with yellow flowers in May and June. Height 25 ft. Spread 18 ft. Full sun. Any soil.

Magnolia grandiflora. Evergreen, large glossy leaves.

Left: A good small tree for town gardens is *Magnolia soulangiana*, with its magnificent wine-flushed white flowers

Right: Not unlike a Lawson cypress *Thuja plicata zebrina* is a handsome evergreen. The leaves of this form are cross-banded with yellow

Globular white flowers, 8 to 10 in. across, lemon scented, produced intermittently from July to September. Height 15 ft. Spread 12 ft. Lime-free soil. Sunny, sheltered position. The best varieties are Exmouth and Goliath.

Magnolia sieboldii. Deciduous. White and crimson, sweetly scented pendent flowers in June. Height 12 ft. Spread 15 ft. Lime-free soil and sheltered position.

Magnolia soulangiana. Deciduous. Large white flowers backed with purple and produced during April and May, before and with foliage. Height 15 ft. Spread 15 ft. Best on lime-free soil. Excellent town tree. There are numerous varieties including *alba superba*, white flowers, and *lennei*, wine purple.

Malus. The crab apples. There are a great many species and hybrids all of which are deciduous and flower in spring. All grow in any reasonably fertile soil. Excellent kinds are *M. floribunda*, the Japanese crab, pink and white flowers, height and spread 15 ft.; *M. lemoinei*, rosy-crimson flowers, purple leaves, height and spread 20 ft.; *M. robusta*, the Siberian crab, white flowers and cherry-like fruits, height and spread 18 ft.; *M.* Golden Hornet, white flowers, yellow fruits, height 20 ft., spread 18 ft. Many more will be found in nursery catalogues.

Metasequoia glyptostroboides. Dawn redwood. Deciduous conifer with feathery, light green leaves turning russet red in the autumn. Very fast growing. Height 40 ft. Spread 15 ft. Will grow much larger eventually. Good, rather moist soil.

Picea pungens glauca. Blue spruce. Evergreen conifer, with blue-grey needles. Height 20 ft. Spread 15 ft. Well-drained soil.

Prunus dulcis (amygdalus). Almond. Deciduous. Pink flowers in March and April before the leaves. Height 20 ft. Spread 20 ft. Well-drained soil. Excellent on chalk.

Prunus avium plena. Double white cherry. Deciduous. Flowers in April and May. Height 25 ft. Spread 25 ft.

Prunus blireiana. Deciduous, purple foliage. Double pink flowers in March before the foliage. Height 15 ft. Spread 15 ft. Any reasonably fertile soil.

Prunus cerasifera pissardii. Purple-leaved plum. Deciduous, foliage changing from ruby red to purple. Pale pink flowers in March and April. Height 20 ft. Spread 20 ft. Any soil.

Prunus persica. Peach. Deciduous. Flowers in April before the foliage. Height 15 ft. Spread 15 ft. The best forms are Clara Meyer, double pink; Aurora, double rose pink, and Iceberg, double white. Well-drained soil. Excellent on chalk.

Prunus serrulata. Japanese cherry. Deciduous. Flowers in April and May. Any reasonably fertile soil. Excellent on chalk. Good varieties are: Amanogawa, pale pink, erect habit 20 ft. by 4 ft.; Fugenzo, pink, late flowering, spreading habit 25 ft. by 30 ft.; Kanzan, very large mauve-pink, 30 ft. by 30 ft.; Kiku-shidare Sakura (Cheal's Weeping), double pink flowers, weeping habit, 15 ft. by 15 ft.; Shirofugen, bronzy foliage, pink flowers, 25 ft. by 30 ft.; Tai Haku, very large single white, 30 ft. by 30 ft.; Shirotae, very spreading, white, 15 ft. by 30 ft.; and Ukon, pale sulphur, 30 ft. by 30 ft.

Prunus subhirtella autumnalis. Winter-flowering cherry. Deciduous. Semi-double pale pink flowers intermittently from November to March. Height 20 ft. Spread 25 ft. *P. s. pendula* is a weeping form, with masses of single pale pink flowers in early April. Height 12 ft. Spread 20 ft.

Pyrus salicifolia pendula. Willow-leaved pear. Narrow silver-grey leaves. Weeping habit. Height 15 ft. Spread 15 ft. Any reasonably fertile and well-drained soil.

Quercus robur fastigiata. Cypress oak. Deciduous. Green leaves becoming russet brown in autumn. Columnar habit. Height 20 ft. Spread 8 ft. Any reasonably fertile soil.

Rhus typhina. Stag's-horn sumach. Deciduous, divided foliage, which turns orange yellow in autumn. Purple fruits on female trees. Height 10 ft. Spread 10 ft. May be hard pruned in spring to produce larger leaves. Variety *laciniata* has leaflets further divided giving an almost fern-like appearance. All like well-drained soil.

Robinia pseudoacacia. Deciduous fast-growing tree with open branching habit, feathery green leaves and white flowers in June. Height 30 ft., spread 25 ft., but will grow much larger in time. Variety Frisia has yellow leaves and is slower growing. Varieties *bessoniana* and *inermis* make much smaller, more densely branched mop-headed trees and are useful in town gardens. Variety *pyramidalis* makes a narrow column only 3 or 4 ft. wide. Well-drained soil suits all kinds.

Salix chrysocoma. Golden weeping willow. Deciduous fast-growing tree with yellowish weeping branchlets, and light green leaves. Height 25 ft. Spread 25 ft. Can grow much larger in time but is worth planting for temporary effect. Best in rather moist soil.

Salix matsudana tortuosa. Corkscrew willow. Deciduous, light green, narrow leaves and curiously twisted branches. Height 25 ft. Spread 15 ft. Best in slightly moist soil.

Sorbus aria lutescens. Whitebeam. Deciduous foliage, white beneath. Flowers white, borne in clusters, followed by red fruits. Height 20 ft. Spread 20 ft. Prefers chalk, but will grow in any well-drained soil.

Sorbus aucuparia. Mountain ash or rowan. Deciduous. White flowers in May, June followed by orange-red berries. Height 20 ft. Spread 15 ft. Well-drained soil.

Sorbus hupehensis. Similar to mountain ash but with grey-green leaves and white berries. Well-drained soil.

Sorbus Joseph Rock. Deciduous. Similar to mountain ash but with yellow berries. Well-drained soil.

Sorbus scopulina. Deciduous. Feathery leaves like a mountain ash but erect habit and larger scarlet berries. Height 15 ft. Spread 4 ft. Ordinary soil.

Thuja plicata. Western red cedar. Evergreen conifer much like a Lawson cypress. Height 25 ft. Spread 18 ft. *T. p. zebrina* is a variety with leaves cross-banded with yellow. Any soil.

Ulmus procera Louis van Houtte. Golden elm. Deciduous, foliage very yellow. Height 20 ft. Spread 18 ft. but will grow much larger than this in time. Any soil.

Opposite: The vibrant colours of evergreen and deciduous azaleas grown beneath a Japanese cherry and a large hardy hybrid rhododendron, enliven a quiet corner. A planting of mixed shrubs gives year-round interest and trouble-free gardening

CHAPTER 9

The Garden Hedge

Avoid too many hedges – Screens of flowering shrubs – Choice of formal hedge shrubs – Privet – Lonicera – Cupressus and thuja – Beech and hornbeam – Laurels and aucuba – Box – Holly and yew – Hawthorn and plum – Sundry shrubs for hedge making – Seaside hedges – Dividing walls – When to plant – Soil preparation – Pruning after planting – Pruning established hedges – Table of hedge shrubs

Hedges can serve a very useful purpose in the garden, but it is probably true that, on the whole, amateurs plant too many hedges rather than too few. This is particularly so in town front gardens, which are often so full of hedge that there is precious little room for anything else. Of course, some sort of permanent barrier may be absolutely essential, but a hedge is not always the best means of providing it. There are many gardens in which a rail fence or a low wall or screen of pierced blocks might be equally effective and far more interesting to look at, especially if used as a support for some not too vigorous climbers such as large-flowered clematis or recurrent-flowering climbing roses.

Informal Hedges. There are other places in which a formal hedge might well be omitted in favour of a more or less informal arrangement of flowering and berry-bearing shrubs. There are plenty of good evergreens to choose from, such as *Berberis darwinii, B. stenophylla, Escallonia* Apple Blossom or Crimson Spire, *Olearia haastii, Mahonia aquifolium, Pyracantha lalandii, Cotoneaster simonsii, Potentilla fruticosa, Spiraea thunbergii* and *S.* Anthony Waterer, and laurustinus (*Viburnum tinus*). These will not only provide a delightful show of flowers (or fruits) which a formal hedge would not, but they will require much less attention, for they do not need regular clipping.

Choice of Formal Hedge Shrubs. Nevertheless, there are places in which a formal clipped hedge is indispensable. The choice of a suitable shrub will depend very largely upon the purpose for which the hedge is required, though the nature of the soil and the relative exposure of the garden must be considered.

Cypresses and Thuja. These are evergreen trees which stand clipping well and so are excellent for large hedges and windbreaks. All have rather feathery foliage. Very fast growing is *Cupressus macrocarpa*, but it is not very hardy and so is most suitable for seaside gardens and other places with a fairly mild winter climate. There are yellow or yellowish-green leaved varieties that are a little hardier but none is as tough as the Leyland cypress (*Cupressocyparis leylandii*), a hybrid which is capable of adding 3 or 4 ft. to its height every year. It is dark green (golden in Castlewellan) and excellent as boundary or windbreak. Lawson

cypress (*Chamaecyparis lawsoniana*) grows at little more than half this rate but is available in a number of varieties – dark green, light green, blue green, grey green and yellow. Varieties also differ in habit, some being narrowly columnar, others broadly conical. All are very hardy.

The thujas closely resemble Lawson cypress in habit and foliage. The best for hedge and screen making is *Thuja plicata,* the western red cedar which in its natural habitat (western North America) grows into a great tree and is the source of the 'cedar' wood used for much garden building. It grows at about the same rate as Lawson cypress but there are not so many useful varieties. However, one named *zebrina* is unique in having its green leaves cross-banded with yellow. *Thuja occidentalis,* another American tree, is more erect in growth than *T. plicata* which, in some cases, is an advantage, but it is a little inclined to get thin at the base.

Beech and Hornbeam. Another grand hedge plant for a tall windbreak is our native beech (*Fagus sylvatica*). A curious thing about this is that, though it loses all its leaves in the autumn when grown naturally as a tree, it retains its dead but delightfully russet-coloured foliage throughout the winter when it is hard pruned as a hedge. The same applies to hornbeam (*Carpinus betulus*), which is as much like beech as *Thuja lobbii* is like *Chamaecyparis lawsoniana*. Both beech and hornbeam will thrive in most soils including those containing a lot of lime or chalk but hornbeam is to be preferred on heavy, poorly drained soils. Both can be pruned hard to form relatively thin yet very strong screens which can be particularly useful in small gardens that require a fairly high screen.

Laurels and Aucuba. The laurel of antiquity is the bay tree (*Laurus nobilis*) of the modern garden, and is not sufficiently hardy to make a hedge in most parts of Britain. When the gardener speaks of a laurel hedge he usually refers either to the cherry laurel, which is a species of prunus (*Prunus laurocerasus*), or to the aucuba, though he may mean the Portugal laurel (*Prunus lusitanica*). All three have their uses, but they are rather big and hungry for the small garden. Two virtues of the aucuba and the cherry laurel are that they will both grow in dense shade and in the smoky atmosphere found in and near big cities. The aucuba is usually seen in its variegated form, the rather pale green leaves being spotted with yellow, but in my opinion the green-leaved variety is much more attractive. There are two sexes, a matter of some importance, for the 'female' bushes will produce delightful red berries in autumn and winter if they have one or two male bushes nearby.

Aucuba will form a hedge 12 ft. in height, but can easily be kept to a third of that. Cherry laurel, if left to its own devices, will grow into a small tree 20 ft. or more in height, but it can be pruned as hard as the aucuba without ill effect. It is poisonous to cattle. Portugal laurel does not like to be cut so hard and is more suitable for a big screen, wide in proportion to its height. It is a hungry shrub that will impoverish the soil for yards around, and is therefore not suitable for the small garden.

Box and Edgings. If left to itself box (*Buxus*) will grow as much as 25 ft. in height; yet it can be clipped to a ridiculously small size. In consequence it is much favoured by topiary artists, who delight us with their fancies in peacocks, dolphins, teddy bears, and other quaint designs. Like beech and hornbeam, box does well on thin, chalky soils in addition to more generous places. For edgings a few inches in height and the neat little hedges used to form the patterned beds and knots so typical of old formal gardens and now coming back into fashion again, a special variety of box is used named *suffruticosa*. This is usually sold by the yard, which means sufficient plants to make a yard of edging when planted about 6 in. apart.

Other shrubs suitable for small hedges and pattern making are lavender (especially suitable for chalk and limestone), rue, rosemary, lavender cotton (*Santolina*) and several small hebes such as *Hebe anomala, buxifolia* and *cupressoides*.

Holly and Yew. Holly (*Ilex*) and yew (*Taxus*) are fine hedging shrubs, and by no means so slow growing as they are often stated to be. Both shrubs have numerous varieties, some with variegated foliage, while there is a type of yew known as Irish yew (*Taxus baccata fastigiata*), which grows stiffly erect and therefore is ideal for forming avenues and screens. Yew is just as good as box for clipping into intricate shapes and the best golden form *T. b. semperaurea* is brighter and retains its colour better than golden box. However, yew is poisonous to cattle, and therefore should not be planted where they might eat it, for they have no instinct to warn them against it. It is, moreover, a hungry shrub – so much so that it is almost impossible to grow anything close to it.

Hawthorn and Plum. Hawthorn, or quick (*Crataegus*), is a favourite with the farmer and is sometimes useful to form an outer barrier to the garden, particularly in rural districts. Its tangled, thorny growth is most effective in keeping out cattle, and its leaves contain no hidden poison. The fact that it loses all its leaves in the winter makes it less desirable within the garden. Similar remarks apply to a form of plum known as Myrobalan or cherry plum (*Prunus cerasifera*) which can be mixed with hawthorn with good effect. The purple-leaved form known as *P. c. pissardii* is also useful and there is a hybrid form named *cistena* which has similar reddish-purple leaves, only grows about 6 ft. high, and by clipping can easily be kept to half that.

Privet. A great deal has been written in abuse of oval-leaved privet (*Ligustrum ovalifolium*), but there are few shrubs that have quite as many good points from the hedging standpoint. It is cheap, almost indestructibly hardy, will grow practically

Top: Where an informal hedge is preferred, the evergreen *Berberis stenophylla* will produce a delightful show of sweet-scented yellow flowers in April

Left: For a tough and fast-growing windbreak the Leyland cypress (*Cupressocyparis leylandii*) is an excellent choice

Top: *Euonymus japonicus*, in either its gold- or silver-variegated form makes an attractive hedge for the seaside garden

Bottom: Cross-section of a double wall, showing the core of soil and the stones set to slope slightly inwards for extra strength. Such walls make very attractive dividers when planted up; if a dry wall is built with soil between the stones instead of mortar, plants can also be inserted in the crevices

anywhere, and will stand any amount of hard cutting. It is sufficiently stiff in habit to stand up by itself in exposed places and suffer little or no harm during heavy rainstorms or even, for that matter, from falls of snow. Moreover, its golden-leaved form *aureum* is bright and effective. So many virtues can hardly be claimed for any other popular hedging shrub.

Lonicera. A rival of the privet is *Lonicera nitida*, a shrubby honeysuckle with neat leaves somewhat resembling those of a box. This is really good for making a small hedge up to about 4 ft. in height, for it is quick growing, hardy, and reasonably

indifferent to soil. Its fault is that it is rather weak in growth, and this becomes very apparent if an attempt is made to form hedges over 5 ft. in height. A much stiffer variety is available named *L. n. fertilis* (it is often wrongly listed as *L. pileata yunnanensis* or *L. ligustrina yunnanensis*), and because of its greater strength it is to be preferred in windy places or in districts in which heavy snow-storms are likely to occur.

Roses. Sweet brier makes an effective prickly barrier on the outskirts of a garden and may even be welcomed in the inner precincts on account of its delightfully aromatic foliage. It does not mind hard pruning and can be kept to a height of 3 ft. and a breadth of 18 in. without difficulty. Any shrub roses and also vigorous free-branching cluster-flowered (floribunda) roses also make attractive informal hedges but must not be constantly clipped into shape as this will prevent them flowering freely.

Seaside Hedges. Other good plants with which to hedge the seaside garden are *Atriplex halimus*, a rather untidy grey-leaved evergreen which can be clipped to improve its habit and which is useful as an outer screen; *Escallonia macrantha* and *E. rubra*, two handsome evergreens with carmine flowers in summer; *Hebe brachysiphon*, another neat evergreen with spikes of small white flowers; *Euonymus japonicus*, which is most attractive in either its gold or silver variegated forms; *Griselinia littoralis*, with larger leaves either light green or variegated with yellow; *Olearia macrantha*, a tall evergreen with holly-like leaves and showy clusters of small white daisy-like flowers in summer, and all species of tamarix.

Dividing Walls. A possible alternative to a hedge in some parts of the garden is a double dry wall with a core of soil. This can be very effective near the house or as a division between one section of the garden and another. In construction it closely resembles the terrace-retaining walls described in Chapter 4, but two walls must be constructed at least 9 in. apart, with good loamy soil rammed between them. A great variety of dwarf trailing plants and alpines can be planted both on top of the wall and also in between the stones themselves.

When to Plant. Hedging shrubs obtained in containers can be planted at practically any time of the year, those lifted from a nursery bed from the middle of October until late March, but it is not wise to do any planting when the soil is very wet or frozen. It is a good general rule to plant nursery-grown evergreens in October or March and to reserve the middle period, particularly November and February, for those shrubs which lose their leaves. Once these have started into growth again in the spring they are rather tricky to transplant satisfactorily, whereas evergreens tend to suffer most check if lifted and replanted when the soil is cold and conditions are unfavourable for root growth. Evergreens should always be lifted with plenty of soil around their roots and sacking or polythene should be tied around this ball of soil

to keep it in place if the plants have to be transported any distance.

Soil Preparation. Do not make the mistake of scamping the preparation of the soil where the hedge is to be planted.

A lot of animal manure is not desirable unless the soil is very light and sandy, very chalky, or so stiff and clayey that it is likely to bake and crack during the summer. In any case the manure used should be strawy and really well decayed and must be mixed thoroughly with the top 10 in. of soil. Peat is a useful soil dressing before planting, forked in at about 3 lb. per yard for a width of 18 in., and bonemeal and hoof and horn meal can also be used at rates of 3 oz. and 2 oz. per yard respectively.

Planting. The simplest way to plant a hedge is usually to dig a trench the whole of the required length and sufficiently deep and wide to contain the roots comfortably. The plants can then be stood in the trench the correct distance apart with the uppermost roots about 1½ in. below soil level. The soil is then shovelled back around the roots and trodden in firmly.

When planting from containers it is essential to remove these first even if they are only of polythene film. This disintegrates very slowly and will keep water from the roots and prevent them growing out into the surrounding soil, so it must be stripped off. In doing this it is important that the soil should not be dislodged from the roots, which should be disturbed as little as possible.

If the site is exposed, a good stake should be provided for each plant. Drive it well into the soil and tie the stem to it. This support can usually be dispensed with after the second year.

Pruning after Planting. Pruning after planting will depend upon what you decide to plant. Privet, Myrobalan plum, tamarisk, and sweet brier should all be cut back rather severely, privet in April or May, and the other three immediately after planting. It will do them no harm if their top growth is reduced by two-thirds. Most other shrubs, including loniceras, cherry laurels, aucubas, yews, hollies, various forms of cupressus and thuja, beech, and hornbeam, should be left unpruned at first. Later on during the summer privet and lonicera will require a little trimming, but the other shrubs mentioned are not likely to need even this much attention until the second year.

Pruning Established Hedges. After the first year most hedges will need to be trimmed or pruned annually according to their character and the purpose for which they are required. Five basic types of pruning can be distinguished, as follows:

(a) Occasional clipping from May to September. Any harder pruning which may be necessary should be done in April–May. Suitable for evergreens with small- to medium-sized leaves.

(b) Prune with secateurs in late spring. Suitable for large-leaved evergreens.

(c) Prune after flowering. Suitable for most flowering or berry-bearing hedges except roses.

(d) Thin or prune in late winter. With roses also shorten flowering stems when flowers fade.

(e) Prune in late summer or autumn. Suitable for most deciduous hedges grown solely for foliage but beech and hornbeam are best left unpruned for the first two or three years until well established.

TABLE OF HEDGE SHRUBS

NAME	MAXIMUM HEIGHT IN FEET	PLANTING DISTANCE IN INCHES	PRUNING
Atriplex	6	21	a
Aucuba	8	30	b
Beech	15	15	e
Berberis darwinii and *B. stenophylla*	8	24	c
Box, Common	8	15	a
Box, Edging	2	6	a
Chamaecyparis lawsoniana (Lawson Cypress)	15	24	a
Cotoneaster simonsii	6	18	c
Cupressocyparis leylandii (Leyland Cypress)	20	24	a
Cupressus macrocarpa (Monterey Cypress)	15	24	a
Escallonia (all kinds)	8	24	c
Euonymus japonicus	10	18	a
Griselinia	10	18	a
Hawthorn (Quick or thorn)	10	9	e
Hebe brachysiphon and small kinds (*H. anomala, H. buxifolia* etc.)	2	12	c
Holly	15	24	b
Hornbeam	15	15	e
Laurel, Cherry	12	24	b
Laurel, Portugal	12	24	b
Laurustinus (*Viburnum tinus*)	10	24	b
Lavender	2	12	c
Lonicera nitida	4	12	a
Mahonia aquifolium	4	18	c
Olearia haastii	5	18	c
O. macrodonta	12	24	c
Potentilla fruticosa	4	18	d
Privet, green	6	12	a
Privet, golden	5	12	a
Prunus cerasifera (Myrobalan or Cherry Plum)	12	18	e
Prunus cistena	6	12	e
Pyracantha (all kinds)	8	18	c
Roses, shrub	6	30	d
Roses, cluster-flowered	5	20	d
Rosemary	3	15	a
Rue	2	9	a
Santolina (Lavender Cotton)	2	12	a
Spiraea (Anthony Waterer and *S. thunbergii*)	4	18	c
Tamarix (all kinds)	10	18	d
Thuja	15	24	a
Yew	15	24	a

CHAPTER 10

Laying a Lawn

*First year or second year? – Seed or turf? –
Selecting seed – When to sow – Quantity of seed
required – Preparation of the soil – How to sow –
Scaring birds – Watering – Rolling and cutting –
Weeding seedling lawns – Lawns from turf –
When to lay turf*

In a new garden it is doubtful whether a lawn should be attempted the first year. Much depends on the state of the soil. If it is very full of perennial weeds and pests you should seriously consider allowing further opportunity for clearing the site before covering it permanently with turf. If the site is sufficiently large it may be a good plan to grow a crop of potatoes to help cleanse the soil. Their wide-spreading leaves smother weed growth, while their roots and tubers, penetrating the soil, break up clods and produce that fine crumbling condition known by the gardener as 'a good tilth'.

If, however, the ground was originally pretty clean or you have succeeded in getting it into good condition by cultivation and possibly the use of a safe non-persistent weedkiller such as paraquat, by all means go ahead with the lawn. It will certainly improve the appearance of your garden and give you a better idea of how your original plans are working out.

Seed or Turf? There are two ways of making a lawn, each with its own advantages and drawbacks. If seed is sown, the mixture can be chosen to suit the soil and position, and there is less liklihood of importing weeds. But a lawn from seed cannot be made in a day, and the soil must be sufficiently well cultivated to allow it to be broken down into a good seed bed.

Turves afford a quicker method of producing a hard-wearing sward and do not call for such elaborate preparation. The difficulties here are that really good, weed-free turves are hard to come by, and there is less choice in the particular grasses obtained and their proportion one to another.

Selecting Seed. This matter of a blended mixture of grasses is rather important. Each variety has its own characteristics and preferences, and it is possible to overcome certain natural disadvantages – such as a very heavy or excessively light soil – by choosing grasses that tolerate such conditions. Seedsmen offer mixtures to suit a great variety of needs. Selected or specially raised turves can also be purchased, but they are usually expensive, and their initial cost may be greatly increased by carriage charges. It is probable that, if you decide on turfing, you will have to be content with some local product stripped from a neighbouring meadow which has fallen into the builders' hands. It is also likely that the turf will then contain more coarse grasses, clover, and weeds than genuine lawn grasses, so that the time and cost of getting it into anything like reasonable condition may be excessive. In view of

this, seed should be your first choice unless you have some very definite reason for rejecting it.

When to Sow and How Much. Grass seed is sown in early autumn or spring, September and April being the two most favourable months. A sowing at the rate of 1 oz. per square yard is usually adequate, though this can be doubled for a quick result. You can obtain a rough guide to the quantity of seed required by counting the strides necessary to cross both the length and the breadth of the lawn site, multiplying the two figures together and dividing the result by 16. This will give the quantity of seed in pounds.

Preparation of the Soil. If you have already dug and cleaned the garden as advised in Chapter 2, it will only remain to give the soil a dressing of a well-balanced garden fertilizer. National Growmore used at 4 oz. per square yard will do well or a proprietary mixture used according to manufacturer's instructions. Fork this in lightly, at the same time breaking down all lumps with the back of the fork. If there is any difficulty in doing this a dressing of peat at from 2 to 4 lb. per square yard will help. After breaking it down, leave the soil for a few days to weather and then, on an occasion when the surface is moist but not sodden, tread it carefully all over, first working backwards and forwards across the breadth of the plot and then in similar manner across its length. This treading will firm it evenly all over and at the same time break up the smaller lumps. Finally, give a light raking to level the surface and remove large stones.

How to Sow. Two or three fairly long planks are a great asset when sowing. If you start at one end and scatter the seed evenly over a narrow strip, you can move the planks backwards across the plot little by little and walk on them throughout, so leaving no footmarks on the soil. Of course, under this method sowing and covering should go on alternately so that one strip is completed before the next is begun. Alternatively, to ensure even distribution, the seed can be spread from a wheeled fertilizer distributor, which will also come in useful when feeding the lawn later on. By running it over a sheet of paper 1 yd. square and weighing the seed that has fallen, it is easy to find the setting that will give the correct distribution.

Grass seed requires to be only just covered with soil, and this you can do either by drawing the rake over the surface at right angles to the direction of the preliminary raking, or else by scattering sifted soil evenly over the surface.

Scaring Birds. Birds must be kept at bay, or they may devour a great deal of the seed. Proprietary preparations are offered by seedsmen with which you can treat grass seed before sowing to make it unpalatable to birds, and some seedsmen pre-treat

Making a lawn from seed. (1) After the initial preparation, the soil should be trodden carefully to obtain an evenly firm seed-bed. (2) A final raking is given to level the surface and clear it of stones. (3) To ensure even distribution of seed, the ground can be measured off in yard-wide strips or squares. (4) Alternatively, a wheeled fertilizer distributor can be used for seed sowing

their grass seed in this way before marketing it. Alternatively black thread can be stretched backwards and forwards across the seed bed a few inches above ground level, or some kind of bird scarer can be used.

Watering. Germination usually takes from a fortnight to three weeks. No watering should be necessary during this period, but if the weather is dry and no grass seedlings appear in the normal period, you can apply water as a fine spray. Excessive watering chills and hardens the soil and hinders germination.

Rolling and Cutting. Nor must you use the roller or lawn mower at first. When the grass is 4 in. in height will be time enough to give it a first cutting, leaving it about 1 in. in length so that it may gain strength. Only light rolling should be practised at first when the lawn is fairly dry.

Weeding Seedling Lawns. Annual weeds such as groundsel and chickweed will disappear with mowing but if more troublesome weeds such as dandelions, buttercups and daisies appear they must be removed with an old knife or small weeding trowel. It is, of course, necessary to deal with perennial weeds before sowing the grass seed by treating them with glyphosate, applying this when the plants are in full leaf.

Fertilizers are best avoided until the seedlings begin to knit themselves together into a close carpet. Then a light dressing of National Growmore can be given, about 2 oz. per square yard, or a proprietary lawn fertilizer used according to label instructions.

Lawns from Turf. If you decide to make a lawn from turves you must prepare the ground in exactly the same way, except that it is not essential to break down the surface quite so finely. Still, if you can get it into seed-bed condition, so much the better, for it is much easier to lay turves dead level on well-crumbled soil than on a lumpy surface.

Turves are usually supplied in rectangular strips 3 ft. long, 1 ft. wide and about $1\frac{1}{2}$ in. thick. For cartage to site the turves are rolled up but if they cannot be laid at once they should not be stored in rolls for more than two or three days or the grass will begin to die. Instead they should be temporarily laid out flat in some convenient place.

Before laying the turves finally, examine them carefully for dandelions, docks, and other tap-rooted weeds. These can be removed much more readily at this stage than later on when they have started to root down into the soil.

The turves are laid in straight lines but staggered in rows like bricks in a wall to get a good bind, similar to the method used by bricklayers to obtain what they describe as a 'bond'.

If the lawn has a curved margin, it is wise to lay the first straight row of turves some distance from the edge, filling in the curve afterwards. Never use very small pieces to finish off the sides. If they are necessary to obtain a fit, place them a row or so away from the edge and complete the job with full-sized turves. Small pieces at the edge are very easily dislodged.

Laying turf. (1) The ground is prepared in the same way as for sowing seed. A garden line will assist in maintaining a straight course. (2) Turves should be laid so that the joints are staggered like bricks in a wall. (3) A wooden turf beater is a useful aid in settling the turf into place. This can also be done with the back of a spade. (4) Soil is sprinkled into the cracks and brushed in to aid the bonding of the turves

As you lay the turves beat them down on to the soil so that no holes or loose places are left. The back of a spade can be used for this, but you will find it easier to do a really good job if you use a wooden turf-beater. This is just a solid, smooth-faced block of wood with a handle conveniently placed for beating.

When all the turves are laid, scatter a little dry, sifted soil and sand over them and brush it down into the cracks with a stiff broom. Then run a light roller across the lawn, first in one direction and then in the other. If the turves are very shaggy and un-tidy, the mower can be used a few days later, but see that the blades are set high. Indeed, it is wise to have the grass a little long throughout the first summer, as this will stimulate root growth.

When to Lay Turf. The best months for turf laying are October and February, but with proper care it is possible to extend this season considerably. Indeed, with the exception of the hot summer months and very frosty periods in winter, there is really no time at which it is impossible to lay turves successfully if a little care is taken both at the time

and afterwards. If dry weather follows laying, you can water the turves freely.

A Lawn from Site Grass. If the natural grass of the site is reasonably good, or in an old garden with neglected turf, it may be possible to make a lawn from it simply by mowing, weeding, feeding and watering. Selective lawn weedkillers such as 2,4-D, MCPA and mecoprop, if watered on to the grass according to manufacturer's instructions, will get rid of a great many weeds, and lawn sand – a mixture of sand, sulphate of ammonia and sulphate of iron which can be purchased ready for dry application – can be used to spot treat more difficult weeds. Regular mowing will kill some weeds and also some of the coarser grasses and generally good lawn management will also help to encourage the better grasses at the expense of those of less desirable character. It may be difficult to deal with irregularities in the surface, for though small holes can be filled with soil and resown with grass seed, larger irregularities must usually be dealt with by removing the turf in strips, adding or removing soil and re-laying the turf.

CHAPTER 11

First Year Vegetable Crop

*Potatoes as a cleaning crop – Planting time –
Summer care of potatoes – Lifting – Spraying
potatoes against disease – Other root crops best
omitted – Peas and beans – Sowing peas for
succession – Support for peas – When and how to
sow beans – Winter green crops – Spring
cabbages – Vegetable marrows*

If you wish to grow vegetables on previously
uncultivated soil, remember that there may be quite
a lot of pests in the soil, particularly if the site was
previously grassland. Millepedes and wireworms,
in particular, can be a great nuisance and may
entirely ruin peas, beans, and carrots. Leatherjackets and slugs have a special partiality for lettuces.

Potatoes as a Cleaning Crop. Far and away the best
crop for newly dug ground is the potato. This has
several advantages. The sets, if well sprouted in
advance, send out shoots strong enough to push
through rough, turfy lumps, and it takes an ab-
normal amount of pest damage to destroy them
entirely. The haulm of the potatoes spreads out well
over the surrounding soil, smothering any weeds
that are missed in the process of earthing up the
rows. It is true that if there are a lot of wireworms
or slugs in the soil there is likely to be damage to the
tubers, but this is rarely bad enough to make the
crop unusable, though it might prove unsaleable.
In rough soil a certain amount of common scab is
likely to occur, especially if there is much chalk
or lime present, but this in no way spoils the cooking
qualities of the potatoes and is therefore not of great
importance.

If you have dug in the turf there is no need to use
any animal manure on the potato plot during its
first season, but if you have stripped the turf off
it will be a great advantage to obtain some well-
rotted manure and dig this in. Keep it away from
the surface as far as possible. It should not come
directly into contact with the newly planted tubers,
but should be well mixed with the soil beneath so
that they may root down into it and find all the
nourishment they need. A barrow load of manure
is sufficient to treat about 10 sq. yd. of ground.
Alternatives to manure are treated sewage sludge,
which can be obtained cheaply in some localities,
treated town refuse, peas and spent hops. In some
places spent mushroom compost is also available
at a reasonable price and is excellent for improving
the texture of both light and heavy soils. Whatever
you use, finish off the surface with a dusting of
bonemeal or superphosphate of lime; these will
supply phosphates, and potatoes can hardly have
too much of these.

Planting Time. Potatoes can be planted during
March or April, but it is customary to start them
into growth by sprouting the tubers some weeks in
advance. If you purchase the 'seed potatoes' or

tubers for planting in February and stand them,
eyes uppermost, in shallow boxes or seed trays
placed in a light room, frost-proof shed or garage,
they will soon begin to make short, sturdy sprouts.
On very cold nights it is advisable to cover them
with sheets of brown paper as a protection against
frost. Then, before planting the tubers out, rub off
any very weak sprouts, retaining from two to five
of the best.

The planting itself is simple. Just chop out with
a sharp spade a trench about 6 in. deep, set the
tubers in this with their shoots uppermost and then
shovel the soil back around them, taking care not
to break off the shoots. The rows for early potatoes
should be 2½ ft. apart, and the tubers themselves
should be 1 ft. apart in these rows. For main crop
and late potatoes it is advisable to allow a little
more space – say, 3 ft. between the rows and 15 to
18 in. between the tubers.

To encourage them to sprout,
seed potatoes should be
stood eyes uppermost in
shallow boxes in a light
frostproof place

Earthing up potatoes. Soil is
drawn up round the potato
shoots into a series of ridges
across the plot

Summer Care of Potatoes. As soon as the shoots appear through the soil scatter a little compound fertilizer all over the plot. For this purpose you can use a mixture of 4 parts superphosphate of lime, 2 parts sulphate of ammonia, and 1 part sulphate of potash well mixed and applied at the rate of 2 oz. per square yard. Alternatively use a good compound fertilizer such as National Growmore at the same rate of application.

Next draw the soil from the centre of each row towards the shoots. This earthing-up process should be repeated a week or ten days later and again a week or fortnight after that, until the soil all over the plot is drawn up into a number of steep ridges with the potato growth along the summit of each.

Lifting. Early potatoes will be ready for digging by the end of June or early in July. You can soon satisfy yourself on this point by scraping a little soil away from around one root and seeing how large the tubers are. Start to dig as soon as they are big enough for use. Main crop and late potatoes should be left longer to ripen properly. The test is to lift a tuber and rub it hard with the thumb. If the skin comes off easily the tuber is not yet ripe, but if the skin holds on firmly the crop is ready for lifting.

Spraying Potatoes Against Disease. It will be worth your while to spray main crop and late potatoes early in July as a protection against late blight, a disease which is so common that few crops escape it completely unless preventive measures are taken. The best spray to use is Bordeaux mixture or one of the proprietary copper fungicides. You can obtain these from any dealer in horticultural sundries, and there will be full instructions telling you exactly how to mix them. You will need a syringe with a fine nozzle to apply the spray properly. The more misty and driving it is the better; it is only wasteful to drench the plants with fungicide. One thing you should be very careful about is to spray the under as well as the upper surface of the leaves.

Peas and Beans. If the soil has been well dug during the autumn or winter the surface can usually be broken down sufficiently in the spring for peas and beans to be sown. It is, however, useless to sow in soil containing many wireworms, as these favour the seeds in preference to any of the baits such as potatoes, carrots, wheat, and oats often put down to attract them. Wireworms can be killed by forking in a soil insecticide such as bromophos or gamma-HCH powder a few weeks before sowing time. Prepare the soil as for potatoes.

Sowing Peas for Succession. Peas should be sown in small successive batches so that plants do not all start to crop at once. If you sow one row every 10 to 14 days from the end of March until the middle of May you should have fresh peas to pick from about midsummer until September. For the earliest sowings choose an early variety. Then go on to a second early or main-crop pea. A few good varieties are as follows – Earlies: Feltham First, Little Marvel, Meteor, Pilot, Gradus, and Kelvedon Wonder. Second Earlies: Kelvedon Monarch, Hurst Green Shaft and Early Onward. Main crop: Onward, Alderman and Show Perfection.

The best way to sow peas is to scoop out, with a sharp spade, a shallow trench about 9 in. or 1 ft. in width and 3 in. in depth. Sow the peas in a double line one on each side of the trench and cover with an inch of soil. The seedlings will then come up

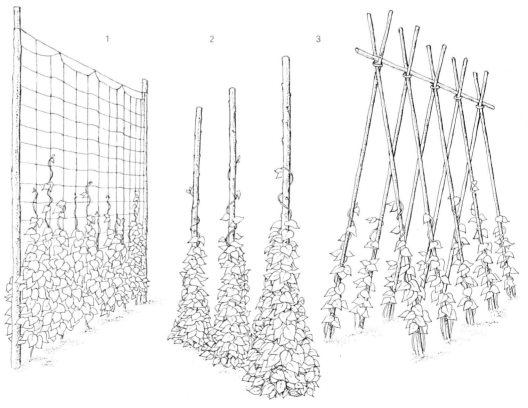

Three examples of training beans. (1) Using coarse-mesh netting as a support. (2) Where space is limited, beans can be trained up a single pole. (3) The conventional method of staking using a double row of poles and a cross-bar

in a slight depression that will afford them shelter.

Sticks for Peas. Even dwarf peas should have some support and it is essential for taller kinds. Brushy hazel branches are best for the purpose, but these are not always easy to buy and netting stretched vertically between posts driven well into the soil can be used instead. The staking should be done early before the peas start to straggle.

When and How to Sow Beans. Runner beans are distinctly tender, and must not be sown outdoors until early in May. Alternatively, they can be sown in boxes in a frame or greenhouse in April and hardened off for planting out at the end of May or early in June. The ground is prepared in exactly the same way as for peas and, if sowings are made outdoors, these are also treated in the same way as peas. The beans themselves should be carefully spaced about 9 in. apart in the rows. Then, when they germinate, you can place one long straight stake to each plant and secure these stakes at the top to a cross-bar running the length of the row. Runner beans can also be trained up netting which needs to be at least 6 ft. high, or they can be trained on wires, string or netting against a wall. The plants are so attractive in flower that many gardeners use them as wall, fence or screen coverings.

The Cabbage Tribe. For later use you may like to have some cabbages, broccoli, brussels sprouts, kale, etc. Seed of all these can be sown in a sheltered border during March or early April, or seedlings ready for planting can be purchased in June or July. If you should decide to try your hand at seed sowing, select a sunny plot, sheltered a little from cold winds by a fence or wall, break the surface down with a

fork to as fine and powdery a condition as possible, and then scatter the seeds thinly in small but distinctly separated patches, each with a clearly written label stating what it is. Cover the seeds very lightly with a little fine soil, which may be sifted over them. Germination should take about a fortnight, and a few weeks later you should transfer the seedlings to another sunny bed in which they can be planted 3 in. apart in rows 6 or 8 in. apart. In this they will grow on into sturdy plants which you can either use to follow on after your peas and potatoes or, if you prefer, can plant out in early summer in any well dug and moderately manured soil.

All these winter green crops like a little well-rotted manure or old mushroom compost dug into the soil. In addition, scatter some bonemeal lightly over the surface before planting and then, when the crops are well established, give two or three very light dressings of nitrate of soda scattered evenly around the plants and stirred into the surface with a dutch hoe. No single dressing must exceed $\frac{1}{2}$ oz. per square yard, and at least a fortnight should elapse between them. If there is no rain after an application, either water it in thoroughly or delay any further use of fertilizers until there has been enough rainfall to wash all the chemical into the soil.

The rows of winter green crops for the final planting should be $2\frac{1}{2}$ to 3 ft. apart and the plants themselves should be about 18 to 24 in. apart in the rows.

In order to obtain a crop of cabbages in the spring to follow the autumn and winter supplies it is necessary to sow seed in July or August. Not all varieties are suitable for this purpose but two of the best are Harbinger and Wheeler's Imperial. The seedlings from these summer sowings will be ready for planting out during September and early October, and they may be planted on ground that has been cleared of peas, beans or potatoes.

Vegetable Marrows. This is a very good first-year crop, for there is nothing that suits it better than decaying turf, unless, perhaps, it is a mixture of decaying turf and decaying manure. Make up a heap of turves in any sunny corner or, better still, dig out a large hole 1 yd. or so in extent each way and at least 1 ft. deep, and fill this with turves. Then purchase some sturdy marrow plants early in June and set them out about 4 ft. apart. If you prefer, you can sow seeds in pairs where the plants are to grow and then thin out the weaker in each case, but you must not sow until the middle of May and even then you should cover the seeds with an inverted flower pot or a cloche to afford them some protection at night. Vegetable marrows are tender and liable to be injured by the least frost.

During the summer all you need do to ensure a good crop of marrows is to water the plants freely when the weather is dry and, if you are growing a trailing variety, to pinch out the point of each 'runner' – long trailing shoot – when it is 2 or 3 ft. in length. Bush marrows need no pinching. Courgette is a variety of marrow which crops very freely if the marrows are cut when 5 or 6 in. long.

Courgettes are an increasingly popular variety of marrow. They will crop freely if gathered when about 5 or 6 in. long

CHAPTER 12

First Year Flowering Plants

Definition of annual, biennial and perennial –
Annuals for a temporary display – Three classes of
annuals – How to sow hardy annuals – Thinning
seedlings – Tender bedding plants – Violas and
pansies – Use of annuals and bedding plants –
Summer treatment – Removal of spent flowers

Before going any further it is, perhaps, necessary to explain that garden plants can be divided into groups defined as annuals, biennials, and perennials.

An annual is a plant that lives for one year only and dies when it has flowered and set its seed. It does not follow that this growth must be within one calendar year from January to December. It is quite possible, and occasionally advisable, to sow seeds of annuals in August so that the seedlings grow slowly during the autumn and winter and flower in spring or early summer.

A biennial differs in taking two growing seasons to complete its cycle, but, like the annual, it dies after flowering and producing seed. This must usually be sown in the spring or early summer in order to produce plants that will flower the following year. As with the annual, it is necessary to practise yearly sowing if there is to be a yearly display of flowers.

A perennial continues from year to year, though it must not be supposed that any one plant will go on for ever. In this respect perennials differ greatly according to their kind and also to the soil and conditions in which they are grown. Some are comparatively short-lived, requiring renewal every few years from seed, while others will continue generation after generation little diminished in vigour.

Annuals for a Temporary Display. Annuals have a special value in new gardens, for they will fill beds and borders with colour throughout the first summer and yet give you the chance for further cultivation in the autumn. In the spring you can sow seed outdoors of such things as sweet alyssum, annual coreopsis, calendula, godetia, bartonia, clarkia, larkspur, sweet scabious, nasturtium, scarlet flax, candytuft, nemophila, phacelia, eschscholzia, nigella, malope, lavatera, cornflower, Shirley and Cardinal poppies, and Virginian stock to produce a blaze of flowers within a couple of months or so, and so keep the garden bright during the first summer. Then, at just the right time, all the plants will conveniently die, and you will have the whole autumn and winter in which to give beds and borders a thorough digging and remove any weeds that were missed the first time.

Three Classes of Annuals. Annuals are divided into three classes: tender, half-hardy, and hardy. With the first you need have no concern at the moment, for tender annuals are suitable only for the greenhouse. Half-hardy annuals can be grown outdoors during the summer, but will not withstand frost. It

is necessary either to sow them in late winter or early spring in a glasshouse, or else to delay sowing outdoors until May, when serious danger of cold weather is usually over. This latter method is quite satisfactory with zinnias, stocks, asters, ageratums, and French and African marigolds, provided the plants are not required to flower early in the summer. But a finer and longer display is obtained by early sowing in a frostproof greenhouse. However, you will have no difficulty in obtaining as many glasshouse-raised half-hardy annuals as you require, for nurserymen make a practice of growing them in hundreds of thousands each year, and the plants are offered for sale during May and June. Do not be tempted to plant too early if you live in a cold district or one known to be subject to late frosts. Local gardeners can usually give advice about local conditions.

How to Sow Hardy Annuals. Hardy annuals (many of which have already been mentioned earlier in this chapter) can be sown outdoors where they are to flower. Sometimes you can make this sowing in August, when the plants will flower during May, June and July, but with most varieties April sowing for summer flowers is most satisfactory.

Seed of all these hardy annuals should be sown very thinly, and is usually best scattered broadcast and not sown in straight drills. A sufficient covering will be given if some soil is shaken over each patch of seeds through a sieve with a $\frac{3}{8}$-in. mesh. A useful general rule to remember is that seeds should not be covered after sowing to more than twice their own depth.

Thinning Seedlings. In a few weeks, the seedlings should be appearing. It is then necessary to thin them out, for even when carefully sown they are almost sure to be overcrowded. Small annuals such as alyssum and scarlet flax may be 6 in. apart, but the bigger kinds should have from 9 to 16 in. each. You will find that full instructions are printed on the packets in which you purchase the seeds.

Tender Bedding Plants. Another group of plants which will be of great service to you during your first summer are the so-called 'summer bedding' plants. These include geraniums (more correctly known as pelargoniums), marguerites, heliotropes, fuchsias, cannas, calceolarias, begonias, and dahlias.

All these bedding plants are perennials, though they are not sufficiently hardy to be grown outdoors during the winter. They must either be taken up at the end of the summer and placed in pots in the greenhouse or, with dahlias and tuberous-rooted begonias, stored in boxes in a frostproof place. Here again nurserymen make things easy by producing big supplies of these useful plants and offering them for sale during May and early June.

If later on you decide to purchase or construct a greenhouse, you will be able to keep many of

Opposite: (1) Sowing annuals broadcast. After a final raking, the bed can be roughly marked out in patches where seeds of each variety are to be sown

(2) Thinning annuals. With most annuals, a certain amount of thinning of the seedlings is necessary to prevent overcrowding

(3) Staking. Twiggy sticks inserted between the young plants will provide support and be fully concealed when the plants have grown

these bedding plants for another season and also raise fresh stock of them from cuttings.

Violas and Pansies. Two other plants that may be of great use for a temporary display during the first summer are violas and pansies. Actually both these are hardy perennials, but they can be purchased so cheaply in the spring and flower so freely and continuously during the summer that they are usually treated as bedding plants, to be thrown away in the autumn if it is not convenient to keep them until the following year. Violas are particularly useful in shady places, in which they flower better than most plants. The low growth of both violas and pansies makes them very suitable for edging and for massing in carpets beneath fuchsias etc.

Use of Annuals and Bedding Plants. With the aid, then, of hardy and half-hardy annuals and bedding plants you can contrive to fill most of your flower beds and borders during the first summer without any permanent planting. There is ample variety in height, colour, and style of growth to make a really good display, no matter what the surroundings. Annuals are particularly useful as a temporary filling for herbaceous borders, in which they can be arranged in informal groups and drifts after the manner followed with perennials.

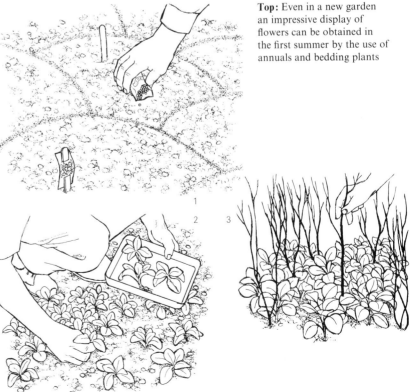

Top: Even in a new garden an impressive display of flowers can be obtained in the first summer by the use of annuals and bedding plants

Left: Petunias and other plants grown in a wooden tub. Such container planting is a welcome change from beds and borders and an effective means of brightening a terrace or patio

Right: Sweet peas trained up a tripod. Of all the annuals, sweet peas are especially rewarding, producing flowers for many weeks provided they are picked regularly

There are other annuals (or plants commonly treated as such) that you can use as a temporary clothing for fences, walls, arches, pergolas, and summer houses. These include Canary creeper, cobaea, climbing nasturtium, ipomoea and Japanese hop.

On the whole, bedding plants are more at home in formal surroundings, though they are not without other possibilities. During your first season you may be very glad of bedding plants as a temporary filling for rose beds. The big decorative dahlias are magnificent at the back of a wide border, while the stocks can be massed in the foreground.

Summer Treatment. The cultivation of all these plants is simple. Seed sowing with hardy annuals has already been described. Half-hardy annuals and bedding plants purchased in late spring or early summer should be planted carefully with a trowel and made thoroughly firm. Subsequently during the summer they and the hardy annuals require little attention, for they are not greatly troubled by pests or diseases, nor do they require much feeding. It is only necessary to hoe the ground between the plants from time to time to destroy weeds and to stake and tie the taller plants as neatly as possible. Trailers such as verbena and ivy-leaved geraniums can be pegged to the soil with advantage.

Removal of Spent Flowers. There is just one other point of some importance in the management of all these plants – namely, that all flowers should be removed as soon as they fade. This will encourage the plants to go on producing more blooms. If the faded flowers are left to produce seeds, the display will soon be over.

TABLE OF HARDY ANNUALS FOR SUMMER BEDS

NAME	COLOUR	HEIGHT	DISTANCE TO THIN
Alyssum (Sweet)	white, purple	4 to 6 in.	6 in.
Bartonia	yellow	$1\frac{1}{2}$ ft.	1 ft.
*Calendula	yellow and orange	1 to $1\frac{1}{2}$ ft.	1 ft.
Coreopsis, annual	yellow and crimson	1 to 3 ft.	1 ft.
*Candytuft	white, lilac and purple	6 to 12 in.	9 in.
*Chrysanthemum (annual)	white, yellow, red, maroon	1 to 2 ft.	1 ft.
Clarkia	white, pink and crimson	$1\frac{1}{2}$ to 2 ft.	1 ft.
Collinsia	white and purple	1 ft.	9 in.
Convolvulus	purple, crimson and white	12 to 15 in.	9 to 18 in.
*Cornflower	blue, rose and white	1 to 3 ft.	9 to 12 in.
Dimorphotheca	orange, salmon etc.	1 ft.	1 ft.
Echium	blue, pink, white	1 ft.	9 in.
Eschscholzia	yellow, orange, carmine and rose	9 to 12 in.	9 in.

NAME	COLOUR	HEIGHT	DISTANCE TO THIN
Godetia	pink to crimson and white	6 to 36 in.	9 to 12 in.
Gypsophila elegans	white, pink and carmine	1½ ft.	9 to 12 in.
Jacobaea	white, mauve, pink and purple	1½ ft.	9 in.
*Larkspur	white, pink, blue and scarlet	1½ to 3 ft.	1½ ft.
Lavatera	white and rose	2½ to 3 ft.	1½ ft.
Layia	yellow and white	1 ft.	9 in.
Leptosiphon	various	3 to 6 in.	3 to 4 in.
Leptosyne	yellow	1½ ft.	9 to 12 in.
Limnanthes	pale yellow	6 in.	6 in.
Linum (scarlet flax)	scarlet	9 to 12 in.	6 in.
Lupin	various	2 ft.	1 ft.
Malope	purple, white etc.	2 to 3 ft.	1½ ft.
Matthiola bicornis	purple, night-flowering (grown for scent)	9 to 12 in.	3 to 6 in.
Mignonette	greenish yellow, white and red	6 to 15 in.	6 to 9 in.
Nasturtium	yellow, scarlet etc.	9 to 12 in. Also climbing	9 to 15 in.
Nemophila	blue	6 in.	6 in.
Nigella (love-in-a-mist)	blue, pink, white	1 ft.	1 ft.
Phacelia	blue	6 to 9 in.	9 in.
Poppy (Shirley and Cardinal)	white, pink, crimson, heliotrope etc.	1½ to 3 ft.	12 to 15 in.
Salvia horminum	blue, pink, white	1½ to 2 ft.	1 ft.
Saponaria	rose, white	1½ ft.	9 in.
Scabious (Sweet)	white, pink, lavender, maroon	1½ to 2 ft.	12 to 15 in.
Sunflower (annual)	yellow and red	3 to 10 ft.	1 to 3 ft.
*Sweet Pea	white, pink, blue, scarlet etc.	1¼ to 10 ft.	4 to 9 in.
Sweet Sultan	white, rose and purple	1½ ft.	9 in.
Virginian Stock	white, pink, lilac to crimson	6 in.	3 in.
Viscaria	white, blue, pink to crimson	1 ft.	6 in.

All these can be sown outdoors during April and May. Those marked with an asterisk may also be sown in September.

TABLE OF HALF-HARDY ANNUALS FOR SUMMER BEDS

NAME	COLOUR	HEIGHT	SOW	DISTANCE APART WHEN PLANTED
Ageratum	blue	6 to 12 in.	March	6 to 8 in.
Amaranthus	purple, greenish yellow	2 to 3 ft.	March	1 ft.
*Antirrhinum	various	6 to 36 in.	February	6 to 12 in.
Aster (annual)	blue, purple, pink, red, white	1 to 2½ ft.	March, April	1 ft.
Begonia semperflorens	pink, red, white, etc.	6 to 12 in.	February, March	9 in.
Celosia	red, yellow	1 to 2½ ft.	March	1 ft.
Cleome	pink	3 ft.	March	1½ ft.
Cosmos	pink, white	2 to 3 ft.	March	1½ ft.
Dianthus (annual)	red, white etc.	6 to 12 in.	February	9 in.
Heliotrope	purple	1½ to 2 ft.	January, February	1 ft.
Hop (annual)	yellow leaves	climbing	March	3 ft.
Impatiens	red, pink, white	6 to 24 in.	February, March	9 in.
Kochia	green foliage turning purple	2 to 3 ft.	March	2 ft.
*Lobelia	blue, purple	4 to 8 in.	March	6 in.
Marigold (African and French)	orange, yellow, crimson	6 to 24 in.	March, April	6 to 24 in.
Mesembryanthemum	red, pink, apricot etc.	trailing	March	6 in.
Nemesia	various	9 to 12 in.	March	6 to 8 in.
Nicotiana	white, pink, crimson, lime green	1 to 3 ft.	March	1 ft.
*Petunia	white, blue, pink, red, purple	1 to 1½ ft.	March, April	8 to 12 in.
Phlox (annual)	red, purple, white etc.	9 to 12 in	March	9 in.

63

FIRST YEAR FLOWERING PLANTS

NAME	COLOUR	HEIGHT	SOW	DISTANCE APART WHEN PLANTED
Rudbeckia (annual)	yellow, red	1½ to 3 ft.	March	1 ft.
Salpiglossis	various	2 ft.	February, March	1 ft.
Salvia splendens	red, purple	6 to 24 in.	January, February	9 to 12 in.
Statice (annual)	various	1½ to 2 ft.	February, March	9 in.
Stocks (ten-week)	various	1½ ft.	March, April	1 ft.
Ursinia	orange, yellow	1 ft.	March	9 to 12 in.
*Verbena	red, pink, purple, blue	1 ft.	March	9 in.
Venidium	orange	2 to 3 ft.	March, April	1½ ft.
Zinnia	red, pink, orange, yellow	6 to 36 in.	March, April	6 to 12 in.

*These are really half-hardy perennials, but modern practice is to treat them as half-hardy annuals.

A TABLE OF SUMMER BEDDING PLANTS

NAME	COLOUR	HEIGHT	DISTANCE APART WHEN PLANTED	METHOD OF PROPAGATION
Begonia (tuberous rooted)	various	9 to 12 in.	9 to 12 in.	Seed in February or division in February or March
Calceolaria (shrubby)	yellow, bronze	1 to 1½ ft.	9 in.	Cuttings in early autumn or spring or seed in spring
Canna	yellow, red	2 to 3 ft.	1 to 2 ft.	Division in the spring
Dahlia	various	1½ to 7 ft.	1 to 4 ft.	Cuttings, seed or division in spring
Fuchsia	pink, red, purple etc.	1 to 4 ft.	1 to 3 ft.	Cuttings in spring or late summer
Gazania	yellow, orange etc.	trailing	9 to 12 in.	Cuttings in early autumn
Heliotrope	blue	9 to 36 in.	9 to 48 in.	Cuttings or seed in the spring
Marguerite	white, yellow	1½ to 2 ft.	1 to 1½ ft.	Cuttings in early autumn or spring
Mesembryanthemum (various)	various	trailing	1 to 2 ft.	Cuttings in the spring or late summer
Pansy	various	4 to 6 in.	6 to 9 in.	Seed in summer to flower the following year
Pelargonium (bedding geranium)	pink, red, white etc.	1 to 3 ft. and trailing	1 ft.	Cuttings in late summer or spring or seed in spring
Penstemon	various	1½ to 2 ft.	1 ft.	Cuttings in early autumn or seed in spring
Salvia (blue)	blue	1½ to 2 ft.	1 ft.	Cuttings or division in spring
Senecio cineraria	silver leaves	1½ to 2 ft.	1 to 3 ft.	Cuttings in spring
Viola	various	4 to 6 in.	6 to 9 in.	Seed in summer to flower the following year

CHAPTER 13

The First Summer

Routine tasks – Keeping down weeds – Hoeing – Mulching – Watering – Summer feeding

During the first summer in your new garden and, for that matter, so long as you continue to keep a garden, there will be a certain amount of routine work to be done. Some of this has already been described in earlier chapters. For example, the faded flowers must be picked off annuals and bedding plants before seed pods begin to form; the long shoots of trailing plants such as verbenas and pansies should be fastened with small pegs to the soil to prevent them blowing about and getting broken off, and some of the taller plants may require staking. Lawns must be cut regularly with a sharp lawn mower. Hedges may require a little trimming, but this should not be overdone the first season, for leaf growth will encourage root growth and so help the shrubs to get established quickly.

Keeping Down Weeds. But far and away the most important task of all during this first summer will be keeping down weeds. Many of these are annuals – that is to say, similar in life style to the ornamental annuals that must be renewed from seed every year. If you can prevent these annual weeds from producing flowers and setting seeds half your battle will be over, for there will only be a few old seeds left in the soil to give further trouble another season – and many of these may get picked up by birds during the winter.

Even perennial weeds such as bindweed, couch, thistle, dandelion, dock, and creeping buttercup will be greatly weakened if they are continually chopped off and prevented from forming any crowns and leaves, though it is even more effective to dig them up, roots and all, as soon as they appear. Some can be spot treated with a safe weedkiller such as paraquat or dichlobenil and bindweed (wild convolvulus) is very sensitive to 2,4-D, one of the chemicals used in selective lawn weedkillers. But if you do use any of these chemicals you must be careful not to get them on any of the garden plants which are likely to be killed by them just as quickly and effectively as the weeds. The safest way is to use a special plastic applicator fitted with a narrow sprinkle bar which will deliver the weedkiller just where it is required.

Hoeing. This is a method of cutting off weeds just below soil level and at the same time stirring the surface soil and so improving soil aeration and keeping beds neat and tidy.

There are many different patterns of hoe, some with long handles to be used standing up, some short handled, necessitating stooping or kneeling. But all can be grouped into two basic types, dutch hoes and draw hoes. The former have a blade set almost in the same plane as the handle to be pushed through the soil, whereas the blade of a draw hoe is set almost at right angles to the handle to be pulled

through the soil and used with a chopping action. Dutch hoes are particularly useful for hoeing crops in straight rows or plants fairly widely spaced; draw hoes are perhaps more controllable where plants are closely spaced at random, and they are also useful for breaking up hard clods and for drawing the soil into ridges or mounds where this is desirable. A short-handled type of draw hoe known as the onion hoe is an excellent little tool for weeding small beds and for thinning out seedlings.

Many people make the mistake of hoeing deeply. This is quite unnecessary, makes hard work, and does not destroy weeds satisfactorily. It may also damage the upper roots of the bed's proper occupants.

Hoeing once a fortnight in late spring and summer is usually sufficient, but if the beds are trodden on for spraying, staking, or picking they must be hoed afterwards. It is also advisable to hoe as soon as all surface moisture has drained off after summer rains as a thin layer of broken soil helps to keep the soil below cool and checks unnecessary loss of water by surface evaporation.

Mulching and Feeding. If you have too much ground to keep hoed regularly there is an alternative method of checking weeds, maintaining a neat, clean appearance and keeping in soil moisture. This is spread peat, composted bark, spent hops (not hop manure, which contains fertilizer and can only be used sparingly) or grass clippings at least an inch deep all over the surface. This is known as a mulch and as it gets drawn in by worms and worked in by hoeing or forking, it improves the texture of the soil. Regular mulching is an excellent way of making heavy and sticky soils more workable.

Plants may also need some feeding during the

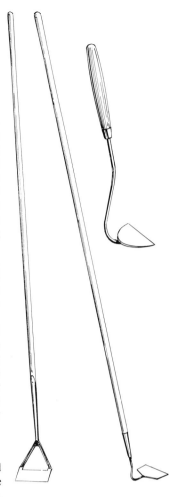

Top: Three types of hoe: a Dutch hoe, a draw hoe and a short-handled onion hoe

Bottom: Applying fertilizer round herbaceous plants. An application of a good compound fertilizer in April, plus a topdressing of bonemeal in autumn, will enrich the soil

summer, and for this purpose a compound garden fertilizer containing approximately equal quantities of nitrogen, phosphoric acid and potash is best. National Growmore is a fertilizer of this kind and can be lightly sprinkled round growing plants two or three times from May to early September just before hoeing so that it is immediately mixed with the surface soil. If the weather is dry, water the fertilizer in, otherwise it will not dissolve and will be useless to plants which can only take from the soil chemicals which are in solution. An alternative is to apply the feed in solution either from a watering can or through a dilutor fitted to a hose feeding a sprinkler. Special liquid or highly soluble fertilizers are available for this kind of liquid feeding.

Watering. If the weather is very hot and dry even hoeing and mulching may not be adequate to keep the soil sufficiently moist, particularly for young plants which have not yet had time to root deeply into the ground in search of the water in the subsoil. Do not be afraid to water, but if you do so be certain to give sufficient to soak down to the roots. It is useless simply to dampen the surface. Individual plants can be watered from a can, preferably directly from the spout and not through a rose, which checks the flow so much that the plants rarely receive enough water. Far better, however, is to use a hose and a sprinkler which delivers a fairly fine rain-like shower and can be left for an hour or so until the soil is properly soaked.

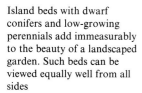

Island beds with dwarf conifers and low-growing perennials add immeasurably to the beauty of a landscaped garden. Such beds can be viewed equally well from all sides

CHAPTER 14

Past Efforts Consolidated

Clearing the ground – A second deep cultivation – Soil fumigation – Where to dig first

By the early autumn after your first summer in a new garden you will be able to clear some of the ground in readiness for a second big onslaught upon weeds and soil pests. As soon as annuals have ceased to flower the plants should be pulled up and either be thrown on the rubbish heap or burned. They are of no use whatsoever for a second year. Similar remarks apply to the old plants of peas and beans when the pods have been gathered. The potato plot, too, will be cleared at latest by the middle of October, and all perennial summer bedding plants such as geraniums, marguerites, and fuchsias must either be thrown away or else removed to a frostproof place, preferably a greenhouse, by about the same date. The tubers of dahlias and begonias can be lifted and stored in boxes filled with dry peat as soon as their foliage and stems have been blackened by frost. These should be cut off just above the tubers. If the boxes are placed in a dry cupboard, room, or frostproof shed or garage and no water is allowed to come near them all the winter, the tubers will keep quite safely until the following spring, when they can be restarted into growth in a frame, greenhouse or even a sunny window.

Having disposed of the plants, rake off all stems, leaves, and other rubbish from the surface of the beds. If disease has been prevalent among the plants during the summer, all this rubbish should be burned at once, but if the plants have been reasonably healthy, all vegetable refuse can be stacked in a heap or placed in a pit in some out-of-the-way place to rot down into manure. If you sprinkle this refuse with sulphate of ammonia or one of the proprietary compost makers it will decay more quickly and the quality of the manure will be improved.

A Second Deep Cultivation. Now dig again every vacant plot exactly as advised for the first cultivation working in well-rotted manure, compost, peat, or any other bulky soil dressing you can obtain. Manure will be most beneficial in places where roses, any further fruit trees, and all vegetables, with the exception of root crops, are to be grown. In all these places manure can be used at the rate of one barrow load to every 10 square yards of ground. A lighter dressing of manure – say, one barrow load to 20 square yards – can be used in places where trees or shrubs are to be planted or herbaceous borders are to be made, but do not give any manure at all to ground you have set aside for rock garden or dry walls. Alpine plants, in general, do not require rich soil which tends to produce rank growth and few flowers and may cause decay in winter.

Soil Fumigation and Liming. As you dig you must watch carefully for all roots of perennial weeds and collect every piece that you can see. This may be the last opportunity you have for thoroughly cleaning out certain parts of the garden. If pests are much in evidence give the soil a good dusting of a soil insecticide as you go along. No harm will result from applying this with manure, but it is not wise to apply lime and manure at the same time. At the very least a few weeks should be allowed to elapse between the two applications.

Since some ornamental plants such as rhododendrons, azaleas, many heathers and lupins, dislike lime it is best not to use it generally in flower beds and borders unless the soil is known to be very acid. It can be used where lime-loving plants such as clematis, lavender and scabious are to be planted and it is also useful in the vegetable garden for peas, beans and all the cabbage family and in the fruit garden for plums, cherries, peaches and other stone fruits. Hydrated lime is the best form to use and it can be dusted quite heavily on the surface (4 to 8 oz. per square yard) and be forked or dug in.

Where to Dig First. The earlier in the autumn the digging can be done the better, for then the ground will have a reasonable time in which to settle and get thoroughly weathered before you start planting again. But you should certainly give preference to any plots on which you are going to grow bulbs or spring bedding plants, for these must be planted early in the autumn (see Chapter 15). Next to these the greatest urgency is to prepare the ground for roses, shrubs and any further ornamental trees you may be contemplating. The vegetable garden and places intended for herbaceous borders, rock gardens, or ornamental pool can be left until last, for spring is the most favourable time for sowing and planting these.

Preparing and boxing dahlias for storing. (1) The foliage and stems are cut back before lifting. (2) The tubers are then clearly labelled and stored in boxes of peat in a dry, frostproof place

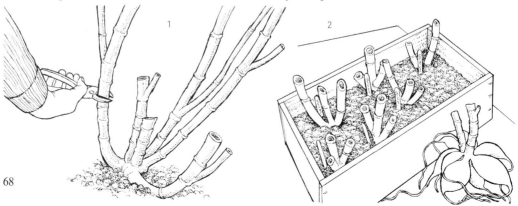

CHAPTER 15

Bulb Planting

Many bulbs replanted annually – Spring as well as autumn planting – What to grow – Preparation of soil – How to plant – Lifting and drying off – Gladioli and montbretias – Bulb selection

When you have cleared and redug some of the ground occupied by temporary summer-flowering plants and summer vegetables one of your first tasks will be the planting of bulbs. If there is any ground that you would like to dig over again at a later date you may well consider planting some bulbs there for a spring or early summer display, for many bulbs are temporary rather than permanent occupants of the ground. Though they are perennials, they have such a marked resting period when their leaves die down that after flowering they are often better out of the ground and in store in a dry, airy shed.

Spring as well as Autumn Planting. Early autumn is not the only bulb planting season, though it is the best time for planting almost all the really hardy bulbous plants such as tulips, daffodils, hyacinths, Spanish, English, and Dutch irises, crocuses, scillas, chionodoxas, muscaris and lilies. But there are a few bulbous-rooted plants which cannot be planted until March or April, as they are not sufficiently hardy to withstand winter weather outdoors. Most important of these are gladioli. Snowdrops are nearly always sold in the shops and garden centres in autumn and so you may have to buy them then, but if you are getting them from a friend or a specialist nursery a better time to plant them is in March immediately after flowering. But at this period snowdrops are in full growth so must not be kept out of the soil an hour longer than necessary.

What to Grow. You will probably not find it very easy to decide just what to grow and what to leave out, so perhaps a few general suggestions may prove helpful.

Hyacinths are especially suitable for formal bedding schemes. They seldom look happy mixed up with other plants in a border, and because of their low stature it is not really practicable to grow anything else with them except perhaps an edging of double daisies or a carpet of aubrieta or arabis.

Tulips are also most suitable for formal places, but are better mixers than hyacinths, and some of the dwarf early tulips and wild species look quite attractive when planted along the margins of borders or in rock gardens.

Narcissi, a name that includes daffodils, are much less formal and are never seen to better advantage than when naturalized in grass, particularly in large drifts around the boles of trees. However, if they are grown in this way the grass should not be cut until the daffodil leaves begin to turn yellow some time in June, otherwise the bulbs will be weakened and may not flower the following year. Of course, when they are grown in this way the bulbs are not

lifted and dried off each summer, but are left undisturbed until a serious falling off in the number and quality of the flowers indicates that they are worn out and must be dug up, divided and replanted. Crocuses and snowdrops also naturalize well and so do colchicums, which look rather like crocuses and flower in the autumn.

There are several different kinds of bulbous iris. The Spanish, English, and Dutch types are about 2 ft. in height and flower in early summer. They are particularly serviceable for cutting, but also look

Top: Narcissi in a small garden. When flowering is over, the bulbs can be lifted and moved to a temporary bed to make room for summer bedding plants.

Bottom: The dwarf *Tulipa kaufmanniana* varieties are especially well suited to planting in the rock garden

Top: A narrow-bladed bulb-planting trowel, showing depth measurements, is a useful aid for planting bulbs. Alternatively, a special bulb-planting tool which lifts a core of soil out of the ground is a great asset if a large number of bulbs are to be planted, especially in turf

Bottom: Table showing the appropriate planting depths for bulbs, corms and tubers.
(a) Ranunculus. (b) Hyacinth.
(c) Gladiolus. (d) Scilla.
(e) Tulip. (f) Crocus.
(g) Narcissus. (h) Anemone.
(i) Bulbous iris. (j) Dahlia.
(k) Lily

charming planted in informal groups in borders or at the front of shrubberies. Dwarf, early-flowering species such as purple *Iris reticulata*, blue *I. histrioides* and yellow *I. danfordiae* should be planted in the rock garden or in a select sunny corner where they will not be swamped later in the year by coarser-growing plants.

Most lilies are seen to best advantage when planted in groups among other plants. There are many kinds that gain considerable advantage from the shade thrown on the soil by fairly low foliage, for lilies as a rule do not like to have their roots baked up, though they are glad to have their heads in the sun. It is possible to create a very pleasing effect by planting lilies between peonies, while some of the tall kinds can be associated with small rhododendrons and azaleas. Some lilies dislike lime and may be unsuitable for your garden if it contains much lime or chalk. Notable exceptions which can be grown in any soil, if it contains a fair proportion of leafmould or peat, are *Lilium candidum, chalcedonicum, croceum, davidii, han-sonii, henryi, martagon, maxwill, monadelphum, pardalinum, pyrenaicum, regale, testaceum, thunbergianum, umbellatum* (also known as *hollandicum*) and the excellent Mid-century Hybrids.

The Dutch crocuses are ideal edging plants and can be used for this purpose in association with other small bulbous-rooted plants. There are also a number of species of crocus that are delightful in the rock garden; notable among these is *Crocus susianus*, aptly known as cloth of gold, *C. tomasinianus*, an early-flowering, lavender variety, and *C. chrysanthus*, a quick-multiplying kind that has a number of varieties including white, cream, yellow, orange, blue and purple.

The muscaris, chionodoxas, and scillas are also at home either in the rock garden or as edgings to beds and borders, but snowdrops are unquestionably children of the wild and do not look happy in any formal setting. Plant them in the rock garden, in groups towards the front of a shrub border, or in select corners of the wild garden, and they are perfectly happy.

Preparation of the Soil. When preparing the soil for bulbs use manure sparingly or not at all, but if the texture of the soil is poor (very light and dry or very heavy and wet) work in peat freely. Also fork in bonemeal at the rate of 3 or 4 oz. per square yard, and then later on, when the bulbs have started to grow and leaves have appeared above ground, give a light dusting of a well-balanced garden fertilizer such as National Growmore.

How to Plant Bulbs. In cultivated soil most bulbs are best planted with a trowel, and special narrow, long-bladed bulb trowels can be purchased and are particularly useful for small bulbs. Some of the larger bulbs, and especially those of lilies, are really best planted with a spade as most like to be in a hole about 7 in. deep with about an inch of peat in the bottom and a mixture of peat and soil round the bulbs. This rather deep planting is necessary because many lilies make roots from the flower stem above the bulb as well as from the base of the bulb itself. It is for this reason also that lilies particularly enjoy a mulch of peat or leafmould while they are growing, into which they can make more roots. But there are exceptions. *Lilium candidum*, the white madonna lily, and *L. testaceum* both like to grow with their bulbs half out of the soil and should be just barely covered when they are planted. They also start to grow very early and are best planted in July or August if bulbs can be obtained then.

The depth at which bulbs are planted is rather important, but this information has been incorporated in the chart on this page, so it is not necessary to go into detail here. Early-flowering tulips should be planted about 6 in. apart, the later May-flowering Darwin tulips 8 in. apart, and a similar spacing will serve for most daffodils and hyacinths. Lilies generally require from 9 to 12 in. apart, though this will depend somewhat on the variety. Spanish, English, and Dutch irises should be about 6 in. apart, but the smaller early-flowering irises do not need more than 2 or 3 in., and this is also sufficient for crocuses, muscaris, chionodoxas, scillas, and snowdrops.

The following table will help you to calculate how many bulbs you will require at these different planting distances.

TABLE FOR CALCULATING NUMBER OF BULBS REQUIRED

Planting distance in inches	2	3	4	6	8	9	12
Bulbs required per square yard	324	144	81	36	20	16	9

If the ground is heavy and inclined to be wet it is a good plan to place a trowelful of silver sand underneath each bulb.

Lifting and Drying Off. If you wish to replace the spring-blooming bulbs in May by summer-flowering plants, you must lift them carefully with as much root as possible and lay them temporarily in a shallow trench in any out-of-the-way place. Cover the bulbs and roots with soil and make it thoroughly

depth in inches

firm. Then leave them undisturbed until the foliage dies down, when they should be lifted again with a fork, shaken out, and laid thinly in seed trays or similar shallow boxes. Place these in a dry, airy, but not sunny place, and a week or so later, clean off the shrivelled leaves and remove any soil sticking to the bulbs. They can then be stored in trays, boxes, or bags in any dry, cool, and airy place until planting time.

If the beds are not required for other plants, leave the bulbs undisturbed until the foliage dies down and then lift them and treat them exactly as above. It is not necessary to lift annually daffodils, lilies, bulbous-rooted irises, crocuses, scillas, muscaris, chionodoxas, or snowdrops. All these can be left to grow and increase until they get overcrowded and the blossoms suffer in numbers or quality. Even tulips and hyacinths can be left to grow on for several years if the soil and position obviously suits them, but in a general way it is better to lift and replant annually. If the bulbs show a great falling-off in size, discard them altogether and purchase new stock in the autumn. Undersized bulbs will not give you any flowers, but can be grown on if space permits.

Gladioli and Montbretias. Some bulbs cannot be planted safely in autumn because they are not hardy enough to withstand the winter except, perhaps, in a few very mild places. Most important of these are gladioli, which can be planted at any time from March until early May. There are innumerable varieties grouped in several different classes according to size and flower formation. The 'large flowered' are the biggest, usually 3 or 4 ft. high; the miniatures are smaller and shorter; the 'butterfly' varieties are usually fairly tall but have flowers of medium size, and the 'primulinus' varieties have small, hooded flowers rather widely spaced on slender stems.

It is worth planting a bed of gladioli in an out-of-the-way place so that you can cut the flowers without spoiling the garden display. Gladioli 'corms', as the solid, food-storing parts are termed, are planted about 3 in. deep and at least 6 in. apart for the smaller types and 8 in. for the large-flowered kinds. All flower during August and September. Montbretias are also planted during March and April to flower in late summer. They have slender spikes of showy flowers, usually in shades of yellow, orange, or crimson. Their corms are smaller than those of the gladiolus and should be planted 2 in. deep and at least 4 in. apart. The common montbretia is fairly hardy and will usually thrive outdoors winter and summer, but some of the large-flowered varieties are a little tender and may need the protection of a cloche or frame in winter.

Top: Bulbs naturalized in grass are a delightful sight in spring. It must be remembered, however, that the grass should not be cut until the bulb foliage has died down

BULB SELECTION

HYACINTHS FOR BEDDING

City of Haarlem, pure yellow.
Delft Blue, mid-blue.
Jan Bos, deep red.
Lady Derby, light pink.
L'Innocence, white.
Myosotis, light blue.
Ostara, deep blue.
Pink Pearl, carmine-pink

EARLY SINGLE TULIPS

Apricot Beauty, salmon and apricot.
Bellona, yellow.
Couleur Cardinal, cardinal red.
General De Wet, golden yellow, heavily flushed
    orange scarlet.
Keizerskroon, bright red, with broad yellow
    margin.
Princess Irene, orange.

EARLY DOUBLE TULIPS

Maréchal Niel, yellow and orange.
Mr van der Hoef, yellow.
Murillo, light rose.
Orange Nassau, deep red.
Peach Blossom, dark rosy pink.
Snow Queen, white.
Vuurbaak, orange scarlet.

EARLY HYBRID TULIPS (Greigii, Kaufmanniana and Fosteriana)

Heart's Delight, carmine and pink.
Oriental Splendour, red and yellow.
Plaisir, cream and vermilion.
Purissima, white.
Red Emperor, scarlet.
Red Riding Hood, scarlet.
Shakespeare, pink and red.

MAY FLOWERING AND LILY-FLOWERED TULIPS

Alladin, red and yellow.
Halcro, carmine red.
Mariette, rose pink.
Mrs John T. Scheepers, yellow.
Orange King, orange with yellow centre.
President Hoover, orange red.
Queen of Sheba, russet red and yellow.
Rosy Wings, satin pink.
West Point, creamy yellow.
White Triumphator, white.

MAY-FLOWERING DARWIN TULIPS

Bartigon, scarlet crimson.
Clara Butt, soft salmon rose.
Niphetos, creamy yellow.
Ossi Oswalda, white and rose.
Pride of Haarlem, rosy carmine, electric blue
    centre.
Princess Elizabeth, soft rose.
Queen of Bartigons, pink.
Queen of Night, maroon black.
Smiling Queen, rose pink.
Sunkist, deep yellow.

The Bishop, violet blue.
William Copland, soft lavender.
William Pitt, scarlet.
Zwanenberg, large white flower.

DARWIN HYBRID TULIPS

Apeldoorn, scarlet.
Golden Apeldoorn, yellow.
Gudoshnik, yellow, pearl and pink.
Holland's Glory, orange red.

VIRIDIFLORA TULIPS

Artist, orange, pink and green.
Golden Artist, yellow and green.
Greenland, pink and green.
Pimpernel, red and green.

PARROT TULIPS

Black Parrot, deep maroon.
Blue Parrot, bluish heliotrope.
Fantasy, soft salmon rose.
Red Champion, cochineal red.
Orange Favourite, orange and green.
Texas Gold, golden yellow.

CROCUSES

King of the Striped, violet and pale lilac.
Jeanne d'Arc, white.
Large Yellow, golden yellow.
Pickwick, palest lavender and purple.
Queen of the Blues, mauve and purple.
Remembrance, sky blue.
Vanguard, violet blue.

DAFFODILS

Actaea, white perianth, scarlet and yellow eye.
Barret Browning, white perianth, orange-red cup.
Beersheba, white perianth and trumpet.
Binkie, lemon perianth, ivory cup.
Carbineer, yellow perianth, orange-scarlet cup.
Carlton, yellow perianth and cup.
Cheerfulness, small double cream flowers.
Eddy Canzony, white perianth, orange cup.
February Gold, golden yellow, reflexed perianth.
Fortune, yellow perianth, orange cup.
Geranium, small white and orange-red flowers.
Ice Follies, white perianth and cup.
Irene Copeland, double creamy-white and
    sulphur flowers.
John Evelyn, creamy-white perianth, soft orange
    cup.
King Alfred, deep yellow perianth and trumpet.
Louise de Coligny, white perianth and apricot-pink
    trumpet.
Mary Copeland, double white and orange-red
    flowers.
Mount Hood, white perianth and trumpet.
Semper Avanti, cream perianth, orange cup.
Texas, double yellow and orange flowers.
Trousseau, white perianth, yellow and white
    trumpet.
Unsurpassable, golden-yellow perianth and trumpet.

CHAPTER 16

Spring Bedding

What is spring bedding? – How plants are produced – Preparation of soil – Arrangement of plants – After flowering

Spring bedding is a term used to describe the use of plants for a temporary display from March until May. As soon as they have finished flowering the plants are removed and their place is taken by summer-flowering plants – chiefly the half-hardy annuals and perennial summer bedding plants already described.

Many of the bulbs mentioned in the last chapter can be used for spring bedding. Tulips and hyacinths are particular favourites, while daffodils, scillas, muscaris, crocuses, and chionodoxas are quite freely employed. But there are also other plants which can be used for this purpose either by themselves or in association with bulbs.

Raising Your Plants. Wallflowers and *Cheiranthus allionii* (Siberian wallflower) are among the most popular of these non-bulbous spring bedding plants. They can be raised easily by sowing seeds outdoors in May or early June. These will germinate in a week or so and as soon as the seedlings have made two or three leaves each they can be transplanted carefully to a 'nursery bed'. This is simply any convenient patch of ground, open and sunny, that can be broken down with a fork to a reasonably crumbly surface. In this well-prepared bed the small seedlings are set out about 6 in. apart in rows 8 or 9 in. apart. By early October they will have grown into sturdy plants which can then be transferred to the beds or borders in which they are to flower. Here they should be set about 1 ft. apart each way.

Forget-me-nots and double daisies are treated in exactly the same way, except that forget-me-nots should not be sown until about the middle of June. If sown in May the plants tend to get too big by the autumn and do not withstand the winter so well. Forget-me-nots are planted about 8 in. apart each way for a massed effect, while double daisies should be about 6 in. apart.

Polyanthus and coloured primroses can also be raised from seeds sown outdoors in late spring, but they do not grow so rapidly as wallflowers and it is really better to sow them in a frame or unheated greenhouse in March. The final planting distance is from 6 to 8 in. according to the size of the clumps.

You may feel that all this seed sowing is out of the question so early on in your garden making. If so you can purchase all the spring bedding plants you may require. Nurserymen make a practice of raising vast numbers of these plants every year and offering them for sale in the early autumn. It is only necessary to plant these out in their flowering quarters and keep the beds clear of weeds in autumn and winter for a good spring display.

Preparation of the Soil. Beyond digging or forking the ground no great amount of preparation is necessary. Animal manure is not desirable, as it will tend to make the plants rot off during the winter. A little bonemeal scattered lightly over the surface and forked in will help the plants along without encouraging soft growth.

Arrangement of Plants. Spring bedding plants can be used in beds or groups of a kind as two or more kinds can be mixed in the same bed.

Forget-me-nots make an ideal groundwork for the May-flowering and Darwin tulips, but are too tall for early-flowering tulips and hyacinths. A very popular arrangement, and one which, though hackneyed, is still delightful, is to plant a bed with forget-me-nots about 8 in. apart each way and interplant these with a pink tulip such as Clara Butt or Mariette.

Double daisies in white, pink, and red are also useful as a groundwork for taller plants, and on account of their low growth can associate well with early-flowering tulips and hyacinths.

Wallflowers are really best by themselves in blocks of different colours. They do not associate particularly well with other plants and in any case are quite adequate on their own. Polyanthus and coloured primroses are also attractive if grown by themselves, and in any case they start to flower rather too precociously for most of the other spring bedding plants with the exception of crocuses and a few other early bulbs.

Good spring displays can also be made with pansies which will continue to flower well into the summer. The so-called winter-flowering pansies actually start to flower about March in most places and finish correspondingly early. Other possibilities are to use white or pink arabis or blue, lavender, pink or carmine aubrieta as a carpet for bulbs such as tulips or hyacinths.

After Flowering. Wallflowers, *Cheiranthus allionii*, double daisies, and forget-me-nots are thrown away after flowering. The treatment of bulbs I have already described. Polyanthus and coloured primroses can be split up into separate crowns or small plants, each with a little root attached, and may then be planted out in a shady, out-of-the-way border to grow on into new clumps for use the following autumn. Arabis and aubrieta will also live from year to year but it is difficult to split them up and better plants are obtained by raising from seed or by taking cuttings of firm young shoots in summer to root in sandy soil in a frame or under a cloche.

CHAPTER 17

A Frame is Added

Autumn a suitable time – The best position – Choice of material and type – Excluding frost – Wintering bedding plants – Bulbs in frames – Seed sowing in frames

At this point it may be wise to turn aside from the primary problem of getting the garden itself into order, and to consider the advisability of adding a frame in which to protect any rather tender plants you wish to carry through the winter for use another year. A greenhouse will do this equally well and also provide a comfortable place in which to work when it is cold or wet outdoors, but you may well feel that you have sufficient on your hands this first year and prefer to consider a greenhouse later. If you do it will still be useful to have a frame as well, as one supplements the other.

It is the slightly tender summer bedding plants such as geraniums, fuchsias, and marguerites that are particularly worth overwintering in a frame or other light place that can be made frostproof as they are fairly expensive to buy and will continue to grow for years so long as they do not get frozen.

The Best Position. A frame to be used for this purpose should be placed in a sunny but sheltered position. The only time that a frame needs to be in a shady site is when it is used solely for propagating cuttings. If you propose to purchase a greenhouse later, you may like to place the frame next to the site it will occupy, or you may prefer to have the frame quite near the dwelling-house so that it can be easily connected to the electricity supply for heating. If you make or buy a portable frame, you can move it about as you wish.

Choice of Material and Type. The walls of frames may be built of metal, wood, concrete, or brick. Metal is certainly more durable than wood and metal frames usually admit a little more light than wooden ones, but against this you must weigh the fact that they lose heat quickly in cold weather and heat up fast when it is warm, and so need careful heating and ventilation.

Ordinary deal is liable to rot unless frequently painted or treated with wood preservative, but western red cedar is highly resistant to decay and so is very suitable for both frames and greenhouses. Frames with very thin wooden walls are no warmer than metal ones.

Brick- or concrete-walled frames are the best of all, but they are comparatively costly to build and are not tenant's fixtures so they cannot be taken away from a rented property.

The height of the frame can vary a great deal, but the slope of the lights should never be less than 8 degrees. If you build it yourself you will find it helpful to make a shallow frame with additional side sections so that depth can be increased at will. In this way you can always have the plants near to the glass without building up the soil inside. Plants grown too far away from the light make weak, straggling growth.

Excluding Frost. To winter tender bedding plants it is essential that the frame should be absolutely frostproof. Except in the milder parts of the south and west of Britain or in particularly sheltered places it is difficult to exclude frost from a completely unheated frame. However, if mains electricity is available the frame can be heated with a soil-warming cable. The cable can be embedded in the soil when it is needed to supply bottom heat, as for rooting cuttings, or it can be fixed with special clips around the inside of the frame sides if it is mainly air warming that is required. If a thermostat is included in the circuit the current will be switched on or off as the temperature of the air or soil falls below or rises above a chosen level, usually about 7 to 9°C. (45 to 48°F.). This means that the cable can be left undisturbed for weeks on end without any current being used unnecessarily.

Wintering Bedding Plants. The plants should be in the frames as soon as the weather shows signs of turning frosty (usually by the second week in October except in the mildest places). Lift all those that you consider worth saving, and shake off some of the soil. Each plant can then be put in a separate pot, or you can plant them into a bed made up in the frame. You will find that separate pots have the advantage that, in the spring, the plants can be transplanted from them with much less root disturbance than from the frame bed. Choose the smallest size of pot into which the roots will go, put plenty of broken crocks in the base to serve as drainage material, and fill up the spaces round the roots with good potting compost. Probably the top growth will have become too large and straggly to be convenient but it can be cut back fairly drastically.

There is no advantage in keeping a high temperature in the frame. During warm spells on sunny, winter days quite a lot of ventilation can be given with advantage, and on all but foggy or frosty days you should give some ventilation by tilting the light up on the side away from the wind. Only a crack of air will be needed on windy days.

The soil should be kept on the dry side, and you should take care not to spill water about unnecessarily as a dry atmosphere is important, the plants being more likely to rot if kept in moist air. If possible you should water in the morning rather than in the evening, and close the lights in time to trap some of the day warmth.

As spring approaches you must try to accustom the plants to the normal outside temperature, only heating sufficiently at night to prevent frost damage. If you do not harden the plants off in this manner you will find that they will be too delicate to plant out in the latter half of May. No tender plants should be put out before this date in any but the mildest areas as there are frequently sharp night

frosts early in May. By the time the plants are ready to plant out they will probably need more room than when you first potted them up.

Bulbs in Frames. A frame is not only of value for overwintering summer bedding plants. If you have any room to spare it can be used for bringing along early pots of bulbs. These should not be placed in the frame as soon as they are potted up or they will start to make top growth before they have made the necessary roots. To be really successful with bulbs you should plunge them for a period of eight to ten weeks under a layer of 4 in. or more of sand or peat. Any out-of-the-way place will do for a plunge bed of this description, and the cooler and more shaded it is the better will be the results. When the pots are getting well filled with roots and the shoots are about an inch or so above the surface of the compost they may be put into the frame, which need only be heated to a low temperature, 10°C. (50°F.) at the maximum. The bulbs, especially hyacinths, tulips, and crocuses, will produce much better blooms in a steady low temperature than in a higher one.

Seed Sowing in Frames. You will find a frame, either cold or warmed, a great help in raising seedlings of vegetables and half-hardy annuals for the next summer. If the frame is unheated you will be well advised not to start seed sowing before early March, or you will find that a particularly cold spell may check the tender seedlings, even if it does not actually injure them. Checks in growth at an early stage are seldom fully outgrown.

In a warm frame with a minimum temperature of about 9°C. (48°F.) you can sow seeds of some hardy and half-hardy plants in March, but a higher temperature is needed for tomatoes.

The amount of room ultimately occupied by the seedlings will be many times that occupied by the seed boxes or pans in the first instance, even if you do not intend to grow on every seedling that germinates. Room must be found to harden the young plants off, for you will not be able to plant them out until May, and there is plenty of time for increase in size between March and May.

When sowing vegetable seeds always bear in mind that all seeds of the same variety of crop sown at the same time in similar conditions will come into bearing more or less simultaneously. Therefore, if you wish to avoid a glut at one time and a scarcity at another, you must make several sowings at intervals of about a fortnight. The individual sowings can be quite small.

Types of garden frame

Interior of a garden frame showing the use of air- and soil-warming cables

CHAPTER 18

Why Not a Rose Garden?

Types for all places – What to plant – The principal types – Bushes and standards – Species and vigorous kinds – Climbing roses and ramblers – Weeping standards – Some exceptions – Colour associations – Associates for roses – The best position – Some points in design – Preparation of the beds – Planting errors to avoid – Care of roots – Pruning after planting – Staking and tying

There can be but few people who do not aspire to grow roses in their gardens, and with very good reason, for, provided suitable varieties are chosen to suit the soil and exposure, there are few other flowers which may be grown with so much satisfaction and success throughout the British Isles. The best results are likely to be obtained where roses can be given a fairly rich soil in a bed to themselves in a sunny, open position.

What to Plant. I am not going to give any advice about the actual selection of varieties, because I think that this is a matter which is best left to personal judgement. Varieties are numerous, and the popular favourites change frequently, but the very fact that competition is so keen means that no rose with any really serious fault can survive for more than a season or so. In consequence, if you make your choice from the standard varieties listed in any nurseryman's catalogue, you can be fairly certain of satisfaction in so far as habit, vigour and freedom are concerned. Colour, shape, and frag-

rance are the only matters of importance that remain, and these are all qualities that affect people so differently that my advice would be as likely to prove misleading as helpful. If you can manage to see the roses you fancy in bloom in a trial ground (The Royal National Rose Society maintains a fine one at St Albans), a public park, a friend's garden or a nursery display garden of established plants (young nursery plants can be misleading), before placing your order, so much the better. Unless you have special knowledge or reliable expert advice it is best to give novelties a miss until they have been well tried out.

The Principal Types. Most of the roses grown nowadays as bushes or standards are either large flowered (hybrid tea type) or cluster flowered (floribunda type). The large-flowered varieties are the ordinary 'roses' of the man in the street. Typically they have fine, full flowers borne singly or in small, rather loose clusters. The cluster-flowered roses have larger clusters of smaller flowers and a much greater range of flower shape including singles, semi-doubles, rosette blooms and shapely flowers similar to those of the large-flowered roses except in size. They make a magnificent display and are ideal bedding roses. Heights vary from about 18 in. to 5 ft. but again there is greater variety in the cluster-flowered roses, most large-flowered kinds being between 2¼ and 4 ft. There are scented varieties in both groups and both flower in a series

The adaptable rose is at home in all types of garden, whether large or small. A better effect is achieved by planting in groups of one colour rather than mixing varieties, which can give a spotty effect

of flushes from June to October, though the cluster-flowered varieties tend to repeat more rapidly than the large-flowered ones.

There is also a smaller class of polyantha roses sometimes referred to as dwarf polyanthas or polyantha pompons. These have small, rosette flowers in large clusters not unlike those of some rambler roses but they are of true bush habit. They are excellent for formal beds.

Bushes and Standards. You should note that any of these types of rose may be grown as bushes, half-standards, or standards. This depends entirely on the way in which they are budded (a form of grafting on to a vigorous root stock) by the nurseryman and in no way upon the variety itself. Bushes are budded low down, and in consequence make branches right from the soil. Half-standards are budded about 2 ft. above ground level and so have a bare 'leg' of that height with the head of branches on top. Full standards are budded 3½ to 4 ft. above ground level and resemble half-standards in all respects except for the greater length of bare main stem. By a skilful blending of all three types it is possible to make tier upon tier of flowers, but you must be careful not to plant so many standards that the bushes beneath are deprived of light. In a general way bushes should be at least 18 in. apart, while half-standards and standards should be at least 4 ft. apart.

Species and Vigorous Kinds. The wild species of rose such as *Rosa moyesii*, *R. willmottiae*, *R. xanthina spontanea* and our fragrant English sweet brier are also grown as bushes, but they need much more room than the hybrid teas and floribundas. The sweet brier makes quite a good hedge surrounding the rose garden, as it can be trimmed to shape without ill effect, but the proper place for most of the species is really the shrub border, for there they can be allowed the room they need for development. Most of the rose species should be planted at least 4 ft. apart.

Similar remarks also apply to hybrid shrub roses, many of which flower in flushes in summer and autumn, whereas most of the true species flower only once each year, usually in late spring or early summer.

Climbing Roses and Ramblers. Climbing roses may also be large flowered or cluster flowered, repeat flowering for most of the summer and early autumn or flowering once only each spring or summer. They also vary greatly in height and in the flexibility of their stems from fairly short, relatively stiff-stemmed varieties to train on pillars or arches 7 or 8 ft. high to enormously vigorous kinds that will scramble to the top of 30- to 40-ft. high trees.

So-called 'rambler' roses are climbers with particularly flexible stems usually about 10 to 15 ft. long, and most are once flowering only in July or August. Ramblers are most suitable for training on large pergolas, screens etc.

For walls climbers of medium vigour are best, and for pillars the shorter climbers are to be preferred. You should bear in mind that no rose is able to cling to a wall, post or pole, though it will scramble through the branches of a large shrub or tree gaining some hold with its thorns. But in general climbing and rambler roses must be tied to wires and poles and this does involve a fair amount of work.

Far left: A half-standard of the delightful white, cluster-flowered rose Iceberg

Left: A climbing rose trained on a pergola makes a charming framework for a garden path

Weeping Standards. Rambler roses are often grown as 'weeping standards'. This simply means that they are budded high up (6 or 7 ft.) on a strong brier stem which makes a support for a large head of branches. These are trained downwards over a wire frame shaped like an open umbrella and make splendid specimens for the centre of a large bed or some other prominent position. A good weeping standard will measure quite 5 ft. through, so obviously it must be allowed plenty of room.

Colour Associations. The best way to group roses is very much a matter of personal taste, but a few general suggestions may prove of service. First of all, do not mix large-flowered, cluster-flowered and polyantha roses in the same beds. Each group is delightful in its own particular way, but they do not mix well. If you want a blaze of colour (summer bedding, in fact) use the cluster-flowered varieties in massed colours. But if you want fine roses to cut for the house, plant the large-flowered roses either in beds of one variety or in small blocks of a colour. Do not go in for too great an assortment of colours or you will get a patchy, ineffective result. Another point to remember is that every different variety of rose has its own idiosyncrasies of growth and habit, and this individuality will necessarily increase the impression of disorder if you mix up too many kinds.

It is quite a good general rule to keep most of the strong colours, such as scarlets, very bright rose pinks, yellows, etc., to the centre of the garden with the paler shades around, but it is possible to adhere too closely even to this excellent rule. You will find that it is usually easier to make effective contrasts (red with yellow, pale pink with crimson, for instance) than it is to make satisfactory blends of closely allied shades, and so I advise you to keep off the latter at first unless you have special knowledge or considerable skill in handling colours.

A garden devoted to roses – a picturesque setting for a period house

Associates for Roses. It is possible to grow roses, particularly the cluster-flowered and shrub varieties, very effectively in a mixed border with herbaceous perennials and, if desired, bulbs and bedding plants. Alternatively roses can be given beds or a section of the garden to themselves and this is a method which particularly suits the less vigorous kinds and those with the shapely, rather formal flowers of the old hybrid tea (large-flowered) type. If you want to extend the flowering period of this part of the garden beyond the normal rose season you can plant tulips, hyacinths or daffodils among the bushes. As these bulbs flower at a time when the rose bushes are at their smallest, after the spring pruning, the only disadvantage is the limit they place upon surface cultivation. Hoeing can, however, be replaced by good surface mulching. An edging of small growing plants, such as forget-me-nots, pinks, or violas, is also delightful and is even less likely to interfere with the quality of the roses, as surface cultivation will not be hindered.

The Best Position. If you can set apart ground for a separate rose garden, this should be in an open and sunny position. Any shelter that is needed is best supplied by a rose hedge or a rose-covered screen. Such a screen, perhaps with rose-covered arches leading into the garden, provides much interest and is strictly in keeping with the enclosed beds and also frequently extends the flowering season.

Some Points in Design. You will naturally shape the garden to suit the site, but you would be wise to make medium-sized beds of fairly simple outline which can either be kept to one kind of rose per bed or used for blocks of roses of one colour. Small beds are difficult to plant satisfactorily, while very large beds are always a nuisance to work. In any case, try to make the beds of such a width that they will take a definite number of bushes spaced at least 18 in. apart, taking care to allow a margin of 1 ft. for spreading branches at the edges, especially if the path is narrow.

The paths can be paved or grassed. Grass is pleasant to look at, but has the disadvantage that it will not stand wear well and will not always be dry and pleasant to walk on.

Preparation of the Beds. It is frequently stated that roses are gross feeders and must, therefore, have deep cultivation and plenty of manure. This is in measure true but it requires some qualification, for there are some places in which deep cultivation, unless carried out with care, may be a real danger. For example roses do not like an excess of lime or chalk in the soil, and so if the subsoil is chalk there is no sense in bringing this to the surface. Under such circumstances the best policy is to cultivate the fertile upper layer as thoroughly as possible, and only break up the chalk sufficiently to ensure good drainage.

The best staple foods for roses are rotting turf and well-rotted manure. If you are in a position to obtain a few loads of top-spit soil and turf from a good meadow or well-kept pasture, or if you

stripped the turf from your plot last year and stacked it to rot, you are in a fair way to making a success of your rose garden. Fresh turf should be buried at least 10 in. beneath the surface, with the grass downwards to make certain that it rots and does not start into growth again. The surface 9 to 10 in. should be of ordinary garden soil or loam well broken up, with a little bonemeal mixed with it for enrichment and a liberal dressing of well-rotted manure if available. Failing this, you can use any of the manure substitutes such as prepared sewage sludge, treated town refuse, old mushroom compost, spent hops etc.

Early November is usually the best time for planting roses from the open ground, but you must take the weather into account and it is possible to plant successfully any time from mid-October to late March. After that roses can be planted from containers without disturbing their roots. It is never wise to plant when the soil is frozen or when it is very wet and sticky.

Planting Errors to Avoid. Probably the commonest mistake made by the novice is that of shallow planting. Not that very deep planting is any more desirable, but this is not an error into which the beginner falls so readily for, whereas common sense warns him of the probable folly of covering obviously green shoots with a considerable quantity of soil, it tells him nothing at all about the necessity for burying the union between stock and scion.

How are you to recognize this union? It certainly sounds a very technical matter, but in reality it should not prove very difficult. All bush roses are budded by the nurserymen low down on a wild rose – in all probability the familiar dog rose of English hedgerows. This part is known as the 'stock'. Subsequently all the top growth of this wild rose is cut off and its place is taken by the shoots that grow from the bud of the garden rose. But there will always be a slight swelling and roughness which marks the point where this bud has been grafted on to the stem of the stock. It is at this point that the stems of the bush start to branch out, while yet another indication of its position is the stump of the old brier growth which was cut off short so that the garden rose might grow. When bush roses are planted this point of union should be just below the surface where it is a little protected from the weather.

Standard and half-standard roses are also budded upon a wild rose stock, but well above ground level and not low down, as in the case of bush roses, so that it is not possible to bury the union beneath the soil. When planting, you should cover the uppermost roots with at least 1 in. of soil.

Pruning after Planting. You must prune the shoots of all newly planted roses severely, whether they are damaged or not, but this is a task that is best delayed until the end of March or, if the winter is long drawn out or your garden is particularly exposed, until early April. It is unwise to prune newly planted roses too early for this might stimulate the basal buds into premature growth and, if this was later killed by frost, there would be no other buds to provide further growth.

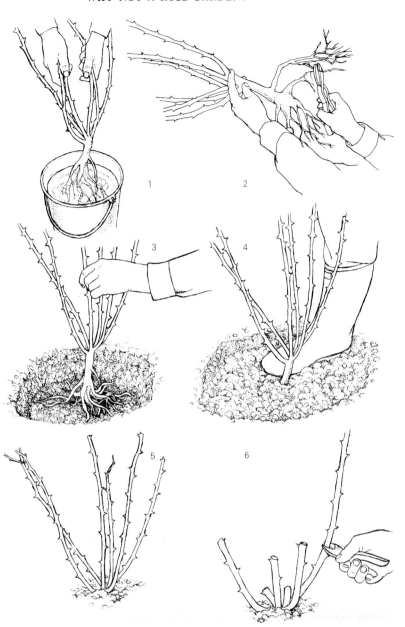

The actual pruning consists in shortening each sturdy shoot of a bush, half-standard, or standard rose to 3 or 4 in. and removing weakly shoots altogether. The shoots of climbers, ramblers and shrub roses, including species, are shortened to about 1 ft.

Staking and Tying. Staking is not usually necessary for bush roses, as these offer little resistance to the wind, but standards and half-standards should be staked as soon as planted. Indeed, to avoid damaging the roots it is better to drive in a stake as soon as a hole has been prepared and before the rose itself has been placed in position.

Even the shoots of rambler and climbing roses, though they are to be shortened severely later on, should be made secure temporarily. If this precaution is not taken, the long canes will inevitably wave about in the wind, dragging at the roots, and breaking many of the slender feeding roots as soon as they are formed.

Planting a rose bush. (1) On arrival from the nursery, the roots should be soaked well before planting. (2) Long, straggling or damaged roots should be removed. (3) The planting hole must be wide enough to accommodate the roots when spread out. (4) Soil should be firmed round the roots as the hole is filled in. (5) The planted rose. The surface of the soil should just cover the top of the union. (6) Newly planted roses should be pruned severely, but this is best delayed until the end of March

CHAPTER 19

Shrubs and Climbers

Preparing the ground – How to use shrubs – Evergreen v. deciduous shrubs – Types for all purposes – Climbers – Soil tolerance – Points in planting – Pruning after planting – A list of the best shrubs – Climbers and shrubs that can be trained on walls

Next to trees shrubs are the most permanent occupants of the garden and so especial care is needed in selecting and placing them and in preparing the ground. That is why I suggest leaving them until the second year if you are not in a particular hurry, for that will give you more time to get the ground really clear of weeds and make up your mind just what you want and where each item should go. But if time is very important then you must bring in the shrub and climber planting earlier in the programme and perhaps make use of a non-persistent weedkiller such as paraquat to clean the soil. This chemical acts through the leaves and is inactivated by the soil. It is most effective in spring and summer when plants are growing fast, and a week or so after it has been applied from a watering can fitted with a sprinkle bar or from a special applicator, the weeds should have turned brown. This is the time to dig or fork them out. Then if you can wait a further three or four weeks to let remaining seeds and roots grow, you can give a second application of paraquat and a second forking, this time working in rotted manure or peat at 3 to 4 lb. per square yard and a compound fertilizer such as National Growmore at 3 to 4 oz. per square yard and go ahead with the planting.

If you are not in a hurry you can buy plants lifted from the open ground between late October and late March. On average they cost a little less than container-grown plants and you will have a wider selection if you go to a good shrub nursery. But if you want to plant directly the soil is ready you may have to use container plants which can be moved even in spring and summer when they are in full growth.

How to Use Shrubs. Shrubs can be planted individually as specimens to be seen from all sides, or they can be grouped in beds and borders with other shrubs, or they can be used in mixed borders with any other kind of plant such as hardy perennials, annuals, bedding plants, roses and bulbs. In modern small gardens it is the first and last of these three methods that are most likely to prove satisfactory as most shrubs take up a fair amount of room and have relatively short flowering seasons so that borders planted exclusively with shrubs tend to be large and to be colourful either patchily or for a fairly short period.

But just a few well-chosen and well-placed shrubs can make a permanent plant framework in the garden into which other plants can be fitted to maintain colour and interest for as long a season as possible.

Evergreen v. Deciduous Shrubs. As with trees, ornamental shrubs can be divided into two groups, evergreen and deciduous. Evergreens can be immensely useful in the garden, for they are interesting and beautiful throughout the year and retain the full value of their contour even in the winter. But too many evergreens will tend to give a heavy, rather oppressive appearance to the garden. In the main they should be well mixed with deciduous varieties, which are constantly changing in appearance and in autumn drop their leaves to reveal the skeleton pattern of their branches. By careful combination of evergreen and deciduous varieties you can have a garden that is always fresh and interesting to the eye and in winter takes on an entirely new look as the evergreens stand out amongst the bare deciduous trees and shrubs.

Another point to remember about evergreen shrubs is that, as they retain their foliage for a long while, they are liable to be covered with soot and grime in big cities and industrial areas. In this respect deciduous shrubs start with an advantage, for they have fresh clothing, so to speak, every spring. I do not mean to suggest for a moment that evergreens will not grow in towns. As a matter of fact, some rank among the most frequently planted of all town shrubs, for they will thrive with considerably less light and fresh air than most other shrubs. But they do become bedraggled and dirty after a while and so should not be overdone.

Types for all Purposes. There are shrubs of all types and sizes ranging from a few inches to a dozen feet and more. Some are grown solely for their foliage, others for their flowers, and others again for their fruits. Many varieties can be trained against walls as well as being grown in bush form in the open. Good ornamental shrubs are far too numerous to mention individually, but I have included many of the best in a table constructed on similar lines to that prepared for ornamental trees.

Climbers for all Purposes. Apart from shrubs that can be trained against walls, there is a whole class of climbers and twiners itself divisible into evergreen and deciduous groups. Unfortunately, really reliable evergreen climbers are not very numerous, many of the most attractive suffering from a regrettable lack of hardiness. However, there are a few that can be recommended with confidence, notably the ivies in very great variety, the variegated honeysuckle (*Lonicera japonica aureo-reticulata*) and a lovely white-flowered clematis named *Clematis armandii*.

Deciduous climbers are much more numerous. Two of the largest families are clematis and the hardy ornamental vines, including the Virginia creepers. The clematises all have abundant and frequently brilliantly coloured flowers, while the vines are notable on account of their delightful

Left: With a mixture of flowers and foliage, both deciduous and evergreen, a well-planned shrub border offers something of interest throughout the year

Bottom: Heeling in shrubs. If the weather is unsuitable for immediate planting, the shrubs should be temporarily placed in a trench and their roots covered with soil, which is lightly firmed

foliage and, in some instances, miniature highly coloured bunches of grapes. Clematises are particularly suitable for planting on chalky soils, for they revel in lime.

A great range of colour and form is also available in modern climbing and rambler roses. These are fully treated in Chapter 18.

There are hardy climbers for sunny places and climbers for shade, varieties suitable for walls, fences, pergolas, arches, screens and, indeed, every conceivable purpose for which you could require climbing plants. In respect of soil, the majority of these are extremely tolerant. Even the many varieties of clematis, though they have a preference for chalky places, will grow quite well in lime-free soil. As for shrubs, I have concentrated all the most essential facts about these plants in a list on page 82, and fuller descriptions can be found in many excellent nursery catalogues.

Soil Tolerance. Most shrubs will grow well in almost any soil that is reasonably fertile and not excessively dry nor very wet. But there are some which have special requirements including quite a number which do not like chalk or lime in the soil. So if you live in a chalk or limestone district it is really best to omit lime-hating plants from your planting scheme. If you do decide to include some, peat can be mixed with sand and lime-free loam to make special beds for them or they can be fed each spring and summer with iron and manganese prepared in a special way known as sequestrated or chelated. Such special

Giving a spectacular display in spring with vigorous growth covered in starry white flowers, *Clematis montana* is an excellent plant for covering a wall

hand as it slips out of the pot. Water the plants thoroughly before planting for if the root ball is planted dry it is unlikely to take up water easily afterwards and will suffer accordingly.

Container-grown plants should be placed in holes just a little larger and about ½ in. deeper than the ball of soil and roots. Soil and peat should then be worked round and over them and made firm. When planting in spring or summer be sure to water the plants in well and keep them watered for several weeks if the weather should be dry.

Pruning after Planting. All trees, shrubs and climbers will require a little pruning after planting. With deciduous varieties, you may do this work in February, shortening strong shoots by about one-third and cutting out weakly growth or shortening it back to a few inches. It is better to leave the pruning of evergreen shrubs and climbers until early May when you should remove all growth that has been damaged by weather and shorten remaining stems or vines just sufficiently to give each plant a good shape.

A LIST OF THE BEST SHRUBS

Only really hardy shrubs suitable for the shrub border are included in this list, which does not include shrubs used only for hedging purposes. The list should be used as a guide rather than an exhaustive selection.

Artemisia abrotanum. Southernwood. Deciduous, grey-green foliage which is aromatic when bruised. Height 3 ft. Spread 3 ft. Sun and well-drained soil.

Aucuba japonica. Japanese laurel. Evergreen. Bright red berries, borne on the female plants if these are planted in the neighbourhood of a male plant. *Crotonifolia* is a good male and Gold Dust a handsome female, both with yellow spotted leaves. Height 7 ft. Spread 8 ft. *Nana rotundifolia* is a green-leaved female only 3 ft. high. All succeed in sun or shade in any soil. Excellent in towns.

Azalea amoena. Evergreen, with tiny leaves and rosy-purple flowers, borne very freely in May. Slow growing. Height 3 ft. Spread 7 ft. Lime-free soil. Best in light shade.

Azalea, deciduous hybrids. Large flowers in May of brilliant shades of orange, rose, salmon and white. Height 5 ft. spread 5 ft. Lime-free soil. Sun or light shade.

Azalea, evergreen hybrids. Low spreading with white, pink, mauve or scarlet flowers in May–June. Height 2 to 4 ft. Spread 3 to 6 ft. Lime-free soil. Sun or light shade.

Berberis buxifolia nana. Evergreen,. dark bluish-green foliage. Can be used instead of box for edging. Height 1½ ft. Spread 3 ft. Any soil. Sun or shade.

Berberis darwinii. Darwin's barberry. Evergreen. Orange-yellow flowers, followed by purplish-blue berries. Height 8 ft. Spread 8 ft. Sun. Any soil.

Berberis gagnepainii. Evergreen, with dark, spear-shaped leaves. Pendent yellow flowers at the end of May. Black berries with blue bloom. Height 5 ft. Spread 4 ft. Sun or shade. Any soil.

Berberis stenophylla. Evergreen, with narrow, dark green foliage and arching stems. Masses of small

fertilizers can be purchased ready for mixing with water according to maker's instructions and are quite safe and easy to use, but they are fairly expensive.

Some Points in Planting. The method of planting will depend on whether you purchase open-ground or container-grown plants. If the former the planting season is restricted to the dormant period from late October to late March. The plants will arrive either with bare roots or balled, that is, with soil around the roots held in place with sacking or polythene. Evergreens are often balled in this way as in general they are more difficult to transplant than deciduous shrubs and balling reduces the shock of being lifted and replanted.

Either way a hole should be prepared for each shrub sufficiently wide to accommodate all its roots without needing to double any up or twist them round. It should be deep enough to allow the uppermost roots to be covered with from 1 to 2 in. of soil. The soil excavated from the hole should be returned a little at a time, well broken up and worked around the roots. It helps to mix a little peat and a peppering of bonemeal with this soil to give the roots a good start. When all the roots are covered the soil should be trodden firmly and then loose soil scattered on top just as when planting trees.

The difference when planting from containers, especially in spring and summer, is that the soil and roots should be disturbed as little as possible. The containers must be removed, unless they are made of compressed peat or paper which will rot in the soil. Polythene containers can be carefully slit and peeled off.

If the plants are in rigid plastic or clay pots, these should be turned upside down and the rims rapped on something solid such as the handle of a spade, while the plant and soil ball is supported with one

orange-yellow, sweetly scented flowers in April and May. Height 10 ft. Spread 10 ft. Sun. Any soil.

Berberis thunbergii. Deciduous, with bright green foliage early in spring and brilliant red colour in autumn. Flowers not showy. Height 6 ft. Spread 7 ft. Variety *atropurpurea* has purple leaves. Sun or partial shade. Any soil.

Berberis wilsonae. Deciduous, usually colouring well in the autumn. Small, pale yellow flowers, followed by masses of coral or salmon-red berries. Height 4 ft. Spread 7 ft. Sun. Any soil.

Buddleia alternifolia. Deciduous, willow-like foliage. Masses of small lilac flowers in June. Height 10 ft. Spread 10 ft. Sun. Any well-drained soil. Excellent on chalk.

Buddleia globosa. Deciduous or semi-evergreen, with balls of orange flowers in June. Height 12 ft. Spread 12 ft. Sun. Any well-drained soil.

Buddleia davidii and its varieties. Deciduous, wide-spreading, arching growths, bearing long spikes of flowers of various shades of mauve or purple, also white, from July to September. Height 10 ft. Spread 8 to 15 ft. May be hard pruned in February for finer flowers. Sun. Any well-drained soil. Excellent on chalk.

Calluna vulgaris and its varieties. Ling, heather. Evergreen. Flowers vary from white, through pink to crimson, single or double; produced in August. Some with yellow foliage. Height $1\frac{1}{2}$ to 2 ft. Spread 2 ft. Sun. Lime-free soil.

Camellia japonica. Evergreen. White, pink, red or crimson flowers, single, semi-double or double in March and April. Height 8 to 10 ft. Spread 8 to 10 ft. Lime-free soil. Best in semi-shade but will grow in full sun. Not suitable for very cold places especially if exposed to east winds. There are a great many varieties, those with small to medium-sized flowers being best for outdoor planting.

Camellia williamsii. Evergreen. White, pink or rose flowers, single, semi-double or double. Height 8 to 10 ft. Spread 8 to 10 ft. Lime-free soil. Best in semi-shade. There are numerous varieties, one of the best being Donation, pink double.

Caryopteris clandonensis. Deciduous. Blue flowers in August–September. Height 3 ft. Spread 3 ft. Sun. Well-drained soil. Can be hard pruned in spring.

Ceanothus burkwoodii. Evergreen, with deep blue flowers, borne from July to October. Suitable for training on walls. Height 8 ft. Spread 8 ft. Sun. Well-drained soil.

Ceanothus hybridus Gloire de Versailles. Deciduous. Powder-blue flowers, borne from July to September. Height 10 ft. Spread 12 ft. Sunny, sheltered position. Can be hard pruned each spring to reduce size.

Ceanothus impressus. Evergreen. Bright blue flowers in May and June. Height 8 ft. Spread 10 ft. Sheltered, sunny site. Well-drained soil.

Ceratostigma willmottianum. Deciduous, with arching growths breaking up from the base. Bright blue flowers in August and September. Height 3 ft. Spread 3 ft. Sunny, warm place. Well-drained soil.

Chaenomeles speciosa. Japanese quince or japonica. Deciduous. Clusters of flowers before the leaves in February and March, followed by large, greenish yellow, scented fruits. Colour of flowers varies with variety, shades of red, coral, pink and white. Height 6 to 10 ft. Spread 12 ft. Does well on wall. Sun or light shade. Any soil.

Chamaecyparis lawsoniana fletcheri. Dwarf form of *C. lawsoniana.* See Trees.

Chamaecyparis pisifera filifera aurea. What a pity that this beautiful evergreen conifer could not have been called Golden Whiplash or something of that kind which would have conveyed a picture of its hanging, whip-like stems closely set with small golden leaves. Height 6 ft. Spread 6 ft. Sun or partial shade. Any soil.

Chamaecyparis pisifera Boulevard. Compact evergreen conifer making neat domes of feathery blue-grey foliage. Height 4 ft. Spread 4 ft. Sun or semi-shade. Any soil.

Chamaecyparis pisifera plumosa. Evergreen conifer with bright green ferny foliage. Height 8 ft. Spread 8 ft. There is also a dwarf golden-leaved form named *aurea nana.* Any soil. Sun or semi-shade.

Choisya ternata. Mexican orange blossom. Evergreen. Clusters of scented white flowers in April and May and again in September. Height 6 ft. Spread 8 ft. Sunny, rather sheltered place. Any reasonably well-drained soil.

Cistus corbariensis. Evergreen. White flowers in June. Height 3 ft. Spread 4 ft. Sun. Well-drained soil.

Cistus crispus Sunset. Evergreen. Magenta flowers in June. Height $1\frac{1}{2}$ to 2 ft. Spread 3 ft. Sun. Well-drained soil.

Cistus cyprius. Evergreen. Large white flowers, with crimson blotch at base of each petal, are produced in June. Height 6 ft. Spread 7 ft. Dry, sunny site.

Cistus purpureus. Evergreen. Rose flowers with maroon blotch in June. Height 3 to 4 ft. Spread 4 ft. Sun. Well-drained soil.

Cistus Silver Pink. Evergreen. Bright, translucent pink flowers during June and July. Height 2 ft. Spread 3 ft. Dry, sunny site.

The graceful, arched branches of *Buddleia alternifolia* are clothed with masses of small lilac flowers in June

Colutea arborescens. Bladder senna. Deciduous, pinnate foliage. Yellow, pea-shaped flowers from June to September, followed by pinkish, bladder-like pods. Height 9 ft. Spread 9 ft. Will grow on dry site. Sun.

Cornus alba spaethii. Deciduous. Fine yellow foliage and reddish-purple stems. Height 6 ft. Spread 9 ft. Does best in moist soil and hard pruned in spring. Sun or partial shade.

Cornus kousa. Deciduous. Valuable for its autumn tints and for the large creamy-white bracts which are produced in May and June. Will form a small tree in time. Height 12 ft. Spread 14 ft. Lime-free soil. Sun.

Cotinus coggygria. Smoke tree, wig tree, or Venetian sumach. Deciduous. Pink flower heads are dense and feathery, produced in June. Height 6 ft. Spread 6 ft. Sun. Well-drained soil. There are purple-leaved varieties of which the best is Royal Purple.

Cotoneaster adpressus. Deciduous. Close-growing shrub suitable for rock garden or edge of shrub border. White flowers in summer followed by red berries in autumn. Height 1 ft. Spread 5 ft. Sun. Any soil.

Cotoneaster conspicuus decorus. Evergreen. White flowers in summer followed by red berries in autumn and winter. Height 4 ft. Spread 6 ft. Sun. Any soil.

Cotoneaster dammeri. Evergreen. White flowers in summer followed by red berries in autumn. Prostrate, spreading indefinitely. Sun or shade. Any soil.

Cotoneaster franchetii. Semi-evergreen. Pinkish-white flowers in May, followed by orange-scarlet berries. Height 7 ft. Spread 8 ft. Sun. Any soil.

Cotoneaster frigidus. Deciduous shrub or small tree. Flat masses of white flowers in June followed by very bright red berries. Height 15 ft. Spread 15 ft. Sun. Any soil.

Cotoneaster horizontalis. Deciduous. Small, pinkish-white flowers in May, followed by red berries. Branches horizontal. Height in open 2 ft., on wall 8 ft. Spread 12 ft. Sun. Any soil.

Cotoneaster microphyllus. Evergreen. Small, dark green leaves. White flowers in summer followed by crimson berries. Weeping habit. Height 3 ft. Spread 6 to 8 ft. Sun. Any soil.

Cotoneaster simonsii. Deciduous. White flowers followed by scarlet berries. Makes good hedge. Height 10 ft. Spread 9 ft. Sun or semi-shade. Any soil.

Cytisus albus. White Spanish broom. Deciduous. Masses of white flowers in May. Height 8 ft. Spread 7 ft. Sunny, well-drained, soil.

Cytisus battandieri. Deciduous. Grey-green leaves. Yellow pineapple-scented flowers in June. Height 12 ft. Spread 12 ft. Can be trained against a wall or screen. Sun. Well-drained soil.

Cytisus beanii. Deciduous. Yellow flowers in May. Height 1 ft. Spread 2 ft. Sun. Well-drained soil.

Cytisus kewensis. Deciduous. Light yellow flowers in May. Height 1 ft. Spread 4 ft. Sun. Well-drained soil.

Cytisus praecox. Deciduous. Primrose-yellow flowers in April. Height 3 ft. Spread 4 to 5 ft. Sun. Well-drained soil.

Cytisus scoparius and hybrids. Common yellow broom and its hybrids. Deciduous. Flowers yellow, yellow and red, cream, pink, mahogany, crimson, produced in May. Height 6 to 8 ft. Spread 6 ft. Sun. Any well-drained soil.

Daboëcia cantabrica (Menziesia polifolia). Irish heath, St Dabeoc's heath. Purple bells from July to October. Height 2 ft. Spread 2 ft. Peaty or sandy, lime-free soil. Sun.

Daphne burkwoodii. Semi-evergreen. Pink scented flowers in May–June. Height 3 ft. Spread 3 ft. Sun. Any reasonably fertile soil.

Daphne mezereum. Mezereon. Deciduous. Fragrant, purplish-red or white flowers before the leaves in February and March, followed by bright red berries. Height 3 ft. Spread 3 ft. Sun or semi-shade. Does well on chalk soils.

Deutzia elegantissima. Deciduous. Sprays of rose-pink flowers in May–June. Height 4 ft. Spread 5 ft. Sun. Any soil.

Deutzia Mont Rose. Deciduous. Sprays of cyclamen-pink flowers in May–June. Height 6 ft. Spread 6 ft. Sun. Any soil.

Deutzia scabra candidissima. Deciduous. Pure white, double flowers in June and July. Height 8 ft. Spread 6 ft. Sun. Any soil.

Elaeagnus pungens maculata (aureo-variegata). Evergreen, with extremely handsome golden variegated leaves. Height 8 ft. Spread 10 ft. Sun or shade. Any soil.

Enkianthus campanulatus. Deciduous, foliage turns yellow in autumn. Creamy-white or buff flowers, shaped like lily of the valley; produced in April and May. Height 7 ft. Spread 5 ft. Lime-free soil. Semi-shade.

Erica arborea alpina. Mountain tree heath. Evergreen, with bright green foliage. Long spikes of scented white flowers in March and April. Height 8 ft. Spread 7 ft. Well-drained, lime-free soil. Sun.

Erica carnea and varieties. Evergreen. Flowers rose, crimson, or white; usually produced in February and March. Height 6 to 18 in. Spread 1 to 2 ft. Any well-drained soil. Sun.

Erica cinerea. Scotch or grey heath. Evergreen. Purple bell flowers from July to September. Height 9 in. Spread 1 to 2 ft. Sunny, well-drained, lime-free soil.

Erica darleyensis. Evergreen. Rose-red flowers from November to May. Height 1½ ft. Spread 2 ft. Sunny, well-drained soil.

Erica mediterranea. Evergreen. White flowers from March to May. Height 3 ft. Spread 3 ft. Any well-drained soil. Sun.

Erica terminalis. Evergreen, deep green foliage. Rose-pink flowers from June to September. Height 6 ft. Spread 6 ft. Any well-drained soil. Sun.

Erica tetralix and varieties. Cross-leaved heath. Evergreen. White, pink or rosy-red flowers from July to October. Height 1 ft. Spread 1½ ft. Lime-free soil. Sun.

Erica vagans and its varieties. Cornish heath. Evergreen. Flowers white, pink, or red; produced from July to October. Height 1 ft. Spread 2½ ft. Lime-free soil. Sun.

Escallonia Apple Blossom. Evergreen. Pink and white flowers in June and July. Height 6 ft. Spread 8 ft. Any soil. Sun.

Escallonia langleyensis. Evergreen, small leaves.

Sprays of rosy-carmine flowers in June. Height 8 ft. Spread 8 ft. Any soil. Sun.

Eucryphia nymansensis. Evergreen shrub or small tree. Large white flowers with conspicuous yellow stamens, produced in July and August. Height 20 ft. Spread 10 ft. Semi-shade, lime-free soil.

Euonymus europaeus. Spindle tree. Deciduous shrub, bearing red and orange fruits in autumn. Height 10 ft. Spread 10 ft. Sun or semi-shade. Any soil.

Euonymus japonicus ovatus aureus. Evergreen, with golden variegated leaves. Height 10 ft. Spread 6 ft. Sun or shade. Any soil.

Euonymus fortunei variegatus. Evergreen, with silver variegated leaves and trailing growth. Useful for edging or training up walls. Spread indefinite. Sun or shade. Any soil.

Euonymus fortunei Silver Queen. Evergreen with cream and green leaves. Height 3 ft. (taller against a wall). Spread 3 ft. Sun or shade. Any soil.

Exochorda grandiflora. Deciduous. Erect stems of pure white flowers in May. Height 8 ft. Spread 10 ft. Sun or semi-shade. Lime-free soil.

Forsythia intermedia Lynwood. Deciduous. Bright yellow flowers, produced abundantly in March and April. Height 7 ft. Spread 7 ft. Sun or semi-shade. Any soil.

Forsythia suspensa sieboldii. Deciduous, very pendulous growths. Flowers yellow, in March and April. Height 8 ft. Spread 10 ft. Can be used to cover banks, also good when trained on wall. Succeeds in any aspect and any soil.

Fuchsia. Deciduous. White, pink, rose, crimson or purple flowers from July to October. There are a great many varieties, not all of which are sufficiently hardy to be grown outdoors. Even the hardier kinds may be killed to ground level in hard winters but will usually shoot up again in spring from the roots. Height 1 to 4 ft. Spread 1 to 4 ft. Sun or semi-shade. Any reasonably fertile well-drained soil. Reliable kinds are *F. magellanica alba*, *magellanica gracilis*, *riccartonii,* Margaret, Mrs Popple, Madame Cornelissen, Tom Thumb and Tennessee Waltz.

Garrya elliptica. Evergreen, green foliage, grey beneath. Long, jade-green catkins on male plants, shorter on female, from November to February. Height 8 ft. Spread 8 ft. Sunny, sheltered. Can be trained against a wall. Any well-drained soil.

Genista aetnensis. Mount Etna Broom. Yellow flowers on slender weeping stems in July–August. Height 12 ft. Spread 10 ft. Sun. Any well-drained soil.

Genista hispanica. Spanish gorse. Deciduous, spiny, cushion-like growth, with yellow flowers in May and June. Height 2 ft. Spread 4 ft. Sun. Well-drained soil.

Genista lydia. Deciduous. Yellow flowers on arching stems in June. Height 1½ ft. Spread 4 ft. Sun. Well-drained soil.

Hamamelis mollis. Chinese witch-hazel. Deciduous. Yellow, fragrant flowers from late December to February. Height 10 ft. Spread 10 ft. Sun or semi-shade. Best in lime-free soil.

Hebe Autumn Glory. Evergreen. Violet-purple flowers from June to October. Height 1½ ft. Spread 2 ft. Sun. Any soil.

Hebe brachysiphon. Evergreen. White flowers in

Evergreen shrubs with pink or carmine flowers, escallonias are a particularly good choice for the seaside garden. Shown here is the variety Donard Seedling

July–August. Height 4 ft. Spread 5 ft. Sun. Any soil.

Hebe Midsummer Beauty. Evergreen. Lilac-blue flowers in slender trails from July to November. Height 4 ft. Spread 6 ft. Sun and a sheltered place. Any soil.

Hebe pagei. Evergreen. Blue-grey leaves and white flowers in May. Height 9 in. Spread 2 ft. Good ground cover. Sun. Any soil.

Hebe salicifolia. Evergreen. White flowers in slender trails, July–August. Height 6 ft. Spread 6 ft. Sun. Any soil.

Hibiscus syriacus. Deciduous. Flowers large, white, purple, blue or rose, single and double according to variety; produced in September and October. Height 8 ft. Spread 6 ft. Full sun. Any reasonably fertile soil.

Hippophaë rhamnoides. Sea buckthorn. Deciduous, linear, grey-green foliage. Female plants, if grown with male, produce bright orange berries. Height 12 ft. Spread 12 ft. Sun. Well-drained soil.

Hydrangea arborescens grandiflora. Deciduous. White flowers in globular heads from July to September. Height 3 ft. Spread 4 ft. Sun or semi-shade. Any soil.

Hydrangea macrophylla. Deciduous. White, pink, rose, purple or blue flowers in globular heads or flat 'lace-cap' clusters according to variety, flowering from July to October. Height 3 to 6 ft. Spread 4 to 6 ft. Sun or shade. Any reasonably fertile soil, but the colour of flowers is affected by the soil, tending to be blue or purple in acid soil and pink or rose in alkaline soil.

Hydrangea paniculata grandiflora. Deciduous. Large panicles of creamy-white flowers, turning pinkish purple, produced during August and September. Can be hard pruned in February. Sun or semi-shade. Any soil.

Hypericum calycinum. Rose of Sharon. Evergreen, spreading and running underground. Large, bright yellow flowers from July to September. Will stand shade. Excellent for covering banks.

Hypericum moserianum. Evergreen, but often killed down to surface in winter, shooting up again in spring. Bright yellow flowers 2 in. across, from July to October. Height 1 ft. Spread 1½ ft. Prefers moist soil.

Hypericum Hidcote. Semi-evergreen. Yellow flowers, produced from July to September. Height 5 ft. Spread 4 ft.

Juniperus communis compressa. A perfect miniature of the Irish juniper. (See Trees.) Height 1 ft. Spread 6 in. Sun. Well-drained soil. Good on chalk.

Juniperus media pfitzeriana. Evergreen conifer making a wide shuttlecock of growth. Height 4 ft. Spread 8 ft. There are also varieties with young leaves yellow or yellow green, the best of which is Old Gold. Sun. Well-drained soil. Good on chalk.

Juniperus sabina tamariscifolia. Evergreen conifer, low-mounded growth. Height 2 ft. Spread 6 ft. Sun. Well-drained soil. Good on chalk.

Kalmia latifolia. Calico bush. Evergreen. Large clusters of shell-pink flowers in June. Height 6 ft. Spread 8 ft. Lime-free soil. Sun or semi-shade.

Kerria japonica flore-pleno. Jew's mallow, bachelor's buttons. Deciduous. Orange-yellow, double flowers in April and May. Height 6 ft. Spread 7 ft. Can be trained on wall.

Lavandula spica and its varieties. Lavender. Evergreen, with grey-green foliage. Flowers various shades of violet or white according to variety. Height 1 to 3 ft. Spread 1 to 3 ft. Sun, well-drained soil. Excellent on chalk.

Lavatera olbia rosea. Tree mallow. Deciduous. Pink flowers, produced from July to October. Height 6 ft. Spread 5 ft. Sunny, well-drained site.

Leycesteria formosa. Deciduous. Stems green. Racemes of rose and white flowers from July to September, surrounded by claret-coloured bracts which last till the reddish-purple berries form. Height 6 ft. Spread 4 ft. Flowers best in full sun, but will grow in shade.

Magnolia stellata. Deciduous. White flowers very freely produced during March and April. Height 5 ft. Spread 5 ft. Sun or semi-shade. Lime-free soil.

Mahonia aquifolium. Evergreen. Holly-like leaves. Yellow flowers from February to May. Height 3 ft. Spread 3 ft. Sun or shade. Any soil.

Mahonia Charity. Evergreen. Handsome leaves composed of numerous holly-like leaflets. Yellow flowers in radiating spikes from October to December. Height 8 ft. Spread 5 ft. Sun or light shade. Fertile, well-drained soil.

Mahonia japonica. Evergreen. Similar to last but wider and with flatter spoke-like pale yellow flower spikes sweetly scented. November to March. Height 5 ft. Spread 7 ft. Sheltered semi-shady place. Fertile, well-drained soil.

Olearia haastii. Daisy bush. Evergreen, box-like leaves. Masses of daisy-like flowers in July and August. Height 5 ft. Spread 4 ft. Sun. Any soil.

Olearia scilloniensis. Evergreen. Grey leaves. Masses of small white daisy flowers in May. Height 4 ft. Spread 3 ft. Warm, sunny place. Well-drained soil.

Osmanthus delavayi. Evergreen, small glossy leaves. Masses of small fragrant white flowers in April. Height 5 ft. Spread 7 ft. Sun or semi-shade. Any reasonably fertile soil.

Pernettya mucronata and its varieties. Evergreen. Small, white flowers, produced in May. Female, in presence of male, grown for its berries, which vary with the variety, and may be white, pink, purple or red. Height 2 to 3 ft. Spread indefinite (by suckers). Sun. Lime-free soil.

Perovskia atriplicifolia. Deciduous. Stems and leaves covered with white down; fragrant of sage. Spikes of small blue flowers in August and September. Height 3 ft. Spread 5 ft. Sunny, dry position. Cut back hard in April.

Philadelphus coronarius. Mock orange. Deciduous. White, scented flowers in June. Height 9 ft. Spread 12 ft.

Philadelphus garden hybrids. Cultivated varieties that differ in the size, form and fragrance of their flowers. Some petals white with purple blotch at base. Among the best are Beauclerk, Belle Etoile, Sybille, Norma and Virginal. Height 3 to 7 ft. Spread 3 to 6 ft. Sun. Any soil.

Phlomis fruticosa. Jerusalem Sage. Evergreen. Grey sage-like leaves. Whorls of yellow flowers in June–July. Height 3 ft. Spread 3 ft. Warm, sunny place. Well-drained soil.

Pieris floribunda. Evergreen, pointed, leathery leaves. Clusters of upright spikes of lily-of-the-valley-like flowers in March and April. Height 4 ft. Spread 4 ft. Sun or shade. Lime-free soil.

Pieris forrestii. Evergreen. Young leaves and stems scarlet, flowers white in sprays in April. Height 4 ft. Spread 4 ft. (but becoming very much larger

Flowering from July to September, *Hypericum* Hidcote is a superb addition to the shrub border

with age). Sun or semi-shade and a lime-free soil.

Pieris japonica. Evergreen. Larger flowers than *P. floribunda* in more spreading sprays. Height 6 ft. Spread 5 ft. Sun or semi-shade. Lime-free soil.

Potentilla fruticosa and varieties. Deciduous. Bright yellow or white flowers from July to September. Height 1½ to 3 ft. Spread 3 to 4 ft. Sun. Well-drained soil.

Pyracantha atalantioides. Evergreen. White flowers in June followed by scarlet berries. Height 8 ft. Spread 6 ft. Any soil. Good on chalk. Can be trained against a wall.

Pyracantha coccinea lalandei. Evergreen. Masses of white flowers in May and June, followed by orange-red berries. Height 8 ft. Spread 8 ft. Sun. Treatment as for *P. atalantioides*.

Pyracantha rogersiana flava. Similar to last but with yellow berries.

Rhododendron. A very large race of evergreen shrubs all thriving most satisfactorily in lime-free soil. They like peat and leafmould, but these are not absolutely essential to their well-being. Many of the most popular varieties are garden hybrids. These, when full grown, have an average height and breadth of 8 ft. but sometimes grow much larger. All flower in May and June. A few good kinds are Betty Wormald, pink; Blue Peter, violet blue; Britannia, scarlet; Cynthia, deep rose; Doncaster, deep red; Elizabeth, scarlet, 3 ft.; *fastuosum flore pleno*, blue mauve; Goldsworth Yellow, apricot and primrose; Gomer Waterer, white, mauve and yellow; May Day, bright red, 4 ft.; Mother of Pearl, pink fading to white; Mrs G. W. Leak, rose and maroon; Pink Pearl, rose pink; Purple Splendour, deep purple; Sappho, white and maroon; Susan, lilac blue; and Temple Belle, rose, 3 ft.

Ribes sanguineum Pulborough Scarlet. Flowering currant. Deciduous. Very deep red flowers in April. Height 7 ft. Spread 6 ft. Sun or shade. Any soil.

Rosmarinus officinalis. Rosemary. Evergreen foliage, grey beneath and aromatically fragrant when crushed. Lavender-blue flowers in May. Height 4 ft. Spread 4 ft. Warm, sunny position. Well-drained soil. Excellent for dry places.

Ruta graveolens. Rue. Evergreen. Blue-grey aromatic leaves. Small yellow flowers in summer. Height 18 in. Spread 18 in. Sun. Well-drained soil. Jackmans Blue has the best blue colouring. This is a good plant for edgings.

Sambucus nigra aurea. Golden elder. Deciduous. Foliage yellow, deepening with age. Prune hard in spring to get best results. Height 8 ft. Spread 8 ft. Less when hard pruned each spring which produces the finest foliage. Sun or shade. Any soil. Good on chalk.

Santolina incana (S. chamaecyparissus). Lavender cotton. Evergreen. Silvery-grey leaves. Yellow flowers in July. Height 1½ ft. Spread 2½ ft. Can be pruned in spring or after flowering for edging. Sun. Well-drained soil.

Senecio Sunshine (formerly known as *greyii*). Evergreen. Grey leaves. Bright yellow flowers in June and July. Leaves larger if pruned back annually in the spring. height 2 ft. Spread 3 ft.

Skimmia japonica. Evergreen. Bright red berries borne on the female plant in the presence of the male, the flowers of which are fragrant. Height 3 ft. Spread 4 ft. Sun or shade. Any soil.

Spartium junceum. Spanish broom. Deciduous. Stems dark green and rush-like. Bright yellow pea-shaped flowers, very fragrant, produced from June to September. Height 6 ft. Spread 5 ft. Sun. Any soil. Good on dry banks. Can be pruned lightly in spring.

Spiraea arguta Bridal Wreath. Deciduous. Masses of white flowers during April and May. Height 5 ft. Spread 4 ft. Sun or semi-shade. Any soil.

Spiraea Anthony Waterer. Deciduous. Flat clusters of deep carmine flowers in July and August. Height 3 ft. Spread 4 ft. Sun or semi-shade. Any soil. Can be pruned hard in spring.

Spiraea thunbergii. Similar to *S. arguta* but even earlier flowering. Height 4 ft. Spread 3 ft.

Spiraea van Houttei. Deciduous; foliage turns bright red in autumn. White flowers in clusters during May–June. Height 6 ft. Spread 7 ft. Sun or semi-shade. Any soil.

Symphoricarpos albus. Snowberry. Deciduous. Valued for white berries. Does well in shade. Height 5 ft. Spreads indefinitely by suckers. Any soil.

Syringa vulgaris in variety. Lilac. Deciduous. Flowers at the end of May, either single or double, all shades of lilac, rosy pink, purple and white. Height 5 to 8 ft. Spread 5 to 8 ft. (but can be double this when mature). Sun. Any soil. Good on lime. Remove suckers from grafted plants.

Tamarix pentandra (T. hispida aestivalis). Tamarisk. Deciduous. Shoots smothered with tiny rosy-pink flowers from July to September. Best results are obtained by hard pruning almost to old wood each spring. Height 8 ft. Spread 8 ft. Dry, sunny site. Good by sea.

A useful shrub for many purposes with its grey-toned leaves and yellow daisy flowers is *Senecio* Sunshine

Thuja occidentalis Rheingold. Evergreen conifer, with golden-yellow summer foliage, turning bronzy red in winter. Height 3 ft. Spread 2 ft. Any soil. Sun or shade.

Viburnum carlcephalum. Deciduous. Ball-like clusters of white flowers in May. Height 5 ft. Spread 4 ft. Sun. Reasonably fertile soil.

Viburnum carlesii. Deciduous. Terminal clusters of very fragrant white flowers during April and May. Height 4 ft. Spread 5 ft. Sun. Reasonably fertile well-drained soil.

Viburnum fragrans. Deciduous. Pinkish-white, fragrant flowers, produced from November to February. Height 7 ft. Spread 5 ft. Sun. Reasonably fertile soil.

Viburnum opulus sterile. Snowball tree. Deciduous. Large balls of white flowers in June. Height 8 ft. Spread 8 ft. Sun or semi-shade. Any soil.

Viburnum rhytidophyllum. Evergreen. Large wrinkled leaves. Yellowish-white flowers in May and June, followed by red berries which turn black. Height 9 ft. Spread 10 ft. Sun or shade. Any soil. Good on chalk.

Viburnum tinus. Laurustinus. Evergreen. Flowers white, tinged with pink, opening from November to April. Bluish-black berries. Height 6 ft. Spread 6 ft. but can double these dimensions in time. Sun or shade. Any soil.

Viburnum plicatum Lanarth. Deciduous. Flat clusters of white flowers along horizontal branches in May–June. Height 4 ft. Spread 7 ft. Sun. Any soil.

Viburnum plicatum. Japanese snowball. Deciduous. Small balls of white flowers in May and June. Height 6 ft. Spread 8 ft. Sun. Any soil.

Vinca major. Greater periwinkle. Evergreen, glossy leaves. Shoots trailing. Bright blue flowers from May to September. Height 1 ft. Spread indefinite. Succeeds in shade. Any soil. Variety *variegata* has cream-edged leaves.

Vinca minor. Lesser periwinkle. As above, but smaller leaves and flowers. Height 6 in. Spread indefinite. Sun or shade. Any soil. There are numerous varieties, some variegated, some with white, purple or double flowers.

Weigela florida. Deciduous. Small, trumpet-shaped flowers in shades varying from pale pink to crimson in May and June. Height 6 ft. Spread 7 ft. Sun or semi-shade. Any soil. Can be pruned after flowering.

Yucca filamentosa. Evergreen, with long, sword-shaped leaves in rosettes. Large spikes of cream, bell-shaped flowers in July and August. Height 4 ft. Spread 2 to 3 ft. Warm, sunny place, well-drained soil.

CLIMBERS AND SHRUBS THAT MAY BE TRAINED ON WALLS, TRELLIS AND SCREENS

Campsis tagliabuana Madame Galen. Trumpet Vine. Deciduous. Clusters of large, trumpet-shaped orange-red flowers in August and September. More or less self-clinging but may need some tying to wires or trellis. Warm, sunny sheltered place. Well-drained soil. Cut out frost-damaged growth each spring.

Ceanothus. See under Shrubs. The evergreen kinds are best for walls.

Chaenomeles speciosa. Japonica. See under Shrubs.

Clematis. Slender but often extensive climbers clinging by tendrils. If possible the roots should be in the shade with the stems trained into a sunny position. *C. jackmanii* and its varieties may be cut hard back each February if small spaces only are to be covered. Other kinds can be thinned or cut back, but rather less severely, immediately after flowering for *C. montana* and other early-blooming kinds, and in February for late-flowering varieties. Clematis may be had in bloom from May until September. The colour range includes white and many shades of blue and red, also a good yellow species, *C. tangutica*, flowering in August–September. All are best in fairly rich soil and like chalk and lime.

Cotoneaster horizontalis. Deciduous. See Shrubs.

Cotoneaster microphylla. Evergreen. See Shrubs.

Forsythia suspensa sieboldii. Deciduous. Good on north wall. See Shrubs.

Hedera helix. Ivy. There are many varieties, all evergreen climbers, either deep green or gold or silver variegated, and differing in size and shape of leaf. They will cover high walls. Succeed in sun or shade and any soil.

Humulus lupulus aureus. Golden hop. Herbaceous twining climber, with gold foliage. Very vigorous. Succeeds anywhere, but colours best in sun. Dies down to the roots in autumn but shoots up again in the spring.

Hydrangea petiolaris. Deciduous, self-clinging climber, with heart-shaped dark green leaves, and white clusters of flowers in June. Vigorous. Sun or semi-shade. Any reasonably fertile soil.

Jasminum nudiflorum. Winter jasmine. Deciduous. Lax growths which require tying to a wall, fence or screen. Yellow flowers, produced from November to February. Succeeds in sun or shade in any soil.

Jasminum officinale grandiflorum (J. o. affine). Jasmine. Deciduous. Vigorous twiner. Fragrant, white flowers from June to September. Sunny position. Any reasonably well-drained soil.

Kerria japonica flore pleno. Bachelor's buttons. See Shrubs.

Lonicera japonica aureo reticulata. Variegated honeysuckle. Evergreen twiner with green leaves in which the veins are picked out in yellow. Twining, bushy growth. Sun or light shade. Any soil.

Lonicera japonica halliana. Evergreen twiner. Pale yellow sweetly scented flowers from June to October. Sun or light shade. Any soil.

Lonicera periclymenum serotina. Late Dutch honeysuckle. Deciduous twiner. Purplish red and yellow, fragrant flowers from July to September. Sun or semi-shade. Any soil.

Magnolia grandiflora Exmouth variety. See Shrubs.

Parthenocissus henryana. Variegated Virginia creeper. Deciduous. Leaves green with silver and pink variegation by the veins. Green parts turn red in autumn. Variegation best on a north or north-west wall. Self-clinging. Any reasonably fertile soil.

Parthenocissus quinquefolia. Virginia creeper. Deciduous, more or less self-clinging. Large five-parted leaves which colour brilliantly in autumn. Sun or shade. Any soil.

Parthenocissus tricuspidata. Ampelopsis, Boston

Far left: *Clematis* Comtesse de Bouchard trained over an old tree stump. The tangled growth and large pink flowers completely conceal the support

Left: A fine self-clinging climber, *Hydrangea petiolaris* will thrive in sun or semi-shade. It flowers in June

ivy. Deciduous, self-clinging, with vine-like leaves which turn scarlet and crimson in autumn. *Veitchii* is a particularly good variety with small leaves. Sun or shade but the leaves colour best in the sun. Any soil.

Passiflora caerulea. Passion flower. Deciduous vigorous climber clinging by tendrils. Blue and white flowers from July to October. Warm, sunny place. Well-drained soil. May be killed to ground level in hard winter.

Polygonum baldschuanicum. Russian vine. Deciduous, very vigorous twiner. Feathery sprays of pinkish-white flowers from July to September. Can be pruned hard in spring. Sun or light shade. Any soil.

Pyracantha. Evergreen. See Shrubs.

Roses. See chapter on roses.

Vitis coignetiae. Deciduous. Ornamental vine, with large leaves which turn scarlet in autumn. Climbs by tendrils. Sunny position. Any reasonably fertile soil.

Vitis vinifera Brandt. Deciduous climber clinging by tendrils. Green leaves turning purple and red in autumn. Sweet, purplish-black grapes. Sun. Any reasonably fertile soil.

Vitis vinifera purpurea. Teinturier grape vine. Deciduous climber clinging by tendrils. Leaves at first claret red, later turning purple. Small deep purple grapes. Sun. Any reasonably fertile soil. Good on chalk.

Wisteria chinensis. Chinese wisteria. Deciduous twiner. Large, pinnate leaves, and long pendulous trails of mauve flowers, produced in May. There are several varieties including *alba*, white and Black Dragon, double, purple. Sun. Any reasonably fertile soil, preferably lime free. Any young growths not required to extend the plant can be shortened to four or five leaves in July.

Wisteria floribunda. Japanese wisteria. Deciduous twiner with scented flowers in May–June. There are numerous varieties including *alba*, white; *W. f. macrobotrys* (also known as *multijuga*), extra long trails of lilac-blue flowers; *rosea*, pink. Soil, situation and pruning as for *W. chinensis*.

Some shrubs which transplant badly are lifted with a large ball of soil which is then wrapped in sacking or polythene. This covering must be removed before replanting, care being taken not to disturb the soil ball round the roots. The shrub is then planted in the usual way, but with the soil ball still intact, so that the roots receive as little set-back as possible

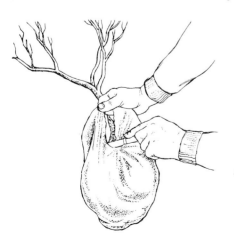

Planting a Fruit Garden

Apples and pears can be wonderfully decorative in the garden as well as providing useful crops and they may well be considered in place of purely ornamental trees or trained in place of hedges or other screens. Cherries and plums are less suitable for small or medium-sized gardens since they take up a great deal of room, but soft fruits such as currants and gooseberries can be entirely satisfactory and so can strawberries.

When to Plant. Fruit trees and bush fruits can be transplanted from the open ground at any time from the end of October until early March, but the most favourable period is early in November just after the leaves have fallen off, and the next best time is in February. Trees and bushes obtained in containers can be planted at any time provided the roots are not broken and the soil around them is not unduly disturbed when the containers are removed.

Apples and Pears on Dwarfing Stocks. The larger fruits such as apples, pears, plums and cherries, are grown on rootstocks to which they are joined by grafting or budding. The rootstock has no influence on the character of the fruit but it does powerfully affect the rate of growth and eventual size of the tree and the age at which it starts to bear. Rootstocks are classed as dwarfing, semi-dwarfing, of medium vigour or vigorous, terms which are self-explanatory, and since the dwarfing and semi-dwarfing stocks not only reduce the ultimate size of the tree but are also the stocks that induce the earliest bearing, they are the ones to choose for garden use, unless large trees are required for reasons of decoration or design.

On suitable dwarfing stocks such as M.9, M.26, M.27 and M.M.106 for apples and Quince A and C for pears these trees can be trained in many ornamental ways. One possibility is to restrict each tree to a single stem, thickly set with fruit spurs from top to bottom. These are known as single-stemmed cordons, and they are a great boon in small gardens since not only do they allow a far greater number of varieties to be grown in the same space than would be possible by any other method, but the fruit is actually of better quality. Pears succeed best in a rather light, well-drained soil, and must have warmth and sunlight to ripen properly.

The most dwarfing rootstock for plums is Pixy, but St. Julien A is semi-dwarfing and suitable for trained trees. The best dwarfing stock for cherries is Colt.

Horizontal-trained Trees, Bushes and Standards. Apples and pears can be grown in many other ways besides cordons. One attractive possibility is horizontal- or espalier-trained trees with regular tiers of branches spread out parallel to the ground. These can be planted against fences or walls, and they also look very handsome at the side of paths or as a narrow division between one part of the garden and another. Then there are bushes, each with a short leg or main trunk, and branches radiating from this roughly in the form of a goblet. This is a favourite form with commercial fruit growers, but as each bush must be planted quite 12 ft. from its neighbour and little can be grown underneath them, you may consider it is an unsuitable form for the small garden. Pyramids look rather like the conventional idea of a Christmas tree with a central trunk and branches radiating all round and tapering towards the top. Dwarf pyramids on suitable dwarfing stocks do not take up a great deal of room and can be very attractive. Standards, which have a big head of branches on a main trunk about 6 ft. in height, require even more space than bushes, and should be planted 25 ft. apart, but it is possible to move freely beneath them and to grow shade-loving plants or vegetables quite close to them. One or two may be magnificent as ornamental features in salient positions if you require some big outstanding object.

Plums and Cherries. Plums and cherries are also grown as bushes and standards. They delight in the greater freedom of growth afforded in this way and make very handsome specimens, but in time they take up a great deal of room. Cherries succeed particularly well on chalky soils.

Currants and Gooseberries. Of the smaller fruits blackcurrants and gooseberries are most serviceable. They are almost always grown as bushes which must be planted from 4 to 5 ft. apart. Red currants and white currants are no more difficult to grow and require the same amount of space, but they are rather more limited in their value. However, red and white currants can be trained, usually as multiple-stemmed cordons, and in this form can be used like small hedges. They are very decorative for a few weeks while the fruit is ripening.

Raspberries. These succeed best in fairly rich soil which is not liable to become very dry in summer. The canes are planted 2 ft. apart in rows about 6 ft. apart, and you will want at least 30 ft. of row if you are to get a reasonable crop. Moreover, you cannot grow anything else in the raspberry plantation, as most of the roots are very near the surface. These are points against the raspberry, but in its favour must be reckoned the fact that it is one of the most delicious fruits of early summer and also that it is quite easy to grow.

Strawberries. Unlike other fruits, strawberries are not planted permanently, the beds being remade every second or third year. Because of this strawberries are often included in the vegetable plot. The ideal time for planting is at the end of August, but the work can be continued until October and resumed in March, though spring-planted strawberries should not be allowed to fruit until the following year. Plants should be spaced 15 in. apart in rows 2½ ft. apart. Since 20 plants is about the minimum from which a useful number of fruits can be picked it will be seen that something like 60 sq. yd. must be allowed for a strawberry bed. An alternative is to grow strawberries in barrels with 3-in. diameter holes about 1 ft. apart in the sides and filled with soil so that plants can be put in on top and in the holes. Large earthenware plant jars with holes in the sides can be used in the same way and either barrels or jars make decorative objects to stand on a terrace or in a patio.

Selection of Varieties. The selection of varieties deserves careful attention. I have prepared a brief list of selections from the most popular kinds and fruit catalogues provide much useful information.

With strawberries it is not enough to get the right variety; you must obtain a good selection from free-cropping, healthy plants. Strawberries are easily infected with virus diseases which are spread by greenflies. This is one reason why it is unwise to attempt to propagate strawberries at home and why plants are best obtained from specialist nurseries.

A similar warning applies to raspberries, which are equally susceptible to virus diseases. Clean stocks, however, exist and are kept healthy by frequent inspection and immediate removal of any diseased plants.

The Sterility Problem. You will notice as you look through my lists that some varieties are marked 'self-fertile', others, 'partially self-fertile', and yet others 'self-sterile'. Any self-fertile fruit tree can, if desired, be planted entirely by itself and will still bear good crops. A self-sterile tree, however, must have a 'mate' nearby of the same *kind* of fruit (plums with plums, pears with pears, etc.), but a different *variety* (cherry Black Heart with cherry Early Rivers and so on). Partially self-fertile trees can be planted alone, but bear heavier crops if they are near another variety of the same kind of fruit. In the list of selections I have indicated suitable pairings for all self-sterile or partially self-sterile varieties. Cross-fertilization is usually effected quite naturally if the trees are not more than 30 ft. apart, the pollen being carried from tree to tree by wind and insects.

RELIABLE VARIETIES FOR THE SMALL FRUIT GARDEN

In the following lists varieties with the same number prefixed to their names can be planted together to ensure proper cross-fertilization and fruiting.

Left: Cordon pears in flower. Trained in this way, fruit takes up little room and is well adapted to a small garden

Bottom: Forms of fruit tree. (1) Espalier-trained. (2) Fan-trained. (3) Cordon. (4) Pyramid

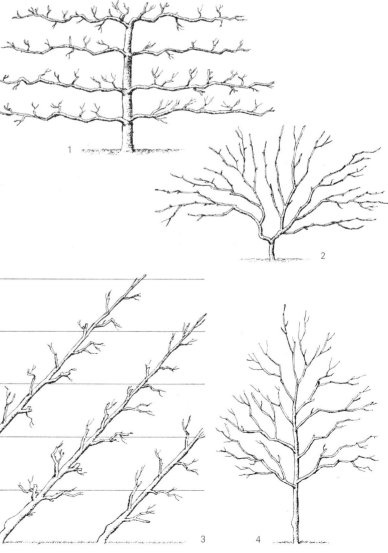

APPLES

(3) **Ashmead's Kernel.** An old apple back in favour for its fine flavour and beautiful blossom. Dec. to Feb. Partially self-fertile.

(2) **Blenheim Orange.** Sound quality and long keeping. Dec. to Feb. Self-sterile. Makes a handsome standard.

(2) **Charles Ross.** A large, handsome fruit. Oct. to Nov. Self-fertile.

(2) **Cox's Orange Pippin.** Acknowledged the premier dessert variety. Oct. to Dec. Partially self-fertile.

(2) **Discovery.** Bright red and well flavoured. Aug. to Sept. Disease-resistant. Partially self-fertile.

(1) **Egremont Russet.** Russet-covered fruits. Oct. to Dec. Resistant to scab. Partially self-fertile.

(2) **Epicure.** An early, handsomely striped apple with food flavour. Aug. to Sept. Partially self-fertile.

(2) **Fortune.** Yellow, striped red. Sept. to Oct. Partially self-fertile.

(3) **Golden Delicious.** Yellow, flecked red. Dec. to Feb. Partially self-fertile.

(2) **Greensleeves.** A fine Cox x James Grieve seedling. Sept. to Nov. Self-fertile.

(2) **James Grieve.** Hardy and prolific. Sept. to Oct. Partially self-fertile.

(3) **Jupiter.** A bright-red high-yielding Cox seedling. Oct. to Jan. Partially self-fertile.

(2) **Laxton's Superb.** Follows Cox's Orange Pippin. Dec. to March. Partially self-fertile.

(1) **Lord Lambourne.** Good in October and November. A handsome apple. Partially self-fertile.

(3) **Orleans Reinette.** Handsome and good flavour. Nov. to Feb. Partially self-fertile.

(3) **Red Ellison.** Rather like Cox's Orange Pippin but earlier and more coloured. Sept. to Oct. Partially self-fertile.

(3) **Spartan.** Deep crimson fruits of excellent quality. Oct. to Dec. Disease-resistant. Partially self-fertile.

(2) **Sunset.** Excellent flavour. Oct. to Dec. Partially self-fertile.

(2) **Worcester Pearmain.** Rich in colour. Sept. to Oct. Partially self-fertile.

(2) **Arthur Turner.** Good early variety. Late July to Sept. Partially self-fertile.

(2) **Bramley's Seedling.** A good apple, large and productive but makes a big tree. Nov. to April. Self-sterile.

(4) **Edward VII.** Shapely green fruits. Late flowering so usually escapes spring frost damage. Dec. to April. Partially self-fertile.

(2) **Grenadier.** Smooth yellow fruits. Aug. to Sept. Disease resistant. Self-fertile.

(3) **Howgate Wonder.** A big, red-striped apple but compact in growth. Nov. to Feb. Partially self-fertile.

(1) **Idared.** Red fruits which can be used for dessert as well as for cooking. Nov. to March. Partially self-fertile.

(1) **Rev. W. Wilks.** Extra large, handsome; crops well. Oct. to Nov. Self-fertile.

CHERRIES

(6) **Bigarreau Napoleon.** Fruit yellow, scarlet next sun; flesh juicy and sweet. Aug. Self-sterile.

(6) **Bradbourne Black.** Large, dark red. July. Self-sterile.

(5) **Early Rivers.** Habit slightly weeping; fruit black, large and tender. End of June. Self-sterile.

(5) **Merton Favourite.** Large, black. June. Self-sterile.

(5) **Merton Glory.** Very large, cream and red. Self-sterile.

(6) **Morello.** Black, flesh soft, juicy and slightly astringent. The best cherry for cooking. Aug. to Sept. Self-fertile.

PEARS

(8) **Beth.** An early variety that can be picked for several weeks. Aug. to Sept. Partially self-fertile.

(9) **Beurré Hardy.** Can be cooked or eaten raw. Strong growing and erect. Oct. Partially self-fertile.

(8) **Conference.** Russet-coloured fruit, good flavour; very hardy and prolific. Oct. to Nov. Partially self-fertile.

(9) **Doyenné du Comice.** Not a regular cropper, but the finest quality pear grown. Nov. Partially self-fertile.

(9) **Fertility.** Large, reasonably good quality fruits. Sept. to Oct. Self-fertile.

(9) **Glou Morceau.** A mid-winter variety. Dec. to Jan. Richly flavoured. Partially self-fertile.

(7) **Louise Bonne of Jersey.** A large and finely flavoured variety. Oct. Partially self-fertile.

(9) **Onward.** Early ripening and of good flavour. Sept. to Oct. Partially self-fertile.

(8) **Williams's Bon Chretien.** Widely known as 'Williams'. It is a finely flavoured variety, ripening in September. Self-sterile.

PLUMS

(12) **Cambridge Gage.** Yellowish-green; superb flavour. Aug. Partially self-fertile.

(11) **Czar.** A good big purple plum for cooking or dessert. Aug. Self-fertile.

(10) **Denniston's Superb.** A prolific dessert variety of good flavour. Mid-Aug. Self-fertile.

(11) **Kirke's Blue.** A very hardy and well-flavoured variety for dessert. Best on trained trees. Sept. Self-sterile.

(11) **Marjorie's Seedling.** Dark purple. Cooking or, when ripened, dessert. Oct. Self-fertile.

(12) **Oullin's Golden Gage.** Yellow. Dessert or cooking. Aug. Self-fertile.

(11) **Merryweather Damson.** Very prolific. Aug. to Sept. Self-fertile.

(11) **Opal.** Red-purple skin and yellow flesh. Excellent flavour. July to Aug. Self-fertile.

(11) **Rivers' Early Prolific.** A heavy and regular cropper. A good early cooking plum. End July. Partially self-fertile.

(11) **Victoria.** The well-known variety and the best of its season. Can be used for dessert and cooking. Aug. to Sept. Self-fertile.

(10) **Warwickshire Drooper.** Yellow. Cooking or dessert. Very prolific. Drooping habit. Sept. Self-fertile.

PEACHES

Hale's Early. A very hardy kind. July to Aug. Self-fertile.

Peregrine. Deeply coloured, fine flavour. Aug. Self-fertile.

Rochester. Flowers late. Good flavour. Ag. Se,f-fertile.

NECTARINES

Lord Napier. Flesh pale green. Very hardy. Early Aug. Self-fertile.

BLACK CURRANTS

Baldwin. Late. A favourite with market growers. Self-fertile.

Ben Lomond. Late. High yielding and mildew resistant. Self-fertile.

Late Jet. Late flowering and so misses frosts. Self-fertile.

Wellington XXX. Mid-season. Good flavour. Self-fertile

WHITE CURRANTS

White Versailles. An old favourite and still justly popular. Self-fertile.

GOOSEBERRIES

Careless. White. Large. Fine for dessert. Mid-season. Self-fertile.

Early Sulphur. Pale yellow. Cooking or dessert. Early. Self-fertile.

Keepsake. Green. Cooking or dessert. Mid-season. Self-fertile.

Leveller. Yellow. Fine for dessert. Mid-season. Self-fertile.

Whinham's Industry. Red. Culinary or dessert. Mid-season. Self-fertile.

RASPBERRIES

Glen Clova. Mid-season. Self-fertile.
Leo. Late. Excellent flavour. Self-fertile.
Malling Jewel. Mid-season. Self-fertile.
Malling Promise. Early. Self-fertile.
Zeva. Autumn. Large fruits. Self-fertile.

STRAWBERRIES

Aromel. Early and late. Heavy cropping. Self-fertile.

Cambridge Favourite. Early. Reliable. Self-fertile.

Gorello. Early. Large berries and good flavour. Self-fertile.

Royal Sovereign. A popular market variety and still one of the best for garden cultivation. Early. Self-fertile.

BLACKBERRIES, ETC.

Oregon Thornless. Good size, well-flavoured berries. No thorns to worry about. Self-fertile.

Thornless Loganberry. A thornless variety of the well-known hybrid between blackberry and raspberry. Fine for cooking. Self-fertile.

DISTANCE APART FOR PLANTING FRUIT TREES

NAME	CORDONS	FAN-TRAINED TREES	ESPALIER-TRAINED TREES	BUSHES	DWARF PYRAMIDS	STANDARDS	CANES	PLANTS
Apples	2 ft. rows 6 ft.	–	12 ft.	15 ft.	3 ft. rows 6 ft.	25 to 30 ft.	–	–
Pears	2 ft. rows 6 ft.	–	12 ft.	15 ft.	3 ft. rows 6 ft.	25 ft.	–	–
Plums	–	12 ft.	–	15 ft.	–	25 to 30 ft.	–	–
Cherries	–	12 ft.	–	15 ft.	–	30 ft.	–	–
Peaches	–	12 to 15 ft.	–	–	–	–	–	–
Nectarines	–	12 to 15 ft.	–	–	–	–	–	–
Apricots	–	12 to 15 ft.	–	–	–	–	–	–
Red and White Currants	1 ft.	–	–	4 to 5 ft.	–	–	–	–
Black Currants	–	–	–	5 ft.	–	–	–	–
Gooseberries	1 ft. rows 4 ft.	–	–	4 to 5 ft.	–	–	–	–
Raspberries	–	–	–	–	–	–	3 ft. rows 6 ft.	–
Blackberries	–	–	–	–	–	–	6 ft. rows 9 ft.	–
Loganberries	–	–	–	–	–	–	6 ft. rows 9 ft.	–
Strawberries	–	–	–	–	–	–	–	1 ft. rows 2½ ft.

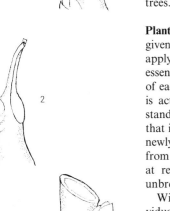

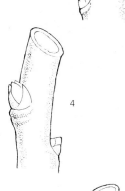

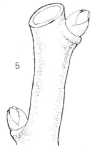

Top: Types of pruning cuts. (1) Cut too close to the bud. (2) Angle too steep. (3) Cut sloping the wrong way. (4) Cut too far from the bud. (5) Correct pruning cut

Right: Summer pruning pears. Each side growth is shortened to four or five leaves

Preparation of the Soil. As with other permanent features of the garden, it is folly to scamp the preliminaries of a fruit plantation. The ground in which trees, bushes or canes are to be planted must be thoroughly dug well in advance and should have some manure or slowly available fertilizer mixed with it. Preparation can be completed with a good dusting of coarse bonemeal forked in lightly to provide a steady supply of phosphates for some years to come – and that may mean a lot to young trees.

Planting and Staking. All the instructions already given for planting ornamental trees and shrubs also apply to fruit trees and bushes and it is equally essential to drive a supporting stake into the centre of each hole prepared for a standard tree before it is actually placed in position. The main stem of standards must be secured to the stake in such a way that it cannot sway in the wind, thus disturbing the newly formed roots, but the tie must be prevented from damaging the bark. Ties should be examined at regular intervals to make sure that they are unbroken and not cutting into the bark.

With espalier-trained trees and cordons individual staking is not usually necessary. Both money and time can be saved by driving in extra strong posts at about 10- or 12-ft. intervals and straining three or four parallel strands of galvanized wire between them. A similar structure can be used for fan-trained cherries, plums and peaches, if these are not planted against a wall or fence. Single-stem cordons are generally planted at an angle sloping along the line of the row so that a greater length of tree can be accommodated entirely within reach from ground level without the need for steps or ladders. The ends of each row can be filled in by training a few branches vertically or horizontally from the first and last trees.

Pruning after Planting. Newly planted fruit trees need to be pruned partly to encourage strong growth, partly to get new branches where they are needed. Whether the trees are planted in summer from containers or in autumn or winter from the open ground, the best time for this first pruning is February or early March.

For the actual pruning you will find a thoroughly sharp pair of secateurs most convenient. Stems of apples, pears, plums etc. which are to be removed completely should be cut right back; any small 'snag' left will only die and may provide a ready entrance for fungal diseases. Make all other cuts just above a bud which is pointing in the direction you want the branch to extend. The cut should slant away from the bud as shown in the illustration above. The main shoots, which are to continue the growth of the tree, should be shortened by about one-third of their length, and side shoots which may bear flowers and fruit should be cut to an inch or so. This will encourage the formation of really sturdy fruit buds during the following summer.

The object of all this pruning is to have new branches roughly 15 to 18 in. apart laterally and 2 to 3 ft. apart vertically. When a main stem is shortened as I have described, it will usually produce two or three new stems instead of one and in this way the branch pattern of the tree is built up. There is, however, one exception to this rule of shortening main stems after planting and that is for cordons which are not required to branch and so should have their leading stem left intact.

Currants and gooseberries are pruned in a similar manner this first year except that branches need to be closer together and raspberries, blackberries and loganberries are cut down to within about 9 in. of ground level to encourage several strong new growths from the base or even, with raspberries, from the roots.

Treatment During the First Summer. During the year after planting it is a good plan to remove all flower buds as soon as you see them opening. This conserves the energies of the plant for root establishment.

Apart from this simple treatment the trees will require little attention during their first summer. It is an excellent plan to spread some very strawy manure on the surface of the soil around each tree to serve as a mulch, but this operation is described in detail in Chapter 13. If the weather is hot and dry, the soil must be soaked thoroughly. Fertilizers are unlikely to be required the first summer if the ground has been properly prepared.

Summer Pruning. Peaches, nectarines, Morello cherries, blackcurrants, and raspberries will not require any summer pruning. Apples, pears, plums, sweet cherries, gooseberries, and red and white currants may need a little attention, especially if they are grown as trained trees or small bushes. You can start work on them early in July and continue to deal with them little by little until the middle of August. All that is necessary is to remove the upper part of each side growth when this starts to get hard and woody at the base. It is shortened to four or five leaves, the purpose being to strengthen the buds at the base and, if possible, make them swell up into fruit buds the following year. Leading shoots that are needed to extend existing branches or to form new ones are not pruned at all at this season.

CHAPTER 21

Making Herbaceous Borders

Are herbaceous borders satisfactory? – Wide borders necessary – Hardy perennials for shade – How to plan a border – Preparation of the soil – When and how to plant – Watering after planting – Summer care

Herbaceous plants differ from shrubs in having relatively soft stems and most, though not all, kinds die down to ground level in the autumn and shoot up again in the spring. So a border entirely composed of herbaceous plants can look pretty bare and uninteresting from November to March, which is one reason why so many gardeners now use herbaceous plants with other plants such as shrubs, roses, bulbs, annuals and bedding plants to make the best possible use of what each has to contribute to the garden.

Hardy Perennials for Shady Places. Many hardy perennials delight in a sunny position, but quite a number succeed in the shade, particularly if it is only the shade cast by a house or a wall and the position is not overhung by the branches of trees. A few good herbaceous plants that can be used in such a shady place are acanthus, aconitum, Japanese anemones, aquilegia, aruncus, astilbe, astrantia, bergenia, brunnera, most of the border campanulas, lily of the valley (convallaria), hardy cyclamen, dicentra, foxgloves (digitalis), epimedium, helleborus, hemerocallis, hosta, inula, lysimachia, meconopsis (but only in peaty, lime-free soil), mertensia, phlox, polygonatum, primroses and polyanthuses, pulmonaria, *Saxifraga umbrosa* (London pride) and mossy saxifrages, tiarella, *Tradescantia virginiana*, trollius and violas.

How to Plan a Border. If you decide to make a plan for a plant border, whether a mixed border containing plants from quite different categories or a border solely of herbaceous plants, this is the best way to set about it. Get a number of small pieces of cardboard or stiff paper and write on these the names of each kind of plant you fancy, together with particulars of colour, height, and season of flowering. All this information can be obtained from any nurseryman's catalogue or from an encyclopedia of plants. Now start to arrange these pieces of cardboard on a large piece of paper, marked out to scale to represent your border. Note very carefully how the colours are associated, and also whether your preliminary arrangement will produce any very bad bare places when several adjacent plants are out of flower at the same time. Also keep a close eye on heights. It will not matter if a tall, late-flowering plant grows up in front of a shorter, early-flowering one, but you must not allow the opposite to occur. Any faults can be

Bottom left: Planning an herbaceous border. To decide on the best combination of colours, heights and flowering times, cut-out cards representing different plants can be moved about on a ground plan

Bottom right: The tranquil atmosphere of this cottage garden owes much to the charm of the traditional herbaceous border

Top: Planting an herbaceous perennial with a trowel. Small plants should be firmed in with the fingers, larger clumps with the foot

Opposite: Soft greens and interesting leaf shapes against a background of cool grey walls and paving create a restful scene. Included here are rheums, epimediums, *Rodgersia aesculifolia* and ornamental grasses

rectified at once by a rearrangement of the cards. As soon as you have adjusted them to your satisfaction stick them down in position and use this chart as a guide when planting.

You should note that, in a general way, large plants growing 4 ft. and more in height should be planted from 2 to 2½ ft. apart; medium-sized plants from 18 in. to 3 ft. or thereabouts in height should be planted about 12 to 18 in. apart; while the small plants used as an edging about 6 to 9 in. apart.

Another point to remember is that straight rows are to be avoided in herbaceous or mixed borders. Arrange the plants in irregular groups, and do not even keep all the tall plants at the back, with those of medium height in the middle, and the dwarf kinds in front. Instead break up the line of the border by letting some of the tall plants come forward and some of the small ones go back, so that when the plants are in bloom, the contour of the border is undulating and split up into a number of bays of varying size.

If you are using shrubs as well as herbaceous plants it may be best to use these to form the bays and to fill in with the other less permanent plants. This way you will have a good background even in winter when the herbaceous plants have died down and bedding plants have been cleared away.

Preparation of the Soil. Even if the ground is to be used solely for herbaceous plants preparation of the soil should be almost as thorough as that of the fruit garden or shrub border, for most of the plants will remain undisturbed for several years and a few for many years. Make sure that the plot is well cleaned and thoroughly dug. You can, with advantage, work a little well-rotted manure or decayed vegetable refuse into the soil and finish off with a dusting of bonemeal at 4 oz. per square yard.

When and How to Plant. Planting of open-ground plants can be done either in autumn or spring, but if the ground is heavy or badly drained, it is best to wait till the latter half of March and the early weeks in April which are usually the best periods. Nowadays a great many herbaceous perennials are grown in containers from which they can be planted at almost any time of year so long as the soil is not frozen or sodden.

Always plant with a trowel or a spade. The essential points are similar to those for other plants, that is holes must be of sufficient size to enable roots to be spread out naturally without any doubling, and soil must be well firmed around the roots. If the ground is rather heavy or lumpy it is an excellent plan to prepare a barrow load of sifted soil mixed with moss peat and to place this around the roots. Small plants should be firmed in with the knuckles of both hands pressed on opposite sides, but large plants are better firmed by foot pressure.

German or flag irises have thick, fleshy root stocks, technically known as rhizomes, which creep along the ground, usually right on the surface, and the roots from these plunge down into the soil. When planting them you must keep the rhizomes as near the surface as possible. Just cover them with sufficient soil to keep them firm while they are rooting into their new quarters. Later on they will work themselves on to the surface.

Watering after Planting. If the weather is dry after planting it may be necessary to water. Do not use a watering can fitted with a rose, but instead tie a piece of sacking loosely around the naked spout to break the force of the water and then give each plant a good soaking close to the roots. Once established, it is unusual for herbaceous plants to require water except in very hot weather and then it is best done with a sprinkler which gives a fine, rain-like spray and which can be left running for an hour or so.

Summer Care. One of the great advantages of herbaceous perennials from the owner-gardener's standpoint is that they require so little attention. Once planted, they can be left undisturbed for three or four years, or even longer if they do not get overcrowded. The only care they need in the meantime, apart from weeding, is a little thinning out and, for the taller kinds, staking in early summer. A topdressing each autumn of bonemeal at the rate of 4 oz. to the square yard, and a scattering of a good compound fertilizer such as National Grow-more at about 3 oz. per square yard in April will keep the soil sufficiently rich. If you prefer to mix your own spring fertilizer you can do so with 4 parts by weight of superphosphate of lime, 2 parts of sulphate of ammonia, and 1 part of sulphate of potash.

HARDY HERBACEOUS PLANTS TO FLOWER THROUGHOUT THE YEAR

In the following lists no attempt has been made to include everything that is in flower during the various months, but only to give a selection of some of the best and most reliable kinds that can be grown without difficulty in all parts of the British Isles.

JANUARY TO APRIL

Bergenia cordifolia. This species has very large, leathery evergreen leaves and racemes of bright pink flowers. It starts to bloom in March. Succeeds in any soil and sunny or shady position. Height 1½ ft. There are several good varieties.

Doronicum plantagineum. Large yellow 'daisies' in April and May. The best tall (3 ft.) variety is Harpur Crewe while *D. cordatum*, 6 in., is a useful dwarf.

Epimedium. Commonly known as barrenwort. Evergreen plants with small flowers and dainty leaves that assume bright autumnal colours. All thrive in shady places. Good kinds are *E. versicolor sulphureum*, pale yellow, and *E. pinnatum*, yellow. Height 1 ft.

Helleborus. Many species of helleborus are in flower during the winter and spring. The best from the gardener's standpoint are *H. niger*, the Christmas rose, and its varieties, white (sometimes red spotted), very early flowering; *H. orientalis*, the Lenten rose,

white, pink, crimson, etc., rather later, and *H. corsicus,* late winter, early spring, with handsome, deeply divided leaves and apple-green flowers. All thrive in partially shady places and dislike root disturbance. Height 1 to 2 ft.

Hepatica angulosa. Blue, anemone-like flowers. Will succeed in sun or partial shade. Does not like root disturbance. Height 6 in. *H. triloba* is still smaller and has pretty pink and double-flowered varieties. Often known as *Anemone hepatica* and *A. triloba.*

Iberis sempervirens. The perennial candytuft. Short spikes of pure white flowers. Evergreen foliage. Height 9 to 12 in. The best form is known as Snowflake. Little Gem is dwarfer.

Primula. Several species of hardy primula may be planted in the herbaceous border to flower in spring. These include the British primrose (*P. acaulis*) in a great number of coloured or double-flowered forms, the hybrids between these and *P. juliae* (of these *P.* Wanda, claret red, is one of the best), and the polyanthus (*P. elatior*) in many varieties. All thrive in partially shady places. Height 4 to 12 in.

Pulmonaria angustifolia. Popularly known as the lungwort or blue cowslip. Pure blue flowers in March and April. Succeeds in shade. Height 1 ft.

Trollius. Popularly known as globe flowers on account of their bright yellow globular flowers. There are numerous varieties, all in shades of yellow. Will thrive in sun or partial shade. Do not mind wet soil. Height 2 to 3 ft.

MAY

Alyssum saxatile. Well named gold dust. Masses of small yellow flowers over greyish foliage. Likes good drainage and sun. Height 9 in. There is a double-flowered variety and another with lemon-yellow flowers.

Convallaria majalis. The popular lily of the valley. Fragrant white flowers. Will succeed in sun or shade. Height 9 to 12 in.

Dicentra spectabilis. Popularly known as bleeding heart. A graceful plant, with finely divided foliage and pendent white and rose-pink flowers. Does well in semi-shade, height 3 ft. *D. eximea* and Bountiful are shorter (1 ft.), have more fern-like leaves and smaller rose flowers in drooping sprays.

Euphorbia griffithii. Striking heads of reddish-orange flowers, 2½ ft. Sun or semi-shade.

Iris pumila. The dwarf or Crimean iris. Like a miniature flag or German iris. The colour range includes ivory white, yellow, and dark blue. All varieties thrive in sun and a well-drained soil. Does well on chalk. Height 9 in.

Polygonatum multiflorum. Solomon's seal. Pendent, ivory-white flowers and graceful arching stems. Succeeds in shade. Height 2½ ft.

Viola. In addition to the many named varieties of viola, most of which make excellent border plants, there are two fine species for border planting, *V. cornuta,* blue, continuous flowering, and *V. gracilis,* violet, neat habit. In the named varieties preference should be given to those of compact tufted habit. Height 4 to 8 in. Succeed in sun or partial shade.

JUNE

Agapanthus Headbourne Hybrids. Clusters of blue flowers on stiff 2-ft. stems. Suitable for a warm, sunny position in well-drained soil.

Anchusa azurea. Like an immensely enlarged forget-me-not. There are several improved varieties, all with flowers in shades of clear blue. Height 4 to 5 ft.

Aquilegia. The columbines. There are numerous races of garden hybrids, mostly with long-spurred flowers, though some are short spurred and some double. All are dainty flowers available in a great variety of colours and readily grown from seed sown outdoors in spring or early summer. Will succeed in any well-drained soil in sun or partial shade. Height 1½ to 3 ft.

Campanula. The peach-leaved bellflower, *C. persicifolia,* will grow well in any reasonably good soil and sunny or partially shady position. There are many varieties, including some with double flowers. All are either white or blue. Height 2 to 3½ ft. Other good kinds are *C. glomerata dahurica,* violet blue, 1½ ft.; *C. grandis,* blue, 3 to 4 ft.; and *C. lactiflora,* pale blue, 4 ft. The last named does well in semi-shade.

Delphinium. There are a great many garden varieties, some with single and others with double flowers. All like an open, sunny position and a rich but well-drained soil. Height 4 to 7 ft. Varieties of *D. belladonna* are shorter and more branching.

Dianthus plumarius. The common pink. This is an indispensable border plant, which does especially well in soils containing a fair proportion of lime or chalk. Must have an open, sunny situation. There are numerous varieties, some with white and others with coloured flowers, single and double, mostly very sweetly scented. Height 9 to 18 in.

Erigeron. There are many varieties in cultivation, most of hybrid origin. All suggest short Michaelmas daisies. The colour range is of shades of blue and pink. Easily grown in any well-drained soil. Height 9 in. to 3 ft.

Gaillardia. Vivid yellow daisy flowers, usually with a broad band of scarlet. In some varieties the flowers are more or less suffused with orange. All must have really good drainage and a sunny position. Will continue to flower all summer. Height 2 to 3 ft.

Geranium. These are the true owners of this name, the tender bedding plants popularly known as 'geraniums' being actually pelargoniums. The hardy perennial geraniums mostly have blue, pink or purple flowers and they thrive in sunny places in most soils including chalk. Recommended are *G. endressii,* pink, 18 in.; *G. grandiflorum,* blue, 18 in.; Johnson's Blue, blue flowers, 18 in., and Russell Prichard, rose, 12 in.

Geum. Like the last-named genus, geums appreciate good drainage, but are not fastidious in other respects. The colour range includes yellow, scarlet, and orange. Will continue to flower for many weeks. Height 1½ to 2 ft.

Incarvillea delavayi. Clusters of trumpet-shaped rose-pink flowers. The roots are fleshy, and should be left undisturbed for as long as possible. Height 3 ft.

Iris germanica. The familiar flag or bearded iris.

A great many garden varieties have been produced in a wide range of colours including shades found in few other plants. All will thrive in any sunny position and well-drained soil, especially relishing lime or chalk. Height 2 to 4 ft.

Lupinus polyphyllus. The well-known herbaceous lupin. It does not succeed well in soils containing much lime, but in other respects is easy to grow, though usually rather short lived. There is a great number of varieties in many colours, including pink, red, lavender, purple, apricot, and white. Height 2 to 4 ft. Raised from seed sown outdoors in spring or early summer.

Paeonia. Both the Chinese and the old English peonies should find a place in every garden. There are many varieties, some with single and others with double or semi-double flowers in a range of colours from white and pale pink to crimson. All thrive in rather rich soil, and should be allowed to grow for a number of years without disturbance. Height 3 ft.

Papaver orientale. The oriental poppy, best known in its flaming scarlet and black forms, though there are many other colours, including pink and white. All succeed best in full sun and well-drained soil. Height 3 ft.

Pyrethrum. These are often termed 'coloured marguerites', or 'coloured moon daisies'. There are many varieties, both with single and double flowers in white, pink or red. All thrive best in a sunny position and rich but light and well-drained soil. Height 3 ft.

Verbascum. The mulleins, with spires of yellow, lilac or purple flowers. There are numerous species and varieties including Broussa, yellow flowers, leaves covered with grey hairs; Cotswold Beauty, pale bronze; Cotswold Queen, salmon bronze; Gainsborough, soft yellow; Harkness Hybrid, deep

Top left: Hostas are a good choice for a shady corner, blending well with other perennials or shrubs. Some kinds have handsome flowers and the foliage of all is an asset to the garden for months on end

Top: A well-planned herbaceous border. Plants are best arranged in irregular groups to avoid uniformity

Left: An invaluable herbaceous plant is the delphinium. Modern hybrids are available in a wide selection of colours

Top: Climbing roses Albertine and Danse du Feu look well on the white wall of this period house. The informal border is planted with easily grown perennials such as achillea, nepeta, heuchera, lysimachia and cerastium

Right: A well-planted herbaceous border. Though the flowering period of many perennials is short, by arranging plants to flower in sequence a continuity of blooms can be maintained all summer. In bloom here are delphiniums, *Thalictrum glaucum*, *Salvia superba*, gaillardias, penstemons and *Campanula lactiflora* with the silver-grey foliage of *Artemisia ludoviciana* for contrast

yellow, and *V. nigrum* (*vernale*), yellow and purple. All thrive in well-drained soil and a sunny or partially shady position. Do not mind chalk. Height 3 to 4 ft. They are usually rather short lived but some kinds can be readily raised from seed sown outdoors in spring or early summer.

JULY

Achillea filipendula. Large, flat heads of yellow flowers on stiffly erect stems. A very hardy and easily grown plant. The best varieties are Coronation Gold and Gold Plate. Height 4 ft.

Anthemis tinctoria. The yellow, daisy-like flowers are very freely produced. There are several forms, including Grallagh Gold, with deep yellow flowers, and E. C. Buxton, with lemon-yellow blooms. All thrive in any sunny position and well-drained soil. Height 3 ft.

Coreopsis lanceolata. Not to be confused with the annual coreopsis or calliopsis. *C. lanceolata* is a true perennial, with bright yellow flowers. Nearly allied plants are *C*. Perry's Variety, with semi-double yellow flowers, and *C. auriculata superba*, with single yellow blooms, marked with crimson. *C. verticillata* has fine, ferny foliage and masses of small yellow flowers. All require sun and good drainage. Height 2½ ft.

Echinops. Globe thistle. Spherical heads of blue flowers. Very hardy and easy to grow in a sunny place and well-drained soil. Taplow Blue, 5 ft., light blue, and *E. ritro*, deep blue, 3 ft., are recommended.

Eryngium. Popularly known as sea holly. Plants with spiky, teazel-like heads of bloom. Good kinds are *E. amethystinum,* amethyst blue; *E. oliverianum,* metallic blue; *E. planum*, blue; *E. alpinum*, steely blue, and *E. tripartitum*, with small blue flowers and one of the easiest to grow. All need a deep, rather light soil and a sunny position. Resist drought well. Height 3 ft.

Galega officinalis. The goat's rue. Small spikes of pea flowers on a large and very bushy plant. Succeeds in any soil and position. Height 5 ft. Good varieties are *G. hartlandii alba*, white, Her Majesty, lilac blue, and Lady Wilson, mauve pink.

Gypsophila paniculata. This is a favourite flower for cutting as well as an excellent border plant. The double-flowered forms are preferable to the single type, and the best of these are Bristol Fairy, white, 3 ft.; Flamingo, lilac pink 3 ft.; and Rosy Veil, pink, sprawling, 18 in. All like a deep, well-drained soil, liberally supplied with lime or chalk.

Hemerocallis. The day lilies, so called because the individual, lily-like blooms only last for one day, though they are constantly replaced. There are numerous kinds, in shades of yellow, orange yellow, salmon, coppery red and crimson. All will thrive in ordinary soil and a sunny or partially shady position. Height 2 to 4 ft.

Heuchera. Graceful plants for the front of the border, with sprays of small pink or scarlet flowers and low clumps of ornamental foliage. Height 1½ to 2½ ft. Any soil. Sun or light shade.

Nepeta faassenii. The popular catmint. An easily grown plant, with spikes of small lavender-blue flowers. Does best in a light, well-drained soil and sunny place. Height 1 to 1½ ft.

Oenothera Fireworks. A very free-flowering perennial with bronze-red buds opening to bright yellow flowers. Height 1½ ft. Needs a sunny place but will grow in any reasonable well-drained soil.

Sidalcea. Graceful spikes of mallow-like flowers. There are many garden varieties, all in shades of pink, rosy crimson or white. Succeeds in any ordinary garden soil and sunny position. Height 3 to 4 ft.

Tradescantia virginiana. Distinctive, rush-like foliage and three-petalled blue, rose, or white flowers. All are very easy to grow in any soil in sun or shade. Height 2 ft.

AUGUST

Aconitum. Popularly known as monkshood. There are many species and varieties, the best for the garden being Bressingham Spire, violet blue, 3 ft.; Barker's Variety, deep blue, 5 ft., and *A. napellus bicolor*, blue and white, 3 ft. All grow well in any reasonably fertile garden soil and sunny or partially shaded position.

Astilbe. Often erroneously known as spiraeas. The kinds commonly grown are hybrids, and they have graceful, feathery plumes of flowers, in colours ranging from white and palest pink to intense crimson. All thrive best in a rather rich, moist soil and sunny or partially shady position. Height 3 to 4 ft.

Chrysanthemum maximum. The familiar Shasta daisy. There are many garden varieties with white flowers of great size. Some, such as Wirral Pride, have semi-double or anemone-centred flowers; some, such as Esther Read, are fully double. All are very easy to grow in any soil including chalk, preferably in a sunny place. Height 2½ to 3½ ft.

Echinacea. Popularly known as the purple coneflower. Large purple daisy flowers on sturdy stems. A good variety is The King, 4 ft. All varieties are easily grown in almost any soil and sunny position.

Helenium. There are many varieties of this easily grown plant, with a height range from 2 to 5 ft. and with yellow to mahogany-crimson flowers. All succeed in any reasonably fertile soil and sunny or partially shady position.

Hollyhock. An indispensable plant for the back of the border. There are single, semi-double, and double-flowered forms, all in a great variety of shades of yellow and red, and also pure white. Height 6 to 7 ft. Well-drained soil and sunny position. Plants are seldom long lived but are readily raised from seed sown outdoors in spring or early summer and are often renewed in this way annually, being sown one year to flower the next.

Kniphofia. The red-hot poker or torch lily. There are many garden forms, some with yellow flowers, others all scarlet, yet others combining both colours and at least one white. All should be grown in rather rich but well-drained soil and a sunny position. Height 3 to 6 ft.

Liatris pycnostachya. Tall, stiff spikes of purplish flowers. These spikes begin to open at the top and continue downwards. Plant in deep, rather moist soil and a position which is sunny. Height 2 to 3 ft.

Macleaya cordata. The plume poppy, also known as bocconia. Large, greyish leaves and loose sprays of small, pinkish-buff flowers on 7-ft. stems. Any reasonably well-drained soil and sunny place.

Monarda. Popularly known as bergamot. Fragrant foliage and heads of hooded flowers. Does well in almost any soil and situation. Good varieties are Cambridge Scarlet, scarlet; Croftway Pink, rose pink; and Blue Stocking, violet. Height 2½ ft.

Phlox paniculata. The popular herbaceous phlox, an indispensable plant, succeeding best in a rather rich soil and cool, partially shady position. There are many garden varieties with a colour range including white, pink, salmon, scarlet, crimson, mauve, and purple. Height 1½ to 3½ ft.

Rudbeckia. Popularly known as coneflowers. There are several good species and garden varieties, including Autumn Sun, yellow, 7 ft.; Goldsturm, yellow and black, 3 ft.; Goldquelle, double, deep yellow, 5 ft.; and Golden Glow, lemon yellow, 5 ft. All are easily grown in any ordinary soil and open, sunny position.

Salvia superba. Slender spikes of violet-blue flowers and bracts. A hardy and easily grown plant. Height 3 ft., but there are shorter varieties such as Lubeca, 2 ft. and East Friesland, 1½ ft. All like well-drained soil and a sunny place.

Thalictrum dipterocarpum. An exceptionally graceful plant, with foliage suggesting a maidenhair fern, and spreading panicles of dainty mauve and yellow. Should be planted in cool, fairly rich, well-drained soil and a sunny position. Height 6 ft. Other good kinds are *T. aquilegifolium*, with finely divided foliage and flattish heads of fluffy pale purple flowers, height 4 ft.; and *T. glaucum*, blue-grey leaves and fluffy heads of yellow flowers. These will grow in any soil in sun or semi-shade.

Veronica longifolia subsessilis. Stout spikes of violet-blue flowers. Height 1½ ft. Other good kinds are Barcarolle, rose pink, 1½ ft.; Shirley Blue, blue, 1 ft. and Wendy, deep blue, grey leaves, 1½ ft. All will thrive in any ordinary garden soil and open position.

The teazel-like grey-blue blooms of this sea holly, *Eryngium alpinum*, provide a striking foil to the warmer colours of the herbaceous border

SEPTEMBER TO DECEMBER

Anemone hybrida. The Japanese windflower. Garden varieties include white, pink, and deep rose forms. All grow freely in any reasonably good soil and sunny or partially shady position. Their roots should not be disturbed unnecessarily. Height 2 to 4 ft.

Artemisia lactiflora. Spreading sprays of creamy flowers. A useful and easily grown plant, thriving in sun or partial shade in most soils. Height 4 ft.

Aster (Perennial). Popularly known as Michaelmas daisies. There are a great number of garden varieties, ranging in height from a few inches to 6 ft., and in colour from white and palest lavender or mauve to violet blue and rosy red. All are easily grown in any ordinary soil and open position, but varieties of *A. amellus* should not be disturbed in the autumn.

Chrysanthemum uliginosum. Like a tall, late-flowering moon daisy. Any soil and position. Height 5 ft.

Helianthus. The perennial sunflowers. Good kinds are Soleil d'Or, with semi-double, golden-yellow flowers, 4 ft.; Monarch, large, single yellow, black-centred flowers, 7 ft. The first is very hardy and easily grown in any soil and sunny place. Monarch needs a warm, sheltered place in well-drained soil.

Sedum spectabile. Flattish heads of rose-pink flowers, which are deeper and brighter in colour in the variety *atropurpureum*. Very easily grown in well-drained soil and a sunny place. Autumn Joy is similar in habit but the pink flowers deepen to russet red as they age.

Solidago. The most imposing variety of Golden Rod is named Golden Wings. Height 6 ft. Will grow in almost any soil and situation. There are dwarfer kinds such as Goldenmosa and Leraft, all excellent.

Stokesia cyanea superba. Very like a single annual aster in flower, but is a true perennial. Should be planted in a sunny position and well-drained soil. Height 2 ft.

Top: *Clematis montana* is a very vigorous climber which has here been trained right across the front of a house. Below is the Japanese quince (chaenomeles) and in the foreground a very highly variegated form of the evergreen *Euonymus japonicus*. Clipped box makes a neat edging for the bed filled with yellow wallflowers

Right: Tulips are invaluable for spring bedding schemes. Here, Darwin varieties, interplanted with wallflowers, make an effective border in front of a wall-trained ceanothus. This is an attractive shrub of which there are both deciduous and evergreen kinds, flowering in spring or summer according to variety

PLANTS GROWN PRIMARILY FOR FOLIAGE

Some herbaceous plants are grown more for their handsome leaves than for their flowers, though these may add to the effect. The following are especially recommended.

Acanthus. Very large, dark green, thistle-like leaves and stiff 4-ft. spikes of hooded, maroon and white flowers in late summer. *A. mollis latifolius* and *A. spinosus* are two of the best varieties. They are easily grown in any soil in sun or shade but they spread by underground stems and can be invasive.

Anaphalis. Popularly known as pearly everlasting because the pearl-white flowers are chaffy and last a long time. The leaves are silvery. Good kinds are *A. margaritacea,* $1\frac{1}{2}$ ft.; *A. triplinervis*, 1 ft., and *A. yedoensis*, 2 ft. All like well-drained soil and a sunny place.

Artemisia. Many kinds have grey or silver leaves. All grow best in sunny places in well-drained soil. Specially recommended are *A. absinthium* Lambrook Silver, a semi-shrubby plant 3 ft. high with aromatic, finely divided leaves, and *A. ludoviciana*, with undivided silver leaves, 2 ft. high.

Hosta. These are the plantain lilies, making large clumps of broad or lance-shaped leaves which may be green, blue-grey or variegated. All produce tubular flowers in loose spikes in July–August and in one or two these are quite decorative. All like rather moist, fertile soil and a shady or semi-shady place. Recommended are *H. albomarginata*, green and white leaves; *H. fortunei*, grey-blue leaves and lilac flowers; *H. lancifolia*, narrow green leaves; *H. sieboldiana*, grey-green leaves and white flowers, and *H. undulata variegata*, green and white wavy leaves.

Rheum palmatum. Leaves like a giant rhubarb and tall, stout stems carrying clusters of small creamy-white flowers. It likes fairly rich, moist soil and a sunny or semi-shady place. Bowles' Crimson has red flowers and red undersides to the leaves, 6 ft.

Rodgersia. Large rounded or deeply divided leaves which are bronze green in some varieties. The flowers are small, pink or white, carried in fluffy-looking clusters on stout stems in July–August. All like rather moist soil and a cool, semi-shady place. Recommended are *R. pinnata superba*, bronzy leaves and pink flowers, 3 ft., and *R. tabularis,* rounded leaves, creamy flowers $2\frac{1}{2}$ ft.

Stachys lanata. The lamb's ears, so called because the oval leaves are densely covered with long, silky grey hairs. It produces spikes of purple flowers in July but these are of little decorative merit and are best cut off. A variety named Silver Carpet does not flower. The plants are prostrate and succeed in any reasonably well-drained soil and sunny place.

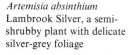

Artemisia absinthium Lambrook Silver, a semi-shrubby plant with delicate silver-grey foliage

CHAPTER 22

Rock Garden and Pool

Soil and foundations – The choice of stone – Setting the rocks – Planting alpines – Pools: formal and informal – Concrete for pools – How to grow aquatics – Oxygenating plants – Snails and fish – When to stock a pool

Rock plants, being mostly small, provide an opportunity for growing a great variety of plants in a very limited space and are often the answer to the problem of the small-garden owner who is deeply interested in plants. Rock gardens themselves can provide a picturesque feature which has decorative possibilities quite distinct from those of any other type of garden making. Water can be introduced in a natural way in the form of a stream, cascades and an irregular pool. However, these methods of using rock plants and water are by no means the only possibilities nor necessarily the best in small gardens where it may be difficult to make such supposedly 'natural' features look convincing. Rock plants grow well in raised beds and water can be used in pools and water basins of regular shape, as well as in fountains, all of which can be made to fit in with even the most sophisticated designs.

Whatever form the rock or water features may take, spring is an excellent time to add them since many rock plants can be established most satisfactorily during the spring months, and May is the best of all months for planting water lilies and other aquatics.

Soil and Foundations. A rock garden is necessarily one of the most permanent features of the garden. Once it has been made and planted it is a labour of Hercules to pull it to pieces again, so do make certain that your preparation is thorough. Good drainage is one of the most essential things. If the subsoil is gravel, sand, or chalk, it is unlikely that any improvement will be necessary, but before making a rock garden on a clay subsoil it is advisable to provide an artificial outlet for surplus water. This can be done by digging out all the good topsoil, removing about 9 in. or 1 ft. of the clay and replacing it by clinkers, brickbats, or any other hard rubble you may have at hand. If you can procure some good turves from a meadow, so much

Rock and water features add a new dimension to garden design, presenting an opportunity to grow many attractive rock or aquatic plants

Top: A well-established rock garden in spring. Bold outcrops of rock provide a solid framework for saxifrages, aubrieta, iberis, alyssum, ericas and dwarf conifers, including the golden-leaved form of Pfitzer's juniper in the background and *Thuya* Rheingold and *Picea albertiana conica* near the summit. In such a setting dwarf conifers offer a refreshing contrast to the brighter colours of the surrounding flowers and provide a variation of height and texture

Right: In a steeply sloping garden a delightful effect can be achieved by the use of terracing to create different planting levels. An ornamental pool and cascade at the lowest level continue the composition of curving walls. The soil is lime-free, permitting planting with rhododendrons, azaleas, camellias and magnolias

the better, for these, laid grass side downwards over the rubble, will prevent the finer soil from silting down into the drainage layer and blocking it up. It may be necessary to construct a soakaway at the lowest part of the garden, but this you must judge for yourself by your experience during the first winter. If waterlogging was not serious then, there should be no need for a soakaway.

Unless the existing topsoil is very sticky and bad, there is no reason why you should not use it as a basis for the rock garden compost, but it must be mixed with plenty of grit in the form of river sand and small stone chippings, plus either leafmould or peat. A good average compost will consist of 6 parts of garden soil, 1 part of sharp gritty sand, 1 part of stone chippings and 2 parts of humus (either all peat, all leafmould, or a mixture of both).

Throw this compost into irregular mounds to represent hills and dales in miniature. While doing this try and visualize the finished appearance of the rock garden. Of course, you will be able to make a lot of readjustment later on as you set the stones, but a good start will save much time and unnecessary labour then.

The Choice of Stone. Good stone is half the battle in making an effective rock garden. It is very difficult to make a satisfactory arrangement with small stones and a few really large pieces can help enormously, as when well sunk into the ground they will give the rock garden a solid appearance. Much of the best rock stone in England is the limestone from the famous Cheddar Gorge in Somerset and from the Westmorland hills, and is removed from the surface, not quarried. This means that the stone will have had centuries of weathering which makes it interesting to look at and more convincing than quarried stone, representing a natural outcrop of rock which is the ideal to be aimed for. But such stone is expensive and requires expert laying.

There are also a number of quarried sandstones that are suitable for rock garden structure, and which are usually much cheaper, and there are other harder stones such as granite and millstone which are occasionally used. Perhaps the best general advice is to work with a local, or near-local, stone and not to introduce rock that is entirely alien to the geology of the district.

Setting the Rocks. It is not easy to explain exactly how the stone should be set. You must, to a large extent, rely upon your own artistic ability, but you can gain useful ideas by inspecting rock gardens constructed by experts and, perhaps even better, from a visit to some hillside or sea cliff where natural outcrops of rock occur. Always remember that the more natural looking the rock garden the better it is. Your aim should be to give the illusion that the rocks you have placed have actually 'grown' on the site, being part of a natural outcrop.

Rock gardens are of many types. Some centre round a few craggy spurs constructed by cleverly building one stone upon another and, maybe, cementing them together in such a way that the mortar is not seen. Others are much softer in character, suggesting undulating alpine meadows or rounded hillsides. It is even possible to make a quite effective rock garden entirely on the flat with stones sunk here and there and just peering through the surface of the soil.

Limestones and sandstones always exist in layers, known by the geologist as strata layers, and these can be seen clearly in many outcrops. It is an excellent plan to follow this idea in the rock garden, and to arrange series of stones, each appearing out of the soil at the same inclination. Following this idea a stage further, successive rows of stones may be used to form irregular shelves of soil in which there will be ample room to establish plants. It is seldom wise to rear stones on end. More frequently they should be set on their broadest face and have at least a third of their bulk sunk into the soil. Only in this way can you give the rock garden an appearance of sufficient solidity and permanence.

Dry Walls and Raised Beds. A 'dry' wall is one that is constructed without mortar. The stones may simply be built one on top of another but in gardens it is better to pack plenty of soil between them as in this it will be possible to establish many plants. Dry walls can be built with any stone or, for that matter, with bricks, but it is easiest to work with roughly dressed stone. The first course should be sunk several inches in the soil for stability and for the same reason some of the largest stones should be used here. Try, so far as possible, to stagger the stones in adjacent courses so that the vertical crevices do not coincide and each course helps to bind the one immediately below it. Pack soil between the stones, ramming it in well so that there are no loose places. If plants are available when you are building the wall you can plant some as you proceed, laying them on or against one stone, spreading soil over the roots and then putting the next stone in place to hold the plant securely. This is a good deal easier than trying to push the roots into narrow crevices after the wall has been built.

Dry walls may be used to retain terraces, to form divisions or boundaries or to contain the soil in raised beds. Terrace walls will have soil behind them and if the bank to be retained is more than 3 ft. high it may be wise to build the wall with a slight backward slope, or batter, to help it hold the weight and thrust of the soil particularly in wet weather.

If boundary or division walls are to be used for growing plants they should be built double sided with a good space (at least 10 in. in width) between them filled with soil. Plants can then be established on top of the wall as well as in the two faces and may in time root right down to the soil beneath the wall.

Raised beds are really an extension of this idea and can be of any size and shape, though it is seldom convenient that they should be more than 3 ft. high or 6 ft. wide or tending the plants can become difficult. The bed is surrounded by a dry wall built in the manner just described and is filled level with the top with a good mixture of soil, sand, grit and peat or leafmould which can be varied to suit the plants to be grown in the bed. Such a raised bed can be a feature even in a very small garden and since

there will be all manner of aspects in the surrounding walls, it can be used for shade-loving as well as sun-loving plants.

Planting Alpines. Many alpines can be planted even in the vertical or horizontal chinks between neighbouring boulders or stones as well as in the wider shelves of soil and on top of walls and raised beds. With care suitable places can be found for every type of plant and the soil can be varied to meet the requirements of those that are fussy. Since most rock plants are sold in containers it is possible to plant at any time of the year, but spring is a particularly favourable time for planting those from the open ground.

Never plant anything in a blind alley. The roots of most alpines will penetrate the soil for a surprising distance, finding their way through crevice after crevice, if need be, until they reach a larger body of soil in which they can find the moisture and nutriment they require. For this reason you should always arrange things in such a way that the narrower crevices lead, either below or behind, to a good volume of soil.

There are miniature shrubs and bushy perennials that can be planted in the higher positions to give an added illusion that these are, in fact, mountains and precipices, while in the valleys you may decide to plant principally low-growing or creeping alpines in keeping with the position.

Sinks, Troughs and Containers. Yet another way to grow rock plants is in old stone sinks or troughs or in modern reproductions of these or in containers. The two essentials are that there must be room for at least a 9-in. depth of soil and a free outlet (or outlets) in the bottom for surplus water. Some pebbles or broken clay pots are placed in the bottom of the container, it is then filled with a good mixture of soil, sand, grit and peat and possibly finished off with a few small pieces of rock bedded in on top and a scattering of stone chippings on the surface. Small alpine plants are most suitable for these troughs and containers and, of course, they must be kept well watered in spring and summer as the small quantity of soil will quickly dry out. Plants well looked after will continue to thrive in such containers for years and they make interesting as well as decorative objects for a paved terrace or patio. It is wise to stand each container on bricks, rocks or a pedestal so that it is off the ground and there is no likelihood of the drainage holes becoming blocked.

Top left: Rock plants inserted into the crevices of a dry stone wall soon cover the surface with flowers and graceful trails of foliage

Top: A collection of sempervivums in a stone trough. Such containers are also an effective way of growing a wide range of small alpine plants

Below: Constructing a rock garden. The rocks should be bedded in the soil to form natural-looking outcrops, leaving irregular shelves of soil in which to establish plants

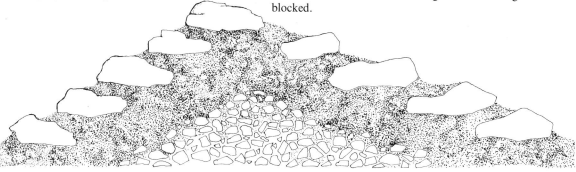

EASILY GROWN ROCK PLANTS

Aethionema. Small bushy plants with narrow leaves and clusters of pink flowers in spring and early summer. Any well-drained soil and sunny place.

Alyssum saxatile. Dense sprays of small golden-yellow flowers in spring. There are double-flowered and lemon-yellow varieties. Any well-drained soil and sunny place. Single varieties usually spread by self-sown seed.

Anemone blanda. A wood anemone with dainty blue, pink, carmine or white flowers in spring. Does well in shady places and cool, slightly moist soil. Excellent on chalk.

Anthemis cupaniana. Sprawling masses of feathery silver-grey leaves and large white daisy flowers all summer. Any well-drained soil and sunny place.

Arabis. Sprawling mats of grey-green leaves. Short spikes of white flowers in spring. There are double-flowered and pink varieties, also one with cream variegated leaves. Any soil and reasonably open place.

Arenaria balearica. Close carpets of tiny emerald green leaves studded with small white flowers in spring. Likes cool, rather moist places. Excellent as a carpet over small bulbs.

Armeria maritima. Close tufts of narrow leaves and pink flowers clustered in globular heads in spring. There are white and carmine varieties. Any well-drained soil and sunny place.

Aubrieta. Carpets of green leaves smothered in purple, lavender, pink or carmine flowers in spring. Any soil, but does particularly well on chalk or limestone. Sunny position.

Campanula. Numerous species, varying from trailing or sprawling to tuft forming. Nearly all have bell-shaped flowers but a few are more open and starry. Most flower in summer and like open places. Not fussy about soil. Especially recommended are *Campanula carpatica, cochlearifolia* (also known as *caespitosa* and *pusilla*), *garganica, poscharskyana* and *portenschlagiana* (also known as *muralis*).

Dianthus deltoides. Trailing mats of narrow leaves and small, single, rose-pink flowers in early summer. There are also deeper carmine flowered varieties. Sunny places and well-drained soil.

Erinus alpinus. Little rosettes of leaves and clusters of small purple or crimson flowers in spring and early summer. Will often sow itself in the crevices of a wall. Likes sunny places.

Erysimum linifolium. Like a little wallflower, but fully perennial and with spikes of purple flowers in late spring and summer. Well-drained soil and sunny places.

Gentiana asclepiadea. Arching stems, each bearing numerous deep violet-blue tubular flowers in summer. Enjoys peat or leafmould and semi-shade.

Geranium sanguineum. Low mounds of small leaves and pink, rose or carmine flowers in summer. Sunny places and well-drained soils.

Gypsophila repens. Slender stems set with narrow grey leaves and bearing sprays of white or pink flowers in summer. Does well on chalk or limestone.

Helianthemum. Known as sun roses because of their love of warm, sunny places. Low bushes of wiry stems covered in yellow, orange, copper, pink or crimson flowers in late spring and early summer. Loves chalk and limestone. Improved by annual clipping after flowering.

Hypericum. Several species including *coris, fragile, repens* and *olympicum*, all with wiry stems, narrow leaves and showy yellow flowers in summer. Any well-drained soil and open position.

Iberis. Two kinds of perennial candytuft are especially recommended, *Iberis saxatilis* and *sempervirens*. Both make bushy plants with dark green, more or less evergreen leaves and clusters or spikes of white flowers in spring, but *sempervirens* makes a larger plant. Both like sun and grow in most soils.

Linum. Two very different kinds are recommended, *Linum flavum*, a tufted plant with light yellow flowers, and *perenne* with long, slender stems, narrow leaves and sprays of light blue flowers. Both flower in late spring and summer and like well-drained soil and sunny places.

Lithospermum Heavenly Blue. Sprawling growth covered in pure blue flowers in May and June. Likes well-drained soil with some peat or leafmould, and a sunny place.

Phlox subulata. Dense carpets of narrow leaves and clusters of lavender, pink, carmine or white flowers in late spring and early summer. Most soils and reasonably open places.

Polygonum. Two species are especially recommended, both making carpets of growth and suitable for most soils and sunny places. *Polygonum affine* has spikes of deep rose flowers and *vaccinifolium* pale pink flowers in late summer and autumn.

Primula denticulata. Globular heads of lavender, purple or rose-pink flowers in spring. The drumstick primrose likes moist soils and open places. Many other primulas are also good bog or rock garden plants.

Saponaria ocymoides. Trailing plants with sprays of rose-pink flowers in summer. All soils and reasonably open places.

Saxifraga. A great many kinds are excellent rock garden plants but especially recommended are the 'mossy' varieties, suitable for cool, slightly moist places, and the 'silver saxifrages', such as *Saxifraga cotyledon* and *aizoon*, with rosettes of silvery leaves and sprays of white or pink flowers. These do best in limy soil and sunny places.

Sedum. Many kinds of stonecrops make excellent rock garden plants in well-drained soil and sunny places. All have succulent leaves but they vary greatly in habit. Especially recommended are *Sedum cauticolum, lydium, reflexum, spathulifolium* and *spurium*.

Sempervivum. These are the houseleeks, so called because some kinds will grow on the roofs of houses on very little soil. They make tight rosettes of succulent leaves in various colours. Especially recommended are *Sempervivum arachnoideum, calcareum* and *tectorum*.

Thymus serpyllum. A mat-forming thyme studded with purple, crimson or white flowers in summer. Excellent on chalk or limestone or in any well-drained soil and sun. Good carpet over small bulbs.

Veronica rupestris. Carpets of growth with short spikes of blue flowers in May and June. Any reasonably well-drained soil and fairly open place.

Opposite: Nothing is so evocative of the new season as a carpet of spring bulbs. In this natural scene wood anemones, grape hyacinths and celandines jostle to form a sweep of colour

Pools: Formal and Informal.

Pools: Formal and Informal. An informal pool can often form a most delightful addition to the rock garden, but if you favour a pool of regular shape you should place it in a formal part of the garden such as a terrace or patio.

Nowadays pools are seldom lined with concrete since it is cheaper, easier and in many ways more satisfactory to line them with plastic or rubber sheeting or to purchase them ready formed in glass fibre. Pools for plants should usually be at least 1 ft. deep but if they are only required for a mirror effect or to contain the water for a fountain they need be no more than a few inches deep. Water plants vary in the depth of water they enjoy, most water lilies liking 1 ft. or more whereas many marginal plants do not want more than 2 or 3 in. over their crowns. To accommodate as great a variety of plants as possible pools are often constructed with a shelf around the edge or at one end where the shallow water plants can be grown, but an alternative to this is to establish all plants in special plastic baskets and support them on bricks or stones to bring them up to the correct level in the pool.

If a ready-made glass fibre pool is purchased all you have to do is to dig a hole of the right size and shape and drop it into position. The edges can be hidden with turf, plants, rocks or paving slabs.

If the pool is to be lined with a plastic or rubber sheet you must excavate a hole of exactly the kind you want and remove all large or sharp stones from the bottom and sides. As an additional precaution against damage to the sheet you can spread a $\frac{1}{2}$-in. layer of builder's sand over the excavation.

The sheet must be large enough to cover the bottom and sides of the pool and overlap by about 1 ft. so that it can be firmly anchored in position. Though sheets are manufactured in standard sizes the makers or suppliers can usually weld two or more together if the pool is so big that even the largest size will not do. Polythene sheets can also be joined on site by overlapping them by at least 6 in. with a special mastic seal between the overlap and a special adhesive tape over the exposed edge. PVC can also be joined with specially prepared adhesive.

Spread the sheet carefully in the pool, bringing it well over the sides and holding it temporarily in place with stones or paving slabs. Then fill the pool with water, the weight of which will settle the sheet down firmly into all hollows and corners. Only when this has been done should the edge of the sheet be finally anchored and concealed by covering it with soil, grass, stones, slabs or whatever else you consider appropriate to the surroundings. This is the technique for polythene, but it can be slightly simplified for PVC or rubber sheeting, both of which stretch slightly. These can be drawn across the pool and held loosely in place with smooth stones or small pieces of paving. Water is then run on to the sheet to drag it down into position.

Fountains and Cascades. If an electrical supply is available the simplest way to operate fountains and cascades is by re-circulating the water in the pool. In this way there is no danger of lowering the

Opposite, top: The plain paving of a patio complements the straight lines of a formal pool

Opposite, bottom: A tiny fountain and pool of crystal-clear water are a refreshing sight on a hot day. Such a feature can be incorporated in quite small garden layouts

Left: Another example of one of the many imaginative ways in which water can be featured in the garden, and again one that takes up little space

Bottom: Constructing a pool with a plastic liner. (1) A hole is excavated to the required size and depth and all large or sharp stones are removed. (2) The plastic sheet is laid in the prepared hole, preferably on a protective bed of sand, the edges held in place by bricks and stones. As the pool is filled, the weight of water helps to mould the liner into the sides and corners. (3) The edge is concealed by laying over it paving slabs, rocks or turf. The water will hold the liner securely in place

temperature greatly or introducing undesirable chemicals as there may be if the water is supplied from the mains. Small fountains and cascades can be operated by submersible pumps, the whole unit, motor, pump and feed pipe being concealed in the pool. Larger installations may require a separately installed motor and pump or, if no electricity is available, a petrol-engined pump. Fountains of many different kinds are available including some which change the pattern of their water play automatically.

Crystal Clear Water. In a pool stocked with plants and fish it is virtually impossible to keep the water clean at all seasons. The conditions that favour the growth of plants also encourage weeds and algae which must be removed from time to time by raking, sweeping or simply by hand. If the main object in having water is to maintain a mirror-like surface and crystal clarity which allows stones in the bottom to be seen, it will be best to exclude plants and fish at least from this section of the pool or water basin and treat the water with copper sulphate at 1 oz. per 500 gal. or some other recommended chemical.

How to Grow Aquatics. There are two methods of growing aquatic plants. One is to spread soil all over the bottom of the pool and plant the roots directly into it, as though you were dealing with a bed in the garden; the other is to plant the roots in pots or baskets and stand them in the pool without any further soil. One advantage of the second

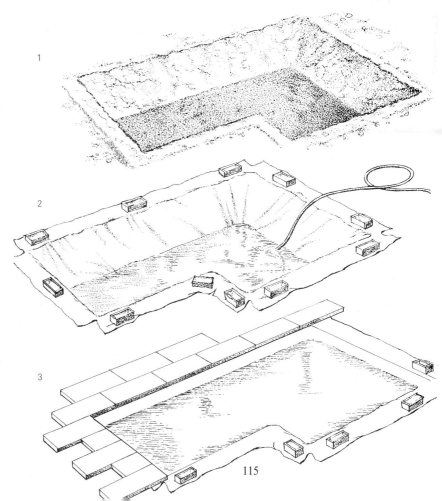

method is that there is less discoloration of the water at first. It is certainly a convenient way of handling plants in small pools. Whichever method you select you should secure some good fibrous loam, rather heavy for preference since aquatics do not like light, sandy soil, and mix bonemeal with it at the rate of 2 oz. to each 2 gal. bucket of soil. If you decide to spread the soil over the bottom of the pool, you can prevent any undue muddying of the water by covering it with about ½ in. of clean, washed gravel.

If the soil is spread planting is carried out without any water in the pool, but if you use baskets they can simply be sunk in position when they have been planted. Firm planting is important. Most of the larger water lilies require a depth of at least 18 in. of water when they are fully grown. Some of the very strong kinds will even succeed in 3 ft. of water, but there are a few dwarf varieties that can be grown in 5 or 6 in. of water, and these are useful for tiny pools. There are a few other aquatics that delight in rather deep water (say, from 1 to 2 ft.), notably the water poppy (hydrocleys), the water hawthorn (aponogeton), and floating heart (nymphoides), but the majority are marginal plants succeeding best with only 2 or 3 in. of water over their roots, which is why it is advisable to build a shelf around the pool. The alternative is to grow these other aquatics in pots, supported on bricks to bring them to the right level.

There are many lovely flowering plants included in this section. A few of the best are the flowering rush (butomus), porcupine rush (*Scirpus tabernaemontani zebrinus*), arrow-head (sagittaria), buck-bean (menyanthes), reed mace (particularly the small forms such as *Typha angustifolia* and *T. minima*), pickerel weed (pontederia), marsh marigold or king cup (caltha), and various water-loving irises such as *Iris laevigata* and *I. pseudacorus variegata*.

Oxygenating Plants. One very important thing is to have plenty of submerged aquatics or oxygenating plants. These produce all their leaves under water, and during sunny weather continually give off bubbles of oxygen which keep the water fresh. They are not planted but are simply dropped into the water. Good varieties for an outdoor pool are the water violet (hottonia), water starwort (callitriche), and the water milfoil (myriophyllum).

Fish. The best ornamental fish for a garden pool are the common goldfish and the golden orfe. These are not simply decorative but are also useful scavengers, devouring the larvae of gnats and mosquitoes which might otherwise become a nuisance. Fish must have plants (including oxygenating plants) for protection and they must be fed. In winter it will also be necessary to prevent the pool freezing right over. The best way of doing this is to suspend a small electric aquarium heater just beneath the surface to keep at least one spot open through which air can enter and foul gas escape. It is also important not to overstock pools with fish. One way of estimating this is to allow a maximum of 4 in. of body length per square foot of water surface.

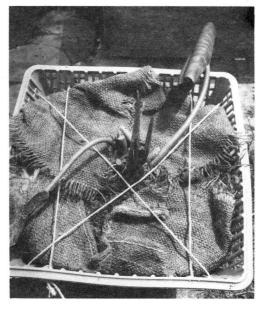

Planting a water lily in a plastic basket. (1) The roots should be trimmed back before planting. (2) The basket is filled with good fibrous loam plus a dressing of bonemeal. (3) A lining of sacking or other porous material will prevent soil from spreading and muddying the water

CHAPTER 23

The Vegetable Garden Established

Potatoes – Peas and Beans – French beans –
Broad beans – Lettuces – Spinach – Root crops
and manure – Parsnips – Carrots – Turnips –
Beetroots – Radishes – Onions – Leeks – Celery –
Outdoor Tomatoes – Parsley – Thyme – Mint –
Rhubarb – Sweet Corn – An Asparagus Bed –
Seakale

Once the ground has been thoroughly cleared of weeds and troublesome pests such as wireworms, millepedes and cutworms, there is no reason why any vegetable you like should not be grown. What the programme should be will naturally depend partly on the space available and partly on personal preference. Where deep freezing is a possibility it may well be wise to consider crops such as peas, beans of all kinds and broccoli which freeze well and special consideration may also be given to quality varieties not normally available in shops.

Potatoes. These, so useful in the beginning as a cleaning crop, are much less attractive as a regular crop because of the large amount of room they require. An early crop may be considered worth while if only because new potatoes taken straight from the garden to the cooking pot always seem to taste so much nicer than any that can be purchased in the shops. But you should, as far as possible, try to grow the potatoes on a different piece of ground each year, not coming back to the same patch for at least three years. You will also probably need to manure more heavily this time and for subsequent crops, as first-year crops will have taken quite a lot of nourishment from the soil. However, there should be no need to exceed the rate of one barrow load of well-rotted manure or composted garden refuse to 10 square yards of ground, though you will be well advised to supplement this by a good dusting of a compound fertilizer such as National Growmore as soon as shoots appear through the soil.

Peas and Beans, etc. These will naturally figure again in your programme, and as the methods of cultivation do not vary I need only refer you once again to Chapter 11.

French or Kidney Beans. French beans, often known as kidney beans, are treated in almost the same manner as runner beans, except that most varieties do not climb, but instead make compact bushes 1 ft. or so in height. For the few climbing varieties culture is identical in every respect with that of runner beans. You must not sow seeds of either kind outdoors until towards the end of April, though you can, if you wish, make a sowing in boxes or pots in a frame early in April and harden off the seedlings to be planted outdoors early in June. If you sow the seeds very thinly in the boxes, or singly in small pots, it will not be necessary to do any pricking out. The rows of French beans should be 18 in. apart, and the plants themselves 6 in. apart in the rows. The seeds should be covered with an inch of soil. A little well-rotted manure dug into the ground when it is prepared in winter will improve both the quality and the quantity of the beans, and may be supplemented by a light dressing of dried blood (about $\frac{1}{2}$ oz. to the yard) when the seedlings have made two or three leaves each, and a second dressing at the same rate about three weeks later. It is important to start to gather pods as soon as they are large enough to use. If you allow them to hang too long they will lose quality and the total crop will not be so heavy. From a late April sowing you should be gathering beans by mid-July.

Broad Beans. Broad beans are much hardier than French beans and can be sown with safety outdoors in March. Sow the seeds 6 in. apart, in rows 2 ft. apart to avoid having to thin the seedlings in any way, and cover them with an inch of soil. The plot you choose for this crop should be well manured in the same way as for other beans and peas, and you should keep the young plants growing freely by hoeing the ground frequently and giving it one or two light dustings of a good compound fertilizer or the mixture of superphosphate, sulphate of ammonia, and sulphate of potash mentioned on page 118. As soon as the beans have set two or three clusters of pods each, pinch out the soft tip of each plant to prevent it growing any taller. Not only will this encourage the pods to swell up quickly, but it will also deter blackfly which is the worst enemy of this crop.

Lettuces. Lettuces are so useful and are so much more palatable when cut and used without delay than when they are allowed to become limp on their way to market, that they may well be a top priority with all garden owners. The secret of success is to encourage rapid growth throughout, and this can only be done by cultivating the soil thoroughly, manuring it well, and taking great care that the lettuces do not go short of water. Dig in plenty of manure or composted garden refuse and rake in a compound fertilizer such as National Growmore or the mixture described on page 118 just prior to sowing.

You can make a first sowing of lettuces in boxes in a frame early in February, pricking out the seedlings into deeper boxes as soon as you can handle them and transferring them to the open ground, after proper hardening off, towards the end of April. You cannot sow with safety outdoors until the second or third week in March, but from that date onwards you should make small successional sowings every fortnight or so until mid-August.

Outdoors sow the seeds thinly in rows 1 ft. apart and cover with $\frac{1}{4}$ in. of soil. When the seedlings have made two or three leaves each thin them out carefully to about 9 in. apart. You can replant the

Intercropping lettuce. To save space, lettuces can be sown between rows of brassicas or other crops. By the time the main crop has increased in size, the lettuces are ready for harvesting

thinnings elsewhere if you wish. They will mature a week or so later than the plants which have not been disturbed. Keep lettuces growing freely by hoeing between the rows frequently and giving occasional dustings of nitrate of soda, but not more than $\frac{1}{2}$ oz. per square yard at any one time. Nor should you give more than one such application every ten days, and if the weather happens to be dry you must water the fertilizer in freely.

Spinach. Spinach is easily grown on any ground that has been well worked and thoroughly manured. During the summer it can be grown well in shady places, so that you can sow rows of spinach between your fruit trees or the rows of tall peas and runner beans. You should make small successional sowings from March until August in rows 1 ft. apart, covering the seeds with $\frac{1}{2}$ in. of soil. For the spring and early summer sowings round-seeded spinach is best but for the last sowing made in mid-August, choose the prickly-seeded spinach because it is hardier. Thin the seedlings to 4 in. and hoe between the rows to keep down weeds. Occasional very light dustings of nitrate of soda, as recommended for lettuce, will improve the crop.

Root Crops and Manure. Animal manures should not be used for any of the root crops (parsnips, carrots, beetroots, turnips, and radishes), as they will encourage forking and disease. However, it will not do to grow these crops on poverty-stricken soil, and so ground should be chosen which is known to be in good condition and be prepared by being given a dusting of a good compound fertilizer such as National Growmore at 3 to 4 oz. per square yard well raked in. Naturally the ground for root crops should be dug as deeply as possible and be well broken up. If the soil is shallow, hard, or lumpy, the roots themselves will be misshapen. Stump-rooted carrots and globe beetroot do not require such deep soil as do long carrots and beetroot, and good turnips can be grown in much shallower soil than parsnips. These are points to bear in mind when choosing the respective places for the various crops.

All seeds of these root crops are sown in shallow drills where the crops are to mature. There must be no transplanting, as this would hinder root development and encourage malformation.

Parsnips. The first sowing to make is that of parsnip seed in March as soon as the soil is in good working condition, and not so wet that it clings to your boots as soon as you walk on it. The seeds should be sown very thinly, 1 in. deep in drills 18 in. apart. Later on, when the seedlings can be seen clearly, they must be thinned out to 6 or 8 in. apart in the rows. At the same time give a light dusting of fishmeal (about 1 oz. per yard), and a few weeks later use a good compound fertilizer or a mixture of superphosphate 4 parts by weight, sulphate of ammonia 2 parts, and sulphate of potash 1 part at the rate of not more than 2 oz. per square yard. You should hoe these dressings in well and keep the bed free of weeds. Parsnips should be ready for digging by the end of September, and you can leave them undisturbed in the beds during the autumn and winter until you actually require them.

Carrots. Carrots are grown in practically the same way, except that three or four sowings should be made from the middle of March until the end of June to ensure a succession of young roots for immediate use as well as mature roots for storing. The quickest growing and most useful in the kitchen are the stump-rooted kinds, and you should certainly make a sowing of these in March for an early crop. The rows should be 9 in. apart and the seed drills $\frac{1}{4}$ in. deep. The earliest roots will be ready in about three months and need not be thinned but main-crop carrots from an April or May sowing should be thinned to about 4 to 6 in. and left until the end of September or early October, when you can lift and store the roots in dry sand or ashes. The best place for the store is a dry shed or cellar. Cut off all the foliage first.

Turnips. Turnips are most palatable when they can be used young directly from the soil. On this account you should make a number of small sowings at approximately fortnightly intervals, starting about the middle of March and finishing in July. In October or early November you can lift some roots from the later sowings and store them in sand or ashes like carrots. The rows for turnips should be 10 to 12 in. apart, and the seedlings must be thinned out to 4 in. apart for early crops and 6 in. for the later crop for storing. Cover the seeds with $\frac{1}{4}$ in. of soil. Feed as advised for parsnips, water freely during hot weather, and, if the turnip flea beetle damages the leaves badly, dust them with lindane or carbaryl.

Beetroots. Beetroots are liable to run prematurely to flower (gardeners call this bolting) if sown too early though varieties differ in their susceptibility to this. Nothing is gained and something may be lost by sowing before late April. The globe-rooted kinds mature more rapidly than the long beetroots and are generally to be preferred for garden cultivation. The rows should be 12 in. apart and the seeds covered with about 1 in. of soil. Thin out the seedlings as early as possible to 4 in. If the ground is in good order and has been dressed with bonemeal, the only subsequent feeding that will be necessary will be a dusting of the compound ferti-

Far left: Twisting off the foliage of beetroot before storing the roots in sand or ashes

Left: In August the tops of onions should be bent over to assist the ripening of the bulbs

lizer mentioned in connection with parsnips. This can be used at the rate of ½ oz. per yard of row after thinning and again at the same rate about three weeks later. Globe beetroot should be ready for use from late July onwards, and any remaining in October can be lifted and stored in sand or ashes in a frostproof shed after *twisting* off the foliage, *not* cutting it off, since if the flesh is damaged the roots may bleed and lose colour.

Radishes. Radishes are very easy to manage. Simply scatter the seed about broadcast, cover it with a light sprinkling of soil, and pull the roots up as soon as they are large enough for use. Make a succession of very small sowings at fortnightly intervals, starting in March and finishing in August. Radishes enjoy very rich soil and are ready for use in about six weeks from the date of sowing.

Onions. Onions also enjoy rich soil with plenty of animal manure provided it is well rotted and thoroughly mixed in. The crop can be further fed with dustings of dried blood at intervals during the growing season and at least one application, at the rate of 1 oz. per square yard, of the mixture of superphosphate, sulphate of ammonia, and sulphate of potash mentioned on page 118 in connection with parsnips. Ash from the garden bonfire is very good for the onion bed and can be dug in freely when it is being prepared.

You should sow onions outdoors early in March in rows 1 ft. apart, covering the seeds with ¼ in. of soil, but if you want an early crop or a few extra big onions for show, you can make a small sowing in a box or pan early in February and place this in a frame to germinate. Heat is not essential, but if you can maintain a minimum of 13°C. (55°F.) germination will be rapid and certain. The seedlings must be pricked out a few inches apart each way into rather deeper boxes when they are about 1 in. in height, and must be gradually hardened off ready for planting outdoors early in April. They should be 9 in. apart in rows 1 ft. apart. A compost of 3 parts of loam, 1 part of leafmould or peat, and 1 part of sand will serve for this seed raising. Seedlings raised outdoors should be thinned to about 6 in. apart. The thinnings make excellent 'spring onions' for use in salads. Bend down the tops of

onions in August to hasten the swelling of the bulbs, and, in September, lift them carefully with a fork, lay them out in the sun so that the skins may dry, and then store in boxes in any dry, airy, and frostproof place.

An alternative method of cultivation especially recommended for soils which are difficult to get into good seed-bed condition by March, is to plant sets in April. These sets are small onions specially grown for the purpose and obtainable from all garden shops in late winter and early spring. They are planted 6 in. apart in rows 1 ft. apart and are barely covered with soil. They grow quickly and are ready for harvesting by August.

Leeks. Leeks are grown in very much the same manner as onions. They delight in a rich, well-worked soil, and are poor in flavour as well as in size if starved. Sow outdoors in March in rows 12 in. apart, covering the seeds with ¼ in. of soil, or, like onions, sow a few seeds during February in a box in the frame and, after pricking out, harden them off for planting out in May. Outdoor raised leeks will be ready for planting in June or July. In either case, make a deep hole with a dibber and drop one plant into each hole until only the green leaf-ends can be seen. Firm the soil around the roots by a second thrust with the dibber. In this way you will ensure well-blanched stems. The plants should be 1 ft. apart. A greater length of blanched stem can be obtained by drawing soil up round the plants as they grow in the same manner as that in which potatoes are earthed up. Leeks are quite hardy and can be left in the ground throughout the winter until required. They grow rather slowly, and something like eight or nine months must elapse from the time of sowing before any are ready for use.

Celery. Seeds should be sown in well-drained pots or boxes in March or early April in a temperature of about 12 to 15°C. (55 to 60°F.). The seedlings should be transplanted, 2 or 3 in. apart, into deeper boxes as soon as they can be handled conveniently, and towards the end of April should be transferred to a frame for hardening off. Meanwhile the trenches in which they are to be grown must be prepared. They should be 18 in. wide and 1 ft. deep,

Earthing up celery to blanch the stems. To prevent soil from working into the hearts the stems can first be tied together or protected with a paper collar

and the bottom of each trench must be thoroughly dug and well enriched with plenty of rotted manure or composted garden refuse. Then spread about 6 in. of good soil without manure in the trench. Plant the celery in June, setting the plants about 9 in. apart. Water freely during dry weather and keep them growing quickly by giving occasional topdressings of nitrate of soda at the rate of $\frac{1}{4}$ oz. per yard. In August start to draw soil into the trenches around the plants, first tying the stems together to prevent the soil from getting into the hearts of the celery. Continue this earthing up until only the uppermost tuft of leaves can be seen. This will blanch the stems, and you can start to dig the celery as soon as blanching is completed. Dig a few sticks at a time as you require them; the plants can remain outdoors all winter if necessary, but it is advisable to scatter some dry straw over the ridges in severe weather.

An alternative is to grow self-blanching celery. This is raised in the same way but instead of being planted in trenches the seedlings are planted 9 in. apart each way in squares so that they get a dense cover of growth from their own leaves. The soil must be rich and the plants should be well watered in dry weather. Self-blanching celery is excellent for summer and early autumn use but it is liable to be damaged later on by frost.

Outdoor Tomatoes. If you have a really sunny border backed by a fence or wall you could utilize this for an outdoor tomato crop. There is no need for the border to be more than a foot in width. In a normal summer quite a profitable crop can be ripened out of doors provided you choose a suitable variety, such as The Amateur, Red Alert or Harbinger. I do not advise you to grow your own plants from seed unless you can be certain of maintaining a constant temperature of from 15 to 18°C. (60 to 65°F.), when seed should be sown in March or early April and the seedlings transplanted into deeper boxes or potted singly in 3-in. pots as soon as they have made two rough leaves each. They should be grown

on, first in the greenhouse and later in a frame, and hardened off ready for planting outdoors early in June. Alternatively plants, well hardened off, can be purchased in the first week of June and put straight into their fruiting place. Make sure that the plants have been well grown or your money will be wasted. The stems should be short and stout with thick blue-green leaves, which should follow closely one after the other, not at long intervals on a spindly stem.

Dig the bed well in advance and, if you can obtain it, work in a little well-rotted farmyard manure. Also give a dressing of bonemeal at the rate of 2 oz. per square yard. Plant the tomatoes 1 ft. apart and at least 6 in. from the fence. You can either put a cane to each plant or train each stem up soft twine attached 4 ft. up the fence. Each plant must be kept to one stem, all side growths being pinched out as soon as they start to grow. You must even pinch out the main growing point as soon as the plant has made four trusses of flowers.

An alternative is to grow a bush variety such as The Amateur, plant it where it has space to spread over a yard-wide circle and allow it to grow naturally without any pinching or removal of side shoots.

Tomatoes need plenty of moisture at their roots (not on their leaves), and you must keep the border well watered in hot weather and preferably mulched with strawy manure. Once the plants are well established and the first truss of flowers has set its tiny fruits you can water with a good tomato fertilizer. You can make your own by mixing 2 parts of sulphate of potash, 2 of sulphate of ammonia, and 3 of superphosphate: of this mixture $\frac{1}{2}$ oz. in each gallon of water can be applied about once a week. If the summer should prove dull and the fruits are slow to ripen, you can pick them as soon as they show the first sign of colouring and ripen them indoors without loss of flavour.

Parsley. Parsley is so useful as a garnishing and seasoning vegetable that you should certainly find a corner for it. It makes a delightful edging to paths in the vegetable garden. You should make three sowings in all, the first early in March, the second about the middle of May, and the third, in a rather sheltered place, about the middle of July. Sow the seed very thinly covering with about $\frac{1}{4}$ in. of soil. Thin out the seedlings to 4 in. apart and later on cut off alternate crowns for use, leaving the remaining plants about 8 in. apart. From these you should pick the leaves, a few at a time, instead of cutting off the whole top. The ground for parsley should be well prepared, with a little well-rotted manure or composted garden refuse worked in, and during the summer you should give an occasional dusting of sulphate of ammonia, but not more than $\frac{1}{2}$ oz. per yard of row each time. Water in freely if the weather happens to be dry.

Thyme. Thyme, like parsley, is always welcome in the garden; and as it makes a charming edging, even in the more ornamental places, you should certainly find room for a few plants. The simplest way of obtaining a supply is to purchase a few roots from a nurseryman in March and plant these

1 ft. apart. Unlike many other crops thyme will thrive quite well on poor soil and it resists drought well, so if necessary you can reserve it for one of the more unfavourable places in the vegetable garden.

Mint. Mint is one of those queer plants that is often rather difficult to establish, but once it gets a hold is apt to take possession of far more than its allotted space. The best method of dealing with it is to prepare a bed by thorough forking and moderate manuring in some out-of-the-way corner where there is little chance of its spreading to any place in which it might overrun other plants. Purchase some roots in March, spread them out thinly, and cover them with about 1 in. of soil. After that you can leave them to take care of themselves, the only attention necessary being an occasional weeding. At first growth may be slow, but once new roots are formed it will be rapid enough.

Rhubarb. Rhubarb is also better planted in some out-of-the-way place since it is best to leave it undisturbed for a number of years and to force growth early by covering the crowns with boxes, drainpipes, or special forcing pots. Rhubarb can be planted at any time from November until early April. Purchase good strong plants from a reliable source, and plant these at least 3 ft. apart each way. The ground should be well dug and moderately manured and should also be dusted with bonemeal. Rhubarb requires very little attention subsequently except for weeding, removal of flowering stems and mulching each February or March with manure or garden compost. The boxes or pots for forcing should be placed in position in January, and every effort made to exclude all light from the crowns. An earlier crop can be obtained by surrounding and almost covering the boxes or pots with dead leaves, while even earlier supplies can be gained by lifting one or two roots in November and bringing them into a warm greenhouse. Here they can be placed under the staging with soil around the roots to keep them moist and sacks hung in front to exclude light. Never force crowns of rhubarb two years in succession, but force some one year and some another, so that they have a chance to recover. In the intermediate years you can pull some sticks from the unforced crowns, but not too many, and not after the end of June.

Sweet Corn

In a warm, sunny place and given fairly rich, well-drained but not dry soil this is an easy crop to grow and a profitable one. It is essential to choose a quick-maturing variety such as Golden Bantam or Earliking and to sow not later than mid-May to give plants plenty of time to mature. In mild places seeds can be sown outdoors during the first half of May 1 in. deep, singly or in pairs, spaced 12 in. apart in rows 3 ft. apart. In most parts of the British Isles it is safer to sow in small peat pots in late April or early May and germinate in a greenhouse, frame or sunny window. Sow one seed in each pot and in late May plant out complete, peat pot and all, spacing as for seeds outdoors. Water freely in dry weather, and

when plants are in flower shake them occasionally to scatter pollen from the male tassels on top of the plants on to the female flowers which protrude from the ends of the cobs forming on the main stems. These cobs are ready to harvest when the female flowers are completely withered and the seeds are well formed but still milky inside.

An Asparagus Bed. Asparagus is one of the most delightful of vegetables, but not one of the easiest to grow. An asparagus bed should occupy a sunny and open position. The practice is to make beds 4 ft. in width, planting these with three rows of asparagus roots 15 in. apart. The soil must be really deeply dug, and plenty of manure should be mixed in both to enrich it and to ensure good drainage. For the same reason it is a good plan to raise the surface of the bed a few inches above the surrounding ground level as this will ensure good surface drainage in the winter. The beds should be prepared as early as possible in the autumn, but must not be planted until the following April. One-year-old roots really give the best results in the long run, but you will probably prefer to start with two-year-old roots, as you will be able to cut a small crop from these two years after planting. With one-year-old plants you must wait three years for a crop. Spread the roots out well and cover them with 4 or 5 in. of good soil. If the natural soil is heavy and inclined to clog mix plenty of sand and leafmould with it. The crowns should be 1 ft. apart in the rows. Subsequently, you should keep the plants growing strongly by dressing the bed with well-rotted dung or composted garden refuse each March. Weeds must be removed carefully so as not to damage the asparagus crowns. In late October all top growth of the asparagus plants is cut off and the bed cleaned. When cutting for kitchen use, the young shoots should be severed 2 or 3 in. below soil level. All cutting must stop by mid-June so that the plants can make plenty of growth during the rest of the summer to strengthen the roots and crowns.

Seakale. This is another luxury vegetable, but it is not everybody's choice. If you like it and decide to have a bed, you should dig the ground deeply and enrich it with well-rotted manure in much the same way as for asparagus. Then obtain some good strong planting thongs in March and plant these with a dibber about 15 in. apart in rows 2 to $2\frac{1}{2}$ ft. apart. For one year the plants should be allowed to grow on uncut, but when they are firmly established you can force them gently in the winter by covering each root with a large flower pot or small box in the same way as for rhubarb. Light must be completely excluded so that the seakale is fully blanched. You can obtain an earlier crop by lifting a few strong roots in the autumn or winter and potting them closely in large flower pots. The side roots can be trimmed off and heeled in temporarily in any sheltered place, for they will make excellent planting thongs in spring. The potted roots can then be brought into a warm greenhouse and kept under the staging, but all light must be excluded or blanching will not be complete.

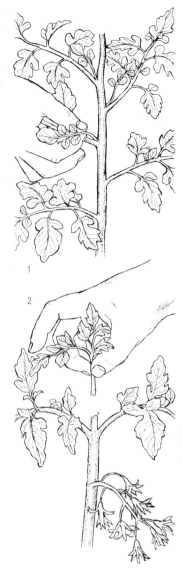

Deshooting tomatoes. (1) The side shoots in the leaf axils should be nipped out as soon as they are seen. (2) When the plants have made four trusses of flowers growth should be stopped by pinching out the growing tip

VEGETABLE SOWING AND PLANTING TABLES

SEEDS TO BE SOWN OR THINNED IN THE ROW

NAME	SEEDS FOR 50 FT. OF ROW	SOW	DISTANCE BETWEEN ROWS	DISTANCE TO SOW OR THIN	DEPTH TO SOW IN INCHES	WHEN READY FOR USE	REMARKS
Beans, broad	$\frac{1}{2}$ pt.	Early Nov. Mar.–Apl.	2 ft.	6 in.	1	June–Aug.	Autumn sowing should only be attempted in fairly sheltered places
French	$\frac{1}{4}$ pt.	Apl.–May	18 in.	8 in.	1	July–Oct.	Gather the beans while still young
haricot	$\frac{1}{4}$ pt.	Apl.–May	18 in.	8 in.	1	Oct. onwards	Leave beans to ripen in pod and then shell out and store dry for winter use
runner	$\frac{1}{2}$ pt.	May–June	8 ft.	8 in.	1	July–Oct.	Plants may be grown as bushes by frequent pinching of runners
Beet	$\frac{1}{4}$ oz.	Apl.–June	1 ft. 15 in.	6 to 8 in.	1	July onwards	Globe varieties are best for early use; cylindrical-rooted kinds for storing
Seakale Beet	$\frac{1}{4}$ oz.	Mar. & Aug.	18 in.	9 in.	1	All the year round	The leaves are cut as required, and boiled in the same way as spinach
Carrot	$\frac{1}{4}$ oz.	Mar.–June	8 in. 15 in.	2 to 4 in.	$\frac{1}{4}$	June onwards	Sow stump-rooted varieties for early use and intermediate kinds for storing
Endive	$\frac{1}{8}$ oz.	Apl.–Aug.	1 ft.	9 in.	$\frac{1}{2}$	Aug.–Mar.	Especially welcome in winter
Kohl Rabi	$\frac{1}{8}$ oz.	Apl.–Aug.	18 in.	1 ft.	$\frac{1}{2}$	July–Nov.	Withstands drought remarkably well
Lettuce	$\frac{1}{8}$ oz.	Mar.–Aug.	9 in. 1 ft.	6 to 9 in.	$\frac{1}{2}$	June–Oct.	Winter supplies obtained by placing seedlings in frames in October
Onion	$\frac{1}{6}$ oz.	Mar.	1 ft.	6 in.	$\frac{1}{2}$	Aug. onwards	Lift in September for storing
Parsley	$\frac{1}{4}$ oz.	Mar.–Aug.	9 in.	5 in.	$\frac{1}{2}$	June–Dec.	Winter supplies obtained by placing seedlings in a frame in October
Parsnip	$\frac{1}{4}$ oz.	Feb.–Mar.	18 in.	8 in.	1	Sept. onwards	Roots may be left in the ground all winter, or lifted and stored
Peas	$\frac{1}{4}$ pt.	Mar.–June	2 to 5 ft.	3 in.	1	June–Oct.	Make frequent small sowings so that a successional supply is maintained
Radish	$\frac{1}{2}$ oz.	Mar.–Aug.	6 in.	—	$\frac{1}{4}$	April–Sept.	Early supplies may be obtained by sowing in February in a frame
Spinach, summer	$\frac{1}{4}$ oz.	Mar.–July	1 ft.	8 in.	1	May–Sept.	Make small successional sowings
winter	$\frac{1}{4}$ oz.	Aug.	1 ft.	6 in.	1	Oct.–April	A sheltered position should be chosen
beet	$\frac{1}{4}$ oz.	Mar.–Aug.	18 in.	9 in.	1	July onwards	Continues to crop for a long time
Swede	$\frac{1}{4}$ oz.	May–June	15 in.	8 in.	$\frac{1}{2}$	Oct. onwards	A wholesale and profitable vegetable
Turnip	$\frac{1}{4}$ oz.	Mar.–July	12 in. 15 in.	4 to 8 in.	$\frac{1}{2}$	June onwards	For summer supplies it is best to sow in a partially shaded position

GERMINATING PERIOD OF VEGETABLE SEEDS

NAME	TIME (DAYS)	NAME	TIME (DAYS)	NAME	TIME (DAYS)	NAME	TIME (DAYS)
Beans, broad	8–12	Cauliflower	7–12	Mustard	4–8	Spinach, summer	10–15
French	10–14	Celery	18–28	Onion, spring-sown	21–25	winter	10–15
runner	10–14	Cress	5–8	August-sown	12–18	beet	18–24
Beet	18–24	Cucumber	5–15	Parsley	28–42	Swede	7–12
Borecole	7–12	Endive	14–21	Parsnip	21–28	Tomato	7–14
Broccoli	7–12	Kale	7–12	Pea	7–12		
Brussels sprouts	7–12	Kohl Rabi	7–12	Radish	6–10		
Cabbage	7–12	Leek	21–24	Savoy	7–12		
Carrot	17–24	Lettuce	10–15	Seakale Beet	18–24		

These germination times are for normal conditions at the usual sowing times and are only approximate. Actual times will vary greatly according to soil, warmth and weather. Given a sufficiently low temperature or dry soil, seeds will remain dormant indefinitely.

SEEDS TO BE SOWN IN SEEDBED AND TRANSPLANTED TO WHERE THEY ARE TO BE GROWN

NAME	SEEDS TO SUPPLY 100 PLANTS SOW		TRANSPLANT	DISTANCE BETWEEN ROWS	DISTANCE BETWEEN PLANTS	DEPTH TO SOW IN INCHES	WHEN READY FOR USE	REMARKS
Borecole (kale)	$\frac{1}{8}$ oz.	Apl.–May	July–Aug.	$2\frac{1}{2}$ ft.	$1\frac{1}{2}$ ft.	$\frac{1}{2}$	Nov.–May	There are numerous varieties, including the well-known curled kales
Broccoli	$\frac{1}{5}$ oz.	Mar.–May	May–July	$2\frac{1}{2}$ ft.	2 ft.	$\frac{1}{2}$	Oct.–June	Varieties can be obtained to give a succession from autumn until late spring
Brussels sprouts	$\frac{1}{8}$ oz.	Mar.–Apl.	May–June	$2\frac{1}{2}$ ft.	2 ft.	$\frac{1}{2}$	Sept.–Feb.	Plant very firmly in soil that has not been over-manured
Cabbage, summer, autumn, winter	$\frac{1}{8}$ oz.	Mar.–Apl.	May–July	2 ft.	$1\frac{1}{2}$ ft.	$\frac{1}{2}$	July–Feb.	Varieties should be chosen to give the required succession
Cabbage, spring	$\frac{1}{8}$ oz.	July–Aug.	Sept.–Oct., Mar.	$1\frac{1}{2}$ ft.	1 ft.	$\frac{1}{2}$	Mar.–June	Not all kinds are suitable for summer sowing. Consult catalogue on this point
Cauliflower	$\frac{1}{8}$ oz.	Feb.–Apl.	May–June	$2\frac{1}{2}$ ft.	2 ft.	$\frac{1}{2}$	Aug.–Dec.	More delicate in flavour than the broccoli, and also more tender
Celery	$\frac{1}{32}$ oz.	Feb.–Apl.	June–July	3 ft.	1 ft.	$\frac{1}{4}$	Sept.–Mar.	Raise the seedlings in a greenhouse or frame
Cucumber (ridge)	100 seeds	Apl.–May	June	4 ft.	3 ft.	1	July–Sept.	Pinch out tips of main runners, to encourage formation of side growths
Leek	$\frac{1}{16}$ oz.	Mar.	June	18 in.	9 in.	$\frac{1}{4}$	Sept.–May	Earlier supplies can be obtained by sowing in a warm greenhouse in January and transplanting outdoors in April
Onion (for transplanting)	$\frac{1}{16}$ oz.	Aug.–Jan. (in frame)	Mid-Apl.	1 ft.	6 in.	$\frac{1}{4}$	June onwards	White Lisbon onions can be sown more thickly in late summer for use as salading in the spring
Savoy	$\frac{1}{2}$ oz.	Apl.–May	June–Aug.	2 ft.	$1\frac{1}{2}$ ft.	$\frac{1}{2}$	Oct.–Mar.	A hardy and profitable vegetable
Tomato	$\frac{1}{4}$ oz.	Mar. (under glass)	June	3 ft.	$1\frac{1}{2}$ ft.	$\frac{1}{4}$	Aug.–Oct.	Earlier plants for cultivation throughout in the greenhouse can be raised from seed sown in January or February
Vegetable marrow	100 seeds	Apl.–May	June	4 ft.	3 ft.	1	July–Oct.	Pinch main runners of trailing varieties to induce formation of side growths

ROOTS AND TUBERS FOR PLANTING

NAME	ROOTS FOR 50 FT. OF ROW	WHEN TO PLANT	DISTANCE BETWEEN ROWS	DISTANCE BETWEEN PLANTS	DEPTH TO PLANT	WHEN READY FOR USE	REMARKS
Artichoke, globe	16	April	3 ft.	3 ft.	–	July–Oct.	The flower heads are cut before they begin to expand
Artichoke, Jerusalem	7 lb.	Feb.	$2\frac{1}{2}$ ft.	15 in.	6 in.	Nov.–March	May be used as a windbreak
Asparagus	40	April	15 in.	15 in.	2 to 3 in.	May–June	Do not cut asparagus for at least two years and never after June
Onion sets	$\frac{1}{2}$ lb.	March	1 ft.	6 in.	Half covered	July onwards	A good method for those who cannot practise autumn sowing
Potatoes, early	8 lb.	March	$2\frac{1}{2}$ ft.	1 ft.	4 to 5 in.	June–July	It is an advantage to sprout the tubers in a light frostproof place before planting
mid-season and late	7 lb.	April	3 ft.	15 in.	4 to 5 in.	Aug. onwards	Dig when the skins are firm
Rhubarb	16	March	3 ft.	3 ft.	–	March–July	Earlier supplies can be ensured by covering the roots with barrels in January
Shallots	2 to 3 lb.	Feb.–Mar.	1 ft.	6 in.	Half covered	July onwards	First class for pickling

CHAPTER 24

A Greenhouse is Added

Types of greenhouse

Span-roofed

Three-quarter span-roofed

Lean-to

Dutch light aluminium

Early summer a good time to start – Unheated or heated? – Methods of heating – Aim at an even temperature – Types and materials – Choice of position – Greenhouse staging – A new use for the frame – Soil, watering, ventilation, feeding – Plants for the greenhouse

Even a small greenhouse can be an immense asset, making it possible to grow many plants that are too tender to be cultivated outdoors in Britain, at any rate in winter, and are too tall to be conveniently accommodated in a frame. Moreover with a greenhouse you can continue to garden in comfort whatever the weather and you will be able to save money by producing from seed or cuttings many of the plants that you would otherwise have to buy.

Early summer is quite a good time to add a greenhouse to your equipment, or at least to make up your mind definitely about it, for it is the time when the seed of many popular greenhouse plants must be sown. If you do not actually complete the greenhouse at once, you can at least make the necessary sowings in boxes in a frame, so that plants may be available later on. In any case the house should be ready by the end of September, when it will be needed for the protection of these seedlings, and it will also be of great service as an addition to the frame for housing half-hardy bedding plants through the winter.

Unheated or Heated? An unheated greenhouse is suitable for storing tender plants only if it can be kept frostproof. This is sometimes possible if the house is a strongly constructed lean-to structure against the wall of a heated dwelling house and the site is sheltered from prevailing winds with no draughts down side entrances. If it cannot be kept frostproof it can still be useful for pans of alpines which do not mind the cold and benefit greatly from the protection from rain. In the spring it can be used for raising seedlings a little later than in a heated house but a few weeks earlier than would be possible out of doors. Nevertheless, an unheated house may prove a snare if it encourages you to start your seed sowing too early in the year or to grow plants that are killed by the slightest frost, since there may be a temptation to plant out the seedlings before all danger of frost is past.

Methods of Heating. If possible, it is undoubtedly wise to have some form of heating apparatus, however temporary, for use in frosty weather. There are plenty of paraffin stoves and electric heaters available and heaters burning natural gas can also be installed inside a greenhouse since, unlike town gas, it mainly gives off carbon dioxide and water vapour, both of which are actually beneficial to plants. Some ventilation is necessary. All three types of heater can be thermostatically controlled which means that fuel will only be consumed when it is really necessary.

TABLE OF HEATING CAPACITY OF TUBULAR ELECTRIC RADIATORS

Note that all these figures are necessarily very approximate, as much depends upon the material of which the house is built and the position in which it stands.

CUBIC CAPACITY OF HOUSE IN CUBIC FEET*	LOADING IN KILOWATTS FOR FROST PROTECTION ONLY	LOADING IN KILOWATTS TO MAINTAIN MINIMUM TEMPERATURE OF 7°C (45°F)
250	0.6	1.25
400	0.75	1.5
600	1.0	2.0
800	1.25	2.5
1,000	1.5	3.0
2,000	2.0	4.0
5,000	5.0	10.0

*The cubic capacity of a greenhouse is calculated by multiplying the length, by the breadth, by the height (measured to a point halfway between eaves and ridge). All measurements must be in feet or fractions of feet if the result is to be in cubic feet.

In large houses it may be better to install hot-water pipes heated from a greenhouse boiler burning solid fuel or oil installed in the wall of the house, with draught holes and stoking door outside, or possibly to connect the greenhouse to the domestic central heating system if this is not too far away. This is probably the most economical method of all if your heating is already on the cheapest tariff.

It is always good policy to install a boiler at least one size larger than the minimum required to heat the house, as then you will be able to maintain the desired temperature without driving the boiler at any time. There is a great difference in the atmosphere of a greenhouse heated by a few pipes that are too hot to touch and one heated by a greater number (or length) of moderately warmed pipes, and plants are quick to show their preference for the latter.

Aim at an Even Temperature. In all greenhouse heating an even temperature should be the aim. You can do far more good with a cool house that has a temperature of 15°C. (60°F.) maximum on sunny winter days and 7°C. (45°F.) minimum on the coldest night than ever you can by raising the day temperature another 5° (10°F.) or so and then letting it drop 15° (25°F.) or more at night. Whatever form of heating apparatus you choose should therefore be capable of easy adjustment and must be big enough to supply that little extra reserve of warmth so necessary when the coldest spells arrive. Any reliable manufacturer of heating apparatus will supply you, without charge, with details of the approximate capacity of the various models which he makes.

Types and Materials. Greenhouses are of four principal types – circular (more accurately octagonal), lean-to, span-roofed, and three-quarter span-roofed. The illustrations make the differences between these types plain. A circular or span-roofed house should always be chosen when the position selected is right out in the open away from houses and walls. Lean-to greenhouses and three-quarter spans must be placed against a wall. The smallest greenhouses measure about 7 ft. in length by 5 ft. in width and are obtainable in sections that you can very readily bolt together for yourself. Similar sectional houses can be purchased up to a maximum of about 30 ft. by 12 ft., beyond which it is really better to build on the spot.

Sectional greenhouses are either made entirely of metal (usually aluminium alloy) or are wood-framed with walls made of weather-board. These are tenant's fixtures, and if erected on rented property should be stood upon a row of bricks firmly bedded into the soil but not mortared together or to the house itself. The points for and against both metal and wood as materials for glasshouse construction are similar to those outlined for frames in Chapter 17.

Choice of Position. The ideal position for a greenhouse depends firstly upon the plants you propose to grow in it. Houses for wintering geraniums, marguerites, fuchsias, heliotropes, and other popular perennial summer bedding plants should be in the sunniest position possible, preferably with some shade or protection from the east and sheltered from strong winds. Such greenhouses will also serve for many popular winter- and spring-flowering plants, such as cinerarias, greenhouse primulas, and calceolarias, cyclamen and winter-flowering stocks if a minimum temperature of 7°C. (45°F.) can be maintained. A house for tropical plants can be in a slightly shaded position, but only propagating houses and ferneries should be placed in fully shaded or northerly situations. It is not advisable for any house to be situated on an east wall, as this makes it very difficult to regulate the temperature. Such houses heat up rapidly early in the morning, and if not ventilated adequately at that time the plants are liable to be scorched. If the house receives little sun late in the day it will be difficult to store natural heat and stove heat must be brought into use rather earlier than normal. So far as possible, span-roofed greenhouses should always be placed in such a way that the ridge bars run as nearly as possible due north and south to give even light.

Greenhouse Staging. Staging in the greenhouse is necessary for almost all pot plants and is often used for cucumbers and tomatoes as well, especially if the house is built on fairly high walls. Commercial growers usually construct their tomato and chrysanthemum houses with low walls and then the plants are set out on the ground. Small greenhouses with glass almost to the ground are available and are excellent for crop cultivation. It is, in any case, quite a good plan to make greenhouse staging portable so that it can be set up or taken away according to the needs of the moment.

A New Use for the Frame. Once you start heating a greenhouse, even occasionally, a frame becomes a necessary link with the open ground. It is rarely possible to acclimatize young plants to the cooler air outside without harming other seedlings, and so the obvious thing to do is to put them in a frame by themselves. There they can be protected at night but ventilated to a greater or less extent during the day until they no longer require protection.

Soil. Standard mixtures for pot plants can be purchased ready for use. These fall into two groups: soil composts, usually based on the John Innes formulae, and soilless composts, usually based on peat plus fertilizers. There are two main John Innes formulae, one for seeds and seedlings known as John Innes Seed Compost, or J.I.S. for short; the other for older plants, known as John Innes Potting Compost, or J.I.P. for short. The amount of fertilizer included in the potting compost can be varied to suit plants according to their age and growth rate. Four standard rates are recognized and are known as J.I.P.1 (4 oz. fertilizer per bushel), J.I.P.2 (8 oz. fertilizer per bushel), J.I.P.3 (12 oz. fertilizer per bushel) and J.I.P.4 (16 oz. fertilizer per bushel). When in doubt always use J.I.P.1 and give extra feed later if necessary. Peat composts are also divided into seed and potting composts but there are no graded strengths for the potting composts and so extra feeding must usually be started after a few weeks of growth.

Watering. The general rule for pot plants is that they should be watered freely while they are in active growth, usually from about April to September, but there are important exceptions, particularly with winter-flowering plants. For the rest of the year, when they are resting, they should be watered moderately or not at all according to kind. When watering you should always give sufficient to wet the soil right through until the water begins to trickle out of the drainage holes in the bottom, but then the soil must be allowed time to get rid of surplus moisture. Overwatering can be as damaging to pot plants as underwatering.

Ventilation. Contrary to popular belief, plants do not have a great need for fresh air. Yet free ventilation is essential in hot weather to prevent the air becoming too hot and scorching foliage and flowers. There must be large ventilators in the roof to allow hot air to rise or extractor fans can be fitted in the ends or sides of the house.

In autumn ventilation may be necessary for another reason, to prevent the air becoming very humid which may encourage disease-causing fungi. Ventilation may then need to be combined with air warming so that a circulation is encouraged and the air is dried a little.

Feeding. Pot plants in full growth can soon exhaust the food in the soil and must then be fed. The best way to do this is to obtain a liquid or readily soluble fertilizer and use this in the water every 7 to 10 days at the rate advised by the manufacturers. It is a mistake to feed plants that are not in active growth

Circular

Span-roofed, glazed to ground level

Dutch light cedar

Span-roofed cedar with brick base

Sowing seed in boxes. (1) Crocks and rough material such as peat are laid over the central crack to prevent soil from running through. This is not necessary with modern plastic seed trays. (2) The box is filled with seed compost. (3) Giving a final firming to the compost with a wooden block to provide an even surface. The level of the compost should be about ½ in. below the rim to allow for watering. (4) Sowing seed on to the prepared compost. A sieve containing fine soil for covering the seeds can be seen in the foreground. (5) Finally, the box should be covered with glass and paper until germination takes place

and also to overfeed which can be even more damaging than not feeding at all.

Plants for the Greenhouse. In these notes I have attempted to give you some useful general advice without too many details. A full discussion of the plants to be grown in a greenhouse and the individual peculiarities of each is a subject for a volume of considerable size, and I should only mislead you if I attempted any such task in the small space available. I have, however, prepared tables of greenhouse plants and half-hardy annuals which will give you much useful information in condensed form, and I have also made a list of plants with which you might start on this new branch of your hobby.

A FEW EASILY MANAGED PLANTS FOR THE NEW GREENHOUSE

Arum lily (Zantedeschia). Purchase dormant roots in September.

Begonia (tuberous-rooted). Purchase dormant tubers in February or March or sow seed in January or February.

Calceolaria (greenhouse). Sow seed in June or July or purchase young plants in early autumn.

Cineraria. Sow seed between April and July or purchase young plants in early autumn.

Cyclamen. Sow seed in August or September or purchase young plants in early autumn.

Freesia. Pot bulbs in August and September and keep in frame until November, or sow seed in February.

Fuchsias. Purchase young plants in the spring or early summer.

Genista fragrans. Purchase plants in spring.

Hyacinths. Pot up bulbs in August and September and keep outdoors under 4 in. of sand or ashes for ten weeks.

Hydrangea. Purchase plants in bud or flower in the spring.

Iris tingitana. Pot up bulbs in September and keep in frame until November.

Lantana. Sow seed in February or March or purchase young plants in spring.

Narcissus (including daffodil). Pot bulbs in August and September and keep outdoors under 4 in. of sand or ashes for ten weeks.

Pelargonium. Purchase young plants in spring or early summer.

Petunia. Sow seed in February or March or purchase young plants in spring.

Primula. All greenhouse kinds, such as *P. sinensis*, *P. sinensis stellata*, *P. obconica*, *P. kewensis*, and *P. malacoides*. Sow seed in spring or early summer or purchase young plants in early autumn.

Schizanthus. Sow seed in spring or late summer.

Tulips. Early-flowering kinds are most suitable. Pot bulbs in September or early October and keep outdoors under 4 in. of sand or ashes for ten weeks.

With the protection of a greenhouse many plants, like these bulbous flowers for instance, can be brought early into flower

GREENHOUSE PLANTS TO RAISE FROM SEED

The temperatures stated are those necessary for quick germination. When in full growth the plants will thrive in a minimum night temperature 5 to 7°C (10 to 15°F.) below these levels.

NAME	SOW	TEMPERATURE CENTIGRADE	HEIGHT	COLOUR	TIME OF FLOWERING	REMARKS
Achimenes	Mar.–Apr.	18 to 20° (65 to 68°F.)	1 to 1½ ft.	blue to red	June–Oct.	Ideal for hanging baskets
*Balsam	Jan.–Feb.	15 to 18° (60 to 65°F.)	1½ to 2 ft.	white to scarlet	June–Sept.	Good strain of seed essential
Begonia (tuberous rooted)	Jan.–Feb.	15 to 18° (60 to 65°F.)	1 to 2 ft.	various	June–Oct.	Cover seed very lightly
*Calceolaria (herbaceous)	June–July	12 to 15° (55 to 60°F.)	2 ft.	yellow and crimson	Mar.–June	Cool, moist conditions required throughout
Canna	Jan.–Feb.	20 to 25° (68 to 77°F.)	3 to 4 ft.	scarlet and yellow	June–Sept.	Soak and chip seeds before sowing
*Celosia	Feb.–Mar.	15 to 18° (60 to 65°F.)	1 to 1½ ft.	crimson and yellow	June–Sept.	Syringe freely
*Cineraria	Apr.–July	12 to 15° (55 to 60°F.)	1 to 2 ft.	white and pink to violet	Nov.–June	Watch plants for the leaf-mining maggot
*Cockscomb	Feb.–Mar.	15 to 18° (60 to 65°F.)	1 ft.	crimson, orange etc.	July–Sept.	A curious form of celosia
Coleus	Feb.–Apr.	15 to 18° (60 to 65°F.)	1½ to 3 ft.	variegated foliage		Small seedlings are frequently the best coloured

127

NAME	SOW	TEMPERATURE CENTIGRADE	HEIGHT	COLOUR	TIME OF FLOWERING	REMARKS
Cyclamen	Aug.–Sept.	12 to 15° (55 to 60°F.)	1 ft.	white to crimson	Nov.–Mar.	Do not bury corms when potting on
Francoa ramosa	Mar.	12 to 15° (55 to 60°F.)	2 ft.	white	July–Aug.	A useful window plant
Freesia	Feb.–Mar.	15 to 18° (60 to 65°F.)	1 to 1½ ft.	various	Jan.–Mar., May–Aug.	Sow thinly in 4-in. pots and do not transplant
Gesneria	Mar.	18 to 20° (65 to 68°F.)	1 to 2 ft.	salmon or orange	July–Sept.	Cover seeds very lightly
Gloxinia	Feb.–Mar.	18 to 20° (65 to 68°F.)	6 to 12 in.	various	June–Sept.	Maintain a moist atmosphere
Humea elegans	Apr.–May	15 to 18° (60 to 65°F.)	3 to 10 ft.	cedar red	June–Sept.	Exceptionally elegant habit
*Impatiens	Mar.–May	15 to 18° (60 to 65°F.)	1 to 2 ft.	pink, scarlet, white	June–Sept.	Make good bedding plants
Lantana	Feb.–Mar.	18 to 20° (65 to 68°F.)	2 to 3½ ft.	white, orange and purple	July–Oct.	Sub-shrubs of bushy habit
Primula kewensis	April	12 to 15° (55 to 60°F.)	1 to 1½ ft.	yellow	Nov.–May	Nearly hardy
Primula malacoides	June–July	12 to 15° (55 to 60°F.)	1 to 1½ ft.	shades of pink	Dec.–Apr.	Plenty of ventilation
Primula obconica	May–June	12 to 15° (55 to 60°F.)	1 to 1½ ft.	various	Nov.–Apr.	Cool treatment throughout
Primula sinensis	May–June	12 to 15° (55 to 60°F.)	9 in.	various	Nov.–Apr.	Careful watering necessary
*Schizanthus	May and Aug.–Sept.	12 to 15° (55 to 60°F.)	3 ft.	various	Apr.–Sept.	Cool treatment throughout
*Stocks (winter flowering)	Aug.–Sept.	12 to 15° (55 to 60°F.)	2 ft.	various	Dec.–Mar.	Cool, airy treatment necessary
Streptocarpus	Jan.–Apr.	15 to 18° (60 to 65°F.)	1 to 2 ft.	pink and mauve to purple	June–Sept.	Cover seeds very lightly

Plants marked with an asterisk are annuals or best treated as annuals.

HALF-HARDY ANNUALS AND BEDDING PLANTS TO RAISE FROM SEED IN THE GREENHOUSE

All these plants can be hardened off for planting outdoors from June till September or, alternatively, may be grown throughout in a well-ventilated greenhouse, unheated in the summer. All should be sown in a temperature of 15 to 18°C. (60 to 65°F.) unless otherwise stated.

NAME	HEIGHT	COLOUR	SOW	FLOWERING PERIOD	REMARKS
Ageratum	6 to 12 in.	blue	March	July–September	Good forms can be raised from cuttings
Amaranthus	2 ft.	crimson, lime green	March	July–September	Known as 'love lies bleeding'
Antirrhinum	6 to 36 in.	various	February–March	June–October	Prefers a limy soil
Aster (annual)	9 to 24 in.	various	March	July–September	Cool treatment throughout
Begonia semperflorens	9 to 18 in.	pink, red	January–March	July–October	Likes cool, leafy soil
Cosmos	2 to 3 ft.	pink, white, orange etc.	March	July–September	Best in rather poor soil
Dahlia (bedding)	1½ to 2 ft.	various	February–March	July–October	Tubers can be stored in winter
Dianthus heddewigii	1 to 1½ ft.	white, pink to crimson	February–March	July–September	Sun and lime loving
Kochia	2 to 3 ft.	ornamental foliage	March		Should be given a very sunny place
Lobelia	3 to 6 in.	blue	March	June–September	Good forms can be raised from cuttings
Marigold	6 to 24 in.	yellow, orange, bronze red	March	July–September	Likes a sunny place
Nemesia	1 ft.	various	March	July–August	Cool, leafy soil and sunny position
Nicotiana	3 to 4 ft.	various	February–March	June–October	Cover seed very lightly. Will grow in shade
Petunia	9 to 18 in.	white to purple	February–March	June–October	Well-drained soil and warm, sunny position
Phlox	1 ft.	various	March	July–September	Peg down or stake straggly shoots
Portulaca	6 in.	various	March	July–September	Very warm, sunny place
Rudbeckia hirta	2 to 3 ft.	yellow, crimson	March	July–October	Sunny place
Salpiglossis	2 ft.	various	February–March	July–September	Cool treatment throughout
Salvia	1 to 1½ ft.	scarlet, purple	February–March	July–October	Warm, moist atmosphere for germination
Statice	1½ to 2 ft.	various	February–March	July–September	'Everlasting' flowers
Stocks (Ten-week)	1½ ft.	various	March	July–September	Cool treatment and free ventilation
Tagetes signata	9 in.	yellow	March	July–October	Excellent as edging
Ursinia	1 ft.	orange	February–March	July–September	Sunny place and well-drained soil
Verbena	1 to 1½ ft.	various	January–February	July–October	Temperature 18 to 21°C. (65 to 70°F.) for germination
Zinnia	1 to 3 ft.	various	April	July–September	Warm, sunny position

PART THREE

The Years Ahead

Keeping Things to Scale

Lawn Management

Looking After the Fruit Garden

Weed Control and Garden Hygiene

CHAPTER 25

Keeping Things to Scale

*Do not over prune – Pruning trees and shrubs –
Some exceptions – Why prune after flowering? –
Pruning for shape – Pruning for strong growth –
Pruning for fruit – Treatment of bush and climbing
roses – Shrub roses – Climbing roses – Climbing
shrubs, twiners, etc. – Thinning herbaceous
perennials*

If you have selected your trees and shrubs wisely,
planned your shrub border on generous lines and
left your specimens ample room, the trees and
bushes will require very little pruning. Sometimes,
however, it is necessary to restrict their growth a
little, to prune out old wood, or even to encourage
more rapid growth. In a small garden it is particularly important to keep everything in scale and not
allow any plant to overrun its neighbour or occupy
more space than it was intended to fill. A great deal
can be done by timely pinching out of shoots that
are straying the wrong way or exceeding their limits
but some heavier pruning will almost certainly have
to be done and some is necessary just to keep plants
in health.

Pruning Trees and Shrubs. The general rule with
flowering trees and shrubs is to prune when necessary immediately after the blooms have faded, if the
blossoms are borne any time up to the end of June,
but to leave the pruning of late-flowering varieties
until the early spring. Thus forsythia (the golden
bell flower), which blooms in March, will need
pruning in April; the weigela and philadelphus
which are May and June flowering, as soon as

practicable in late June or early July; but the purple
buddleia, which flowers on into September, is best
left till February.

Some Exceptions. There are, of course, exceptions
to this pruning rule, the most important being
those shrubs which are grown for the beauty of their
fruits. If hard pruned after flowering the autumn
display would be badly spoilt.

Evergreen shrubs do not, as a rule, like to be cut
severely either early or late in the year. In consequence, if they get so overgrown that drastic
reduction is essential, this is best done in late April
or early May.

Pruning for Shape. The actual pruning is a comparatively simple matter. First remove any very
weak, straggly growth and any branch which
crosses another that is better placed. If the shape of
the bush would be improved by a strong shoot where
at present there is only a weak one, do not cut it
right out, but leave one or two buds at the base. If
the bush is well fed and is in good health one of
those buds will probably give you the stem you
require. The uppermost bud of each pruned stem
should point in the direction in which you wish the
new shoot to grow and the cut must be made just
above it and sloping down on the opposite side of
the stem to the bud. If you cut an inch or so above
the bud, this piece will die, and once decay starts it
is difficult to stop it.

The majority of shrubs are not suitable for
clipping or making into topiary specimens and it is
a mistake to try to turn each shrub in a border into
a neat bush, perfectly smooth in outline. Any
pruning that destroys the natural habit of the tree
or shrub is to be deprecated. The term 'pruning
for shape' means the normal habit of the shrub and
refers to balanced growth on all sides. This allows
the stems to stick up spikily or fall in graceful
cascades instead of being clipped back into a
characterless mop-head.

Pruning for Strong Growth. To encourage the
formation of strong new growth anywhere you must
prune hard – cut almost all of the shoot away.
Purple buddleias, *Hydrangea paniculata* and other
shrubs that bloom on new wood produce much
finer blossoms if hard pruned for all the sap is
concentrated in a few strong growths on which the
flowers form terminally. Hard pruning is also
necessary when the tree or shrub is grown for its
foliage or young bark, as these are almost always
finer on the strong growth produced as a result.
Shrubs that merit this treatment for their foliage
include the golden elder and purple hazel, while
among trees the golden-leaved form of the Indian
bean tree (*Catalpa bignonioides aurea*) and hardy
species of eucalyptus are commonly treated in this
way. The red-barked dogwoods (cornus) and
willows (salix) with coloured bark give much

Forsythia is pruned in April
immediately after flowering.
Some of the flowering
branches are cut out to
encourage development of
the young shoots which will
bear next year's flowers

brighter colour on the young shoots, and their strength should therefore be confined to these by removing the previous year's to within a few inches of their base in February.

Pruning for Fruit. If the tree or bush is to carry fruit, a certain amount of summer pruning can often be accomplished. Thus you can shorten any side shoot which is not carrying fallen blossom or embryo fruits and even those that have fruits can be cut back to within a leaf or so of them. This way you can keep a pyracantha trained against a wall neat without losing any of its decorative potentiality. During the late winter or early spring you can make any further reduction in branches that may be necessary, but loss of blossom will result unless you are sufficiently experienced to be able to distinguish flower from growth buds at sight. Flower buds are usually fatter than those which will produce only leaves. Where it is possible to distinguish between the two kinds you can prune away the portion at the end bearing only growth buds.

Pruning Large Trees. As the years pass, some trees, both ornamental and fruit bearing, may become too big for their allotted space or too crowded with branches for other plants growing beneath them. When this happens do not lop them back thoughtlessly but look very carefully at them and then remove completely branches that you see can be spared without spoiling the natural outline of the tree. If when you have done this the tree is still too big, cut back some of the longest branches to a point at which there already is another branch. In this way you will leave no ugly amputated stumps and very soon the tree will be reclothed and it will be difficult to see where the pruning has been done. This kind of pruning is best done in winter and all large wounds should be painted with a wound dressing.

Treatment of Bush and Standard Roses. All the large-flowered (hybrid tea) and cluster-flowered (floribunda) roses are recurrent flowering, which means that they flower on and off from about June until October or even later, according to the weather. The only pruning that can be done during the summer, therefore, is to remove the flowers or flower clusters as they fade and when doing this it is desirable to cut back a few inches to a good leaf (there will be a growth bud where it joins the stem) or to a young shoot if one has already started to grow.

But the main pruning of these roses, whether they are grown as bushes or as standards, is done in February or March just before growth restarts in the spring and it is an essential annual operation as these roses depend on a constant renewal of growth. First you should cut out all growth that has been damaged during the winter. Some stems may actually be dead and some may be ringed by brown or purple patches. Also, as the plants get older, try to cut out some of the old wood which you can recognize by its comparatively thick, dark, rough bark. But in doing this do not sacrifice any of the strong young growth made the previous year

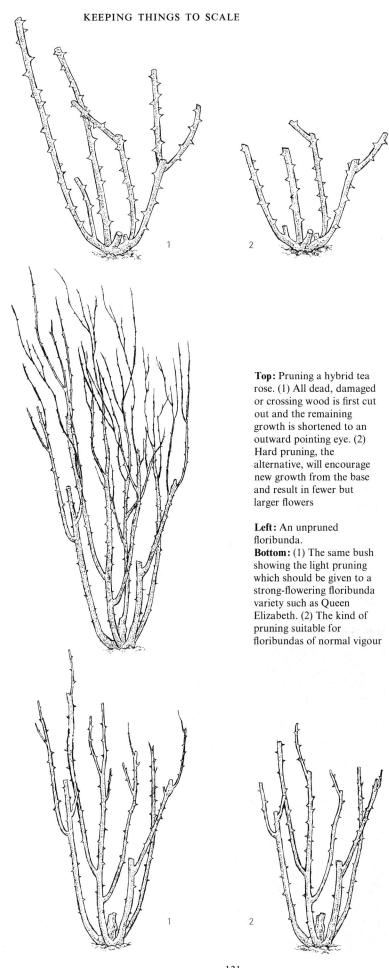

Top: Pruning a hybrid tea rose. (1) All dead, damaged or crossing wood is first cut out and the remaining growth is shortened to an outward pointing eye. (2) Hard pruning, the alternative, will encourage new growth from the base and result in fewer but larger flowers

Left: An unpruned floribunda.
Bottom: (1) The same bush showing the light pruning which should be given to a strong-flowering floribunda variety such as Queen Elizabeth. (2) The kind of pruning suitable for floribundas of normal vigour

because it is this that will bear the best flowers this year.

When all this thinning out of old and damaged growth has been completed the plants will probably look a great deal simpler than they did before you started to work on them. It only remains to shorten the remaining stems and how hard you do this depends a good deal on whether you want a few large flowers or a lot of smaller ones. Hard pruning, which means shortening even good strong stems to 4 or 5 in. and weaker ones to about 1 in., will give the big blooms. Light pruning, which means leaving strong stems up to 12 in. long and weaker ones from 4 to 6 in., will give a bigger plant with lots of flowers of medium size.

All growth coming directly from the roots below the budding point must be removed as soon as it is seen, winter or summer, unless the rose is on its own roots, that is, grown from a cutting or layer, in which case these sucker growths will be of the same character as the rest of the plant, will produce good flowers and can be retained.

The main stem of a standard rose must be kept entirely free of growth, only the head of branches on top being retained and pruned.

Shrub Roses. These branch more freely and do not need such a regular renewal of growth as do bedding

Flowers of exceptional size will be produced if *Clematis jackmanii* and its varieties are cut back each February to within 1 ft. of the ground

roses. In consequence pruning can be lighter, consisting mainly in the removal of damaged stems and old branches that are carrying little new growth. Some varieties bloom once only each spring or summer and you can, if you wish, prune these as soon as they have finished flowering unless they are varieties that carry decorative crops of heps in the autumn. Some shrub roses are recurrent flowering like bedding roses and these are best pruned in February–March, a safe time for all roses.

Climbing Roses. These also fall into two groups, one flowering once only each summer, the other recurrent flowering. Ramblers belong to the first group. Some varieties, such as American Pillar, annually make a great number of strong new cane-like growths from the base. With these you should untie all growth after flowering and remove completely as many as possible of the old canes which have flowered. It is not always possible to cut out all this wood each year, but it is unwise to keep the old canes for more than two years. If a cane has already flowered, but cannot be spared, you should hard prune the side shoots, leaving two or three buds only at the base of each, from which the new growths for the following year's flowers will be formed. Having retained sufficient shoots to cover the allotted space, you should re-tie them to their support in such a manner that the young canes can go on growing in length and ripening in the sun. In the spring you may need to remove the tips of some of the less well ripened canes.

Other vigorously growing ramblers, such as Emily Gray, François Juranville, and Albéric Barbier, flower profusely on wood of almost any age and therefore require little pruning. Where the growth is becoming too crowded you should, of course, remove old wood in preference to new shoots. Mermaid, that magnificent hybrid bracteata, is another rose which should be treated in this way.

Recurrent-flowering climbers are best pruned in February or March when damaged shoots can be removed together with as much of the old wood as can be cut out without losing the strong new growth made the preceding summer, since it is from this that the best blooms will be produced. If some old stems which have already flowered have to be retained, the side shoots which have carried the flowers (you will still be able to see the old withered flower trusses, perhaps carrying some heps) should be shortened to about 1 in.

Climbing Shrubs, Twiners, etc. Shrubs trained as wall climbers require rather careful pruning. The general rules that you must observe are the same as those for shrubs grown in the open, but you will probably need to be considerably more severe on side shoots and in particular upon any that stick forward from the wall or fence. Sometimes you may be able to tie such side shoots in neatly, but you need not hesitate to shorten them back immediately after flowering in the case of the early-flowering kinds, in February or March with late-flowering deciduous varieties, or in May with late-flowering evergreen shrubs.

True climbers do not as a rule require a great

deal of pruning. If honeysuckles get very over-crowded you can thin them out or shorten them back a little immediately after flowering. The many species and varieties of clematis can also be left unpruned so long as there is room for development, but if they grow too big for their place the summer-flowering kinds can be pruned in February, and the early-flowering kinds immediately after flowering. Pruning consists in shortening back the younger growths to within a few inches of the main 'vines'. With *Clematis jackmanii* and its varieties it is even possible to cut all growth back each February to within a foot or so of ground level. This results in a few strong growths carrying flowers of exceptional size, as with hard-pruned buddleias (see page 130).

The flowering shoots of overgrown winter-blooming jasmines may be cut back fairly hard as soon as the flowers fade, and the summer-flowering jasmines may also be thoroughly thinned after flowering. Ivy will benefit from an annual trimming with shears in March, and you will find it a good plan to brush all growth with a stiff broom at the same time, so getting rid of a great many snails, a lot of dead leaves and other rubbish. The Russian vine (*Polygonum baldschuanicum*) should be cut hard back every autumn if it grows too big and can also be thinned during the summer as much as necessary to keep it within bounds.

Herbaceous Perennials. Even these may require some thinning out of young growth, particularly very free-growing kinds such as the perennial asters. But more important than this is the division of old roots essential to keep many kinds in full health. After three or four years most herbaceous perennials have made such large clumps that the central parts become starved and may even begin to die, only the outside of the clump producing satisfactory growth. Before this stage is reached the whole plant should be dug up and split into a number of portions, the best of which (this usually means the younger pieces from the outside of the clump) should be replanted and the rest thrown away. This will also give you the opportunity of passing on some plants to your friends and very likely when they have to divide their own plants they will be able to provide you with some varieties you want.

However, not all herbaceous perennials benefit from biennial or triennial division. Some dislike disturbance so much and take so long to settle down again that it is best to leave them for many years until a definite falling off in the number and quality of flowers produced makes a new start essential. Prominent among such plants are peonies, Japanese anemones and hellebores (but *Helleborus corsicus* often increases itself by self-sown seedlings which transplant well while young.)

Dividing herbaceous perennials. Plants should be lifted and the roots teased apart, or a knife can be used for separating tough clumps. To divide larger clumps, two garden forks can be inserted back to back and forced apart

CHAPTER 26

Lawn Management

Mowing your lawn – When to feed – Watering – Keeping weeds down – Slitting and raking – Rolling

Grass is such an important feature of most British gardens that it is worth paying considerable attention to it. To preserve its quality you must mow it regularly but not too severely, feed it wisely, keep it free of weeds and from time to time get rid of the accumulation of dead grass and roots that nearly always forms under the green surface.

Mowing. This not only keeps the lawn tidy, it also keeps it free of some weeds and tends to discourage the coarser, less desirable grasses. But over-close mowing can actually kill the good grass as well and may leave you with little but moss and a few ground-hugging weeds. In general, lawns should be cut to about $\frac{3}{4}$ in., perhaps to as close as $\frac{1}{2}$ in. if they are to be used for ball games, or to as long as 1 in. if the grass is merely to be a green setting for fairly large shrubs and trees. Mowing is most necessary from mid-April until early October and should be rather lighter in hot dry weather when a fairly good cover of grass helps to protect the roots from scorching.

It does not matter at all whether you cut with a cylinder- or a rotary-type mower provided the blades are sharp and do not drag or bruise the grass. Rotaries can deal with longer, wetter grass than most cylinder mowers but a well-geared, multi-bladed cylinder mower is difficult to beat for quality of finish. If you have a lot of grass you may well decide that you need one of each type, the cylinder machine for the finer lawns near the house, the rotary for the rougher lawns in the outlying parts and for emergency use in wet weather or when grass has been temporarily neglected.

Feeding. Grass needs feeding just as much as any other plant and will show a quick response to nitrogen in spring and summer. You will get the best from your lawn by feeding at least three times each year, first in April with a compound fertilizer fairly high in nitrogen (there are plenty of proprietary lawn fertilizers to choose from), again in June or early July with the same fertilizer at a slightly reduced rate, and finally in September with a special autumn lawn fertilizer which should have very little nitrogen but quite a lot of phosphoric acid and potash. At the same time you can put on a dressing of fine peat at about 1 lb. per sq. yd. and work it well down into the turf with a broom or the back of a rake.

Watering. Lawns can suffer rapidly from shortage of water in hot, dry weather and then regular watering can improve them immensely. The best method of watering is from a sprinkler that can be left playing for an hour or more so that the water has time to soak right in to the roots.

Weeds. Nowadays, thanks to the perfection of selective lawn weedkillers, these should present no problem. You should make it part of your normal routine to treat all the lawn area each spring, a few

Right: Regular mowing, feeding and weeding are well worth the effort in order to maintain a smooth, green lawn

Right centre: A cylinder mower gives the closest finish, but the blades must be sharp to avoid dragging the grass

Far right: Left in place for more than an hour, a sprinkler will ensure that the ground becomes thoroughly soaked

days after the application of fertilizer, with a selective lawn weedkiller. There are a number of brands on the market, some prepared to kill clover as well as other weeds, some, at a slightly lower price, without the clover killer. Which you should choose will depend on what weeds have invaded your lawn.

This one annual application should be sufficient but if some weeds do appear you can remove them with a knife or spade or spot treat them with selective weedkiller or lawn sand. Lawn sand will also kill moss or you can buy special mercurized lawn sand for the purpose. But if moss does become a serious problem it is almost certainly because something has gone wrong; probably the surface soil has become hard through wear or the soil is starved. The remedy then is to spike the surface with a fork or special tool and then to brush in peat or fine sand to improve the porosity of the soil and perhaps give an extra dose of fertilizer as well.

Slitting and Raking. Special tools can be purchased which will cut down vertically through the turf and slice up the mat of dead material that can collect beneath it. Then this dead matter can be dragged out with a spring-toothed grass rake. Slitting and raking can be done at any time but is usually most effective in early autumn.

Rolling. This is hardly ever necessary on purely amenity lawns. Rolling is only of value where a very true surface is essential for putting, croquet, tennis etc. and then should be no heavier or more frequent than is necessary to achieve this object. Roll your lawn, if you must, when it is just moist. Rolling will have no effect when it is very dry and can be positively harmful when it is very wet.

1 2
3 4

Some methods of dealing with lawn weeds. (1) Applying lawn sand, particularly effective for broad-leaved weeds such as plantains. (2) Cutting weeds out with a knife. (3) Spot treating with a brush dipped in weedkiller. (4) Spiking the lawn with a fork to improve porosity

CHAPTER 27

Looking After the Fruit Garden

Growth of fruit – Pruning apples – Feeding and spraying apples – The treatment of pears – Plums – Cherries – Peaches and nectarines – Some general observations – Pruning small fruits – Blackcurrants – Raspberries and bramble fruits – Manuring small fruits – Surface roots – The strawberry bed

Once fruit trees and bushes are well established their management falls into a regular routine which is only slightly modified with the passing years. With the larger fruits, particularly plums and sweet cherries, fruit production is not important for the first four or five years during which the trees will be building up a sound foundation of branches.

Small fruits such as gooseberries, currants, raspberries, and bramble fruits and also cordon-trained apples and pears on very dwarfing stocks may all start to bear in their second year, and Morello cherries that are growing well and strong peaches and nectarines may also carry some fruit by then. It will simplify matters if I deal with the various kinds of fruit individually.

Pruning Apples. The regular winter pruning of apples will vary in severity according to the amount of growth that has been made during the summer. If the trees have made new main shoots a foot and more in length, it will be sufficient to shorten these by two-thirds and to cut back all side shoots (new growths not actually required to extend existing branches or form new ones) to about 1 in. each or to a fruit bud near the base.

There are only two exceptions to this general rule. One is made for cordons and applies to the main central shoot only. This is not pruned at all unless growth has been very unsatisfactory, in which case it should be cut back really hard to start a new and more satisfactory leader.

The other exception concerns espalier-trained apples and again applies only to the main central shoot. If you wish to add a new tier of horizontal branches, you must cut this central shoot off about 15 in. above the last tier. Then you will be able to retain the three uppermost new shoots that grow next year, training one vertically as a new leader, and bending the other two to the left and right as new horizontal arms. If you do not wish to add any more tiers, simply cut the young central shoot right out close above the last pair of horizontal branches.

It is quite likely that young apples will not have averaged new young shoots 1 ft. and more during their first full summer. Even with the most careful treatment transplanting is always bound to give fruit trees a considerable check and the result may be little or no growth for a year. In that case you must harden your heart and prune them hard. Examine each branch carefully and search for a good, plump-looking growth bud. Cut the shoot off just above the uppermost sturdy growth bud that you find. Do not make the mistake of cutting back

Top right: Winter-pruned cordon apples

Bottom: Branch of fruit tree showing the types of buds and shoots

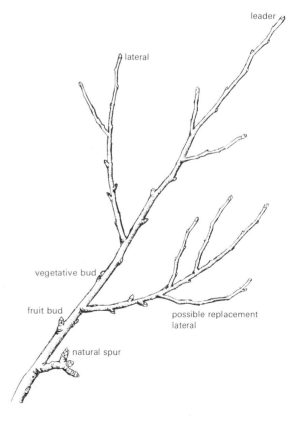

leader

lateral

vegetative bud

fruit bud

possible replacement lateral

natural spur

to a fruit bud instead of a growth bud. It is not really very difficult to tell the difference between the two types since fruit buds are much larger and more globular but a glance at the illustration on page 136 will help far more than a lengthy description. If growth has been poor you must also treat side shoots a little more severely, leaving fewer fruit buds to act as a possible drag on progress.

This winter pruning must be supplemented by summer pruning exactly as described in Chapter 20.

Feeding Apples. Bad growth may be a sign that the soil is poor or that the roots have been disturbed. You should, therefore, feed the trees rather liberally and make quite certain that the soil is well firmed around the roots and that the trees are themselves made quite secure to their supports. Well-rotted manure or garden refuse properly composted can be spread liberally around the trees in late winter and in March a good compound fertilizer such as National Growmore can be used at 3 to 4 oz. per square yard. These routine dressings should be used whether growth has been good or bad, but if bad, they should be supplemented by two applications of nitrate of soda or Nitro-chalk each at the rate of 1 oz. per square yard, the first to be applied in April and the second in June.

Spraying Apples. It is always rather a nuisance to have to spray against pests and diseases but many apples, including the popular Cox's Orange Pippin, are so susceptible to a disease called scab (it causes brown scabs and cracks on the fruit as well as black blotches on the leaves) that it really is wise to adopt a routine preventive programme. Captan and benomyl are the pleasantest chemicals to use, and it is a good idea to alternate them. At least two annual applications will be needed, the first in April when the flower buds are well formed and the second in late May or early June as soon as the blossom has fallen. Give a third in July if necessary.

The Treatment of Pears. Pear trees are treated in practically the same way as apples. If anything they can be pruned even more severely, for their natural habit is to produce most of their best fruits on stumpy side growths known as 'spurs'. Summer pruning, as described in Chapter 20, is also necessary. Feeding is the same as for apples.

Plums. Plums can usually be pruned a little more lightly, for their natural tendency is to make long shoots with fruit buds almost throughout their length. If growth has been satisfactory, it will be sufficient to shorten main shoots or those required to form new branches by about one-third their length and to thin out side growths where overcrowded. But if very little growth has been made it may be necessary to cut leaders back hard and shorten side growths to an inch or so.

Summer pruning is only necessary for trained plums and consists of pinching out the soft tips of side shoots from mid-June until early August to prevent a superabundance of growth which could not conveniently be trained in. Feeding is the same as for apples.

Cherries. For the purpose of pruning, cherries may be divided into two classes, one composed of all the 'sweet' varieties and the other of the Morello cherry alone. Pruning of the sweet cherries is the same as the pruning of plums, but this will not serve so well for Morello cherries. If these have made plenty of strong new growth, you can preserve some of the best side shoots at full length; tie them in neatly if the trees are trained fanwise against walls, fences, or wire trainers. Other side growths that are less sturdy or are badly placed for tying in may be cut right out. You must shorten all the leading shoots by about half their length to encourage further strong growth the following year. Only if progress has been really unsatisfactory during the first summer should young wood be pruned at all severely, and this should be supplemented by liberal manuring to hasten growth the next summer.

Winter pruning of Morello cherries must be followed by a rather specialized form of summer pruning. Instead of pinching back the young side shoots when they have made seven or eight leaves each, you should thin them out, leaving one at the tip and one at the base of each old side shoot to grow unchecked and removing most of the remainder except where they are required to fill unoccupied space. Do not do this pruning all at once, but little by little from June until August. A glance at the illustration of the summer pruning of a peach on this page will probably help you grasp this process, for the pruning of peaches and Morello cherries is practically identical.

Feeding of cherries is the same as for apples.

Peaches and Nectarines. Peaches and nectarines are treated in the same manner as Morello cherries, both in winter and in summer. Feeding for these is the same as for apples.

Some General Observations. In all this pruning you should keep in mind the shape you want the fully grown trees to assume. Then you can remove any misplaced branches and make all your cuts in such a way that the new shoots will tend to grow where you want them without a lot of tying and training

Top: Thinning Morello cherries. The summer pruning of Morello cherries is almost exactly the same as for peaches

Summer pruning a peach. Secondary side shoots on the laterals are removed to leave only two or three, at least one of which should be near the top and another at the base of the lateral

Top: Pruning gooseberries. Young shoots at the ends of branches are cut back by about one-third, and side shoots are shortened to about 1 in.

Right: The fruiting canes of summer-ripening raspberries are cut out at ground level after the crop is gathered

during the summer. Bear in mind throughout that the principal new shoot will come from the growth bud immediately beneath each cut and that it will tend to grow in the direction in which the bud is pointing. It is advisable, therefore, so far as possible to make all cuts just above buds that are pointing in approximately the direction you intend the new shoot to take.

The Care of Small Fruits. The pruning of gooseberries and both red and white currants is very much like the pruning of apples. The young shoots at the end of the branches are cut back to about one-third of their present length, and side shoots are shortened to about 1 in. each unless there happens to be room, here and there, for one to remain as a new branch, in which case it is treated like the terminal growths. Only very occasionally, with exceptionally backward bushes, is it necessary to prune really hard. All sucker growths, shooting up from the roots, should be removed in their entirety. On no account must the bushes be allowed to become crowded with a thicket of wood that would keep out light and air and make it wellnigh impossible for you to gather the crop.

Blackcurrants. These do not resemble red and white currants in their manner of bearing fruits, and in consequence are not pruned in the same way. At the end of the first summer, if growth has been fairly good and new shoots 15 in. or more in length have been produced, they can be left entirely unpruned. But if growth has been poor, some, or even all, the branches should be cut hard back to within 6 in. of soil level. Unlike red and white currants, strong sucker growths are desirable in blackcurrants as they usually produce the best fruits. In subsequent years as much as possible of the growth that has borne fruit should be cut out any time after the crop has been gathered and all the young stems that have not yet fruited should be retained at full length for fruiting next year.

Some gardeners make picking easy by cutting the fruit-bearing stems when the fruit is ripe and stripping them indoors. If this is done carefully no further pruning will be necessary.

Raspberries and Bramble Fruits. At the end of the first summer raspberries are treated very much like blackcurrants, that is, if they have made strong new canes 3 or 4 ft. in length, they will not require any pruning but if growth has been poor, some or all of the canes must be cut back to within 6 in. of the soil. In subsequent years all the fruiting canes of summer-ripening raspberries are cut out at ground level when the crop has been gathered. Autumn-fruiting raspberries are not pruned until February when all growth is cut to within about 6 in. of ground level.

Loganberries, blackberries and other bramble fruits bear their best crops on strong canes made the previous year, so they too must have all the old fruiting canes cut out as low down as possible when the crop has been gathered, and then the young canes that have not yet borne any fruit are trained in their place.

Manuring Small Fruits. Correct manuring is as necessary for these small fruits as it is for the larger ones. Red and white currants and gooseberries need plenty of potash so a high potash compound fertilizer should be sprinkled around the bushes each March as advised by the manufacturers, or alternatively, an ordinary fertilizer of the National Growmore type can be used at about 3 oz. per square yard plus sulphate of potash at 1 oz. per square yard. Growth can be further stimulated by spreading some animal manure around the bushes in late winter or early spring.

Blackcurrants do not need so much potash but a good deal more nitrogen which helps them to make the vigorous growth which is essential for heavy and regular cropping. Manure is very valuable and generous dressings of this or of well-composted garden refuse can be spread round the bushes in late winter or early spring. Even this should be supplemented by a compound fertilizer of the National Growmore type at 4 oz. per square yard in March plus sulphate of ammonia or Nitro-chalk as a topdressing in May at 1 oz. per square yard.

Manure or composted garden refuse is also valuable for raspberries which, like blackcurrants, appreciate anything that helps to keep the soil moist in summer. They, too, can have National Growmore in early spring plus sulphate of potash at 1 oz. per square yard.

Surface Roots. Never dig or fork deeply in the raspberry plantation. Mix the fertilizer with the surface soil by hoeing lightly or simply leave it to be washed in by rain. Most of the valuable feeding roots are just below the surface and it is easy to destroy them by well-meant cultivation. Similar remarks also apply to cultivation near cherry trees; indeed, in any part of the fruit plantation you must always proceed with caution, never cultivating more than a few inches deep, and stopping altogether at the first intimation that you are disturbing roots.

The Strawberry Bed. Spread some well-rotted manure or composted garden refuse in the rows between strawberry plants each March or April and at the same time give them 3 oz. per yard run of National Growmore or, alternatively, 2 oz. of superphosphate of lime and $1\frac{1}{2}$ oz. of sulphate of potash. Cut off all runners during the summer months unless you decide to peg down one or two per plant to root and provide young plants for a new plantation. In this case you should only peg down one plantlet on each runner, and that the nearest to the parent plant. The remainder should be cut off. Pegging down is done in July and the plantlets should be rooted and ready for removal to new beds by the end of August or early September (see Chapter 20). However, there are dangers in propagating one's own strawberries in this way, economical though it may seem, because in a garden it is almost impossible to keep the plants free of virus diseases which are spread by greenflies. Even nursery plants can be suspect unless they come from specialist firms where the plants are grown in isolation, are regularly sprayed and are constantly watched for the first indications of infection.

Top left: Pegging down strawberry runners. Only one plantlet should be pegged down on each runner

Top: Laying straw round and between strawberry plants to protect the fruit from soil and dirt

CHAPTER 28

Weed Control and Garden Hygiene

Hoeing – The use of herbicides – Hand weeding – Garden hygiene – Systemic fungicides – Some common pests

Any plant growing where it is not welcome can be a weed, and since the conditions of a garden favour the growth of plants, weeds soon take over if they are not dealt with regularly.

Weeding. Hoeing is one of the best ways of disposing of weeds as it not only cuts them off but also loosens the surface soil so letting in health-giving air and leaving beds looking very neat and tidy. But hoeing takes time, is virtually impossible on hard paths and can be very difficult where plants are growing closely together.

Path weeds can be dealt with by watering or dusting them with safe herbicides such as simazine, dichlobenil, glyphosate and paraquat. The first three are slow acting but last a long time – as much as a year – from a single application. Paraquat will even kill quite large weeds in a few days but will not prevent the emergence of new seedlings as simazine does, nor does it kill strong roots. So some manufacturers make mixtures of herbicides for path weed-killing which combine both the quick effect and suppressors of emergent seedlings. Glyphosate acts much more slowly than paraquat but is more effective in killing strong roots.

It is possible to use glyphosate and paraquat to kill weeds around plants but it needs care in application as these herbicides are not selective. However, they only kill through the leaves and soft stems. Keep them off these and they do no harm and they have no effect through the soil. The best method of application is from a sprayer fitted with a hood to prevent drift. This is held close to the ground where the spray is directed on to seed leaves but is kept off the leaves of garden plants. This is quite easy with trees, including fruit trees, shrubs and roses, but more difficult around herbaceous plants for which a small one-hand sprayer may be necessary.

Garden Hygiene. In an earlier chapter I referred to the necessity of carrying out routine spraying of some varieties of apples because of their susceptibility to a disease known as scab. Fortunately for the gardener there is not a great deal of such regular disease or pest control that need be done, certainly far less than in market gardens and commercial fruit orchards where, because of the great concentration of one kind of plant, pests and diseases can build up at a speed and to a degree that would be unlikely in the much more mixed plant population of a garden. Still, there are some exceptions and even when one does not plan any regular control programme there are some pests and diseases that appear with sufficient frequency to make it wise to keep the appropriate remedy at hand ready for immediate use if required.

Except in areas where there is a good deal of sulphur in the air from industrial pollution, black spot attacks some varieties of rose so regularly and severely that it is wise to carry out preventive spraying every year. The disease, like so many that attack plants, is caused by a fungus, the minute spores of which float about in the air ready to germinate on any rose leaf where the conditions are right. The fungus destroys the tissues, causing round black spots which rapidly increase in size until the leaf drops off. Some varieties can be completely defoliated by mid-July if adequate protection is not given. Fortunately there are a number of chemicals, known as fungicides, which will prevent the spread of black spot, the best being those, such as benomyl and thiophanate-methyl, known as 'systemic' fungicides, because they actually enter the tissues of the leaf, where the fungus is growing, and do not simply make a film on the surface of the leaf. Systemic chemicals cannot be washed off by rain and so are usually effective for several weeks. Five sprayings between mid-May and mid-September should be sufficient to keep all your roses free of black spot and also of mildew, another disease that attacks some varieties much more than others.

Some Common Pests. Various species of aphid, known as greenfly or blackfly according to their colour, or sometimes simply as plant lice, attack many different kinds of plant, sucking sap from the young leaves and shoots and causing them to become distorted or even to die. As a rule there is no need to practise routine spraying against these pests but simply to keep watch for them, particularly from May until August, and spray with an insecticide directly they are seen. (Note the difference: fungicides are for diseases caused by fungi, insecticides are for insects such as greenflies and caterpillars.) Again, it is possible to buy systemic insecticides and I think these are to be preferred to non-systemic insecticides for ornamental plants because of their efficiency and relative persistence. For food crops I prefer to use an insecticide such as derris, malathion, permethrin or pirimiphos-methyl, which remains on the surface and so can be washed or wiped off before the crop is eaten.

Caterpillars, being relatively large, can often be dealt with by hand, simply being picked off and destroyed if they appear. But this may take too long if there is a severe attack and then one must spray or dust with an insecticide.

Some caterpillars live in the soil and eat the roots or crowns of plants and so do some other pests such as wireworms, millepedes and leatherjackets. Special insecticides are obtainable prepared in powder form which can be forked or raked into the soil to deal with these pests.

Then there are slugs and snails to be found in almost every garden ready to destroy seedlings and small plants and disfigure larger ones by eating large pieces of their leaves. They are most active in warm damp weather and feed principally at night, which is why new gardeners are often mystified as to what can be causing the damage. Poison baits containing metaldehyde or methiocarb can be purchased ready to be sprinkled or placed in small heaps wherever slugs or slug damage have been seen.

Mice can eat bulbs, corms and the larger seeds such as peas and beans and, if they prove troublesome, must be poisoned or trapped.

Birds can be both a delight and a nuisance in the garden. They do a lot of good by eating insects but they can also do a lot of harm by stripping the growth and flower buds from trees and shrubs, tearing off the flowers of crocus, polyanthus etc. and pulling up seedlings. In some country gardens it is essential to protect fruit and vegetables with nets or even to build a permanent bird-proof cage over the fruit and vegetable sections of the garden. Town gardeners have a bonus here as birds seldom do much damage to their plants.

Finally, though it is excellent policy to rot down all clean garden refuse into compost to be used as a substitute for manure, it is unwise to compost diseased plants nor any that may carry the eggs of harmful insects. When in doubt burn such material and use the ashes as fertilizer. In that, at least, you will be perfectly safe.

Tidy beds, healthy plants and a velvet lawn call for constant vigilance but the serene beauty of a well-kept garden is the ultimate reward

Index